SOUL EATER NOT!

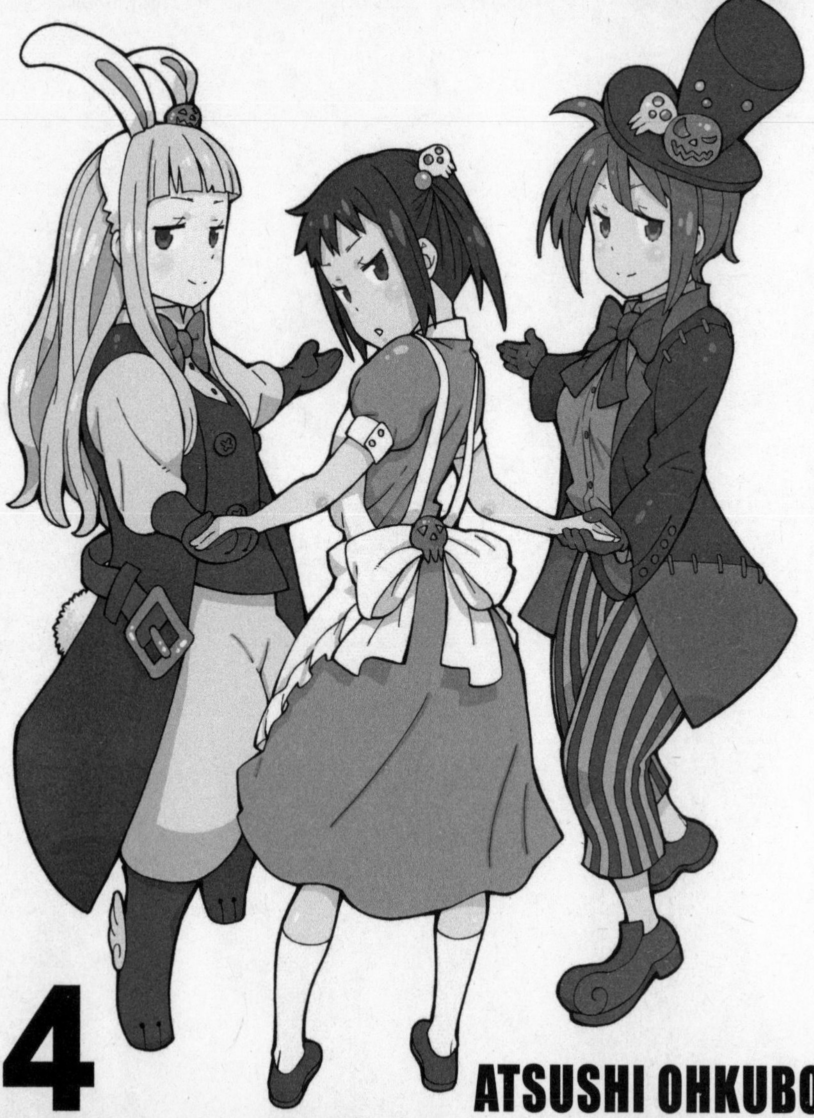

4

ATSUSHI OHKUBO

EATER

ATSUSHI
OHKUBO

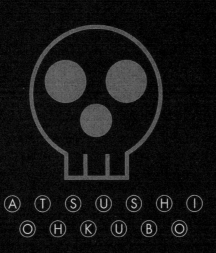

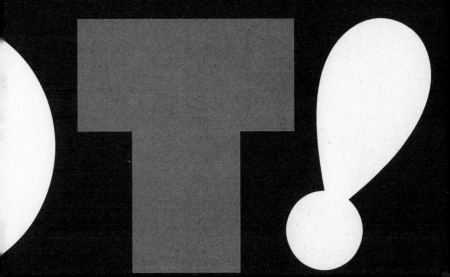

SOUL

04

NO

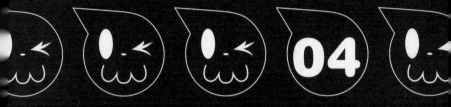

S O U L   E A T E R   N O T !

04

CONTENTS

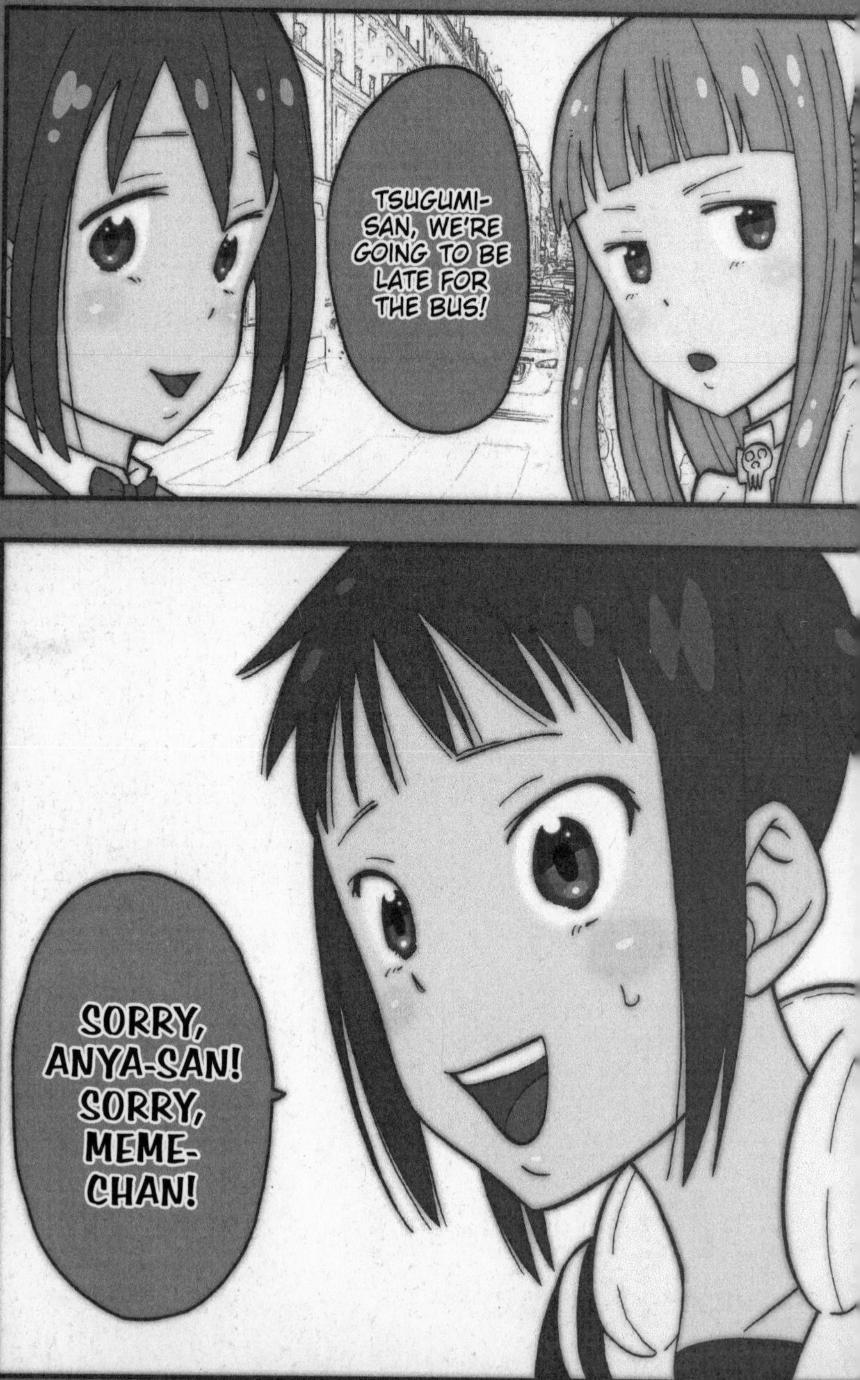
TSUGUMI-SAN, WE'RE GOING TO BE LATE FOR THE BUS!
SORRY, ANYA-SAN! SORRY, MEME-CHAN!

CHAPTER 21: FIRST DAY!

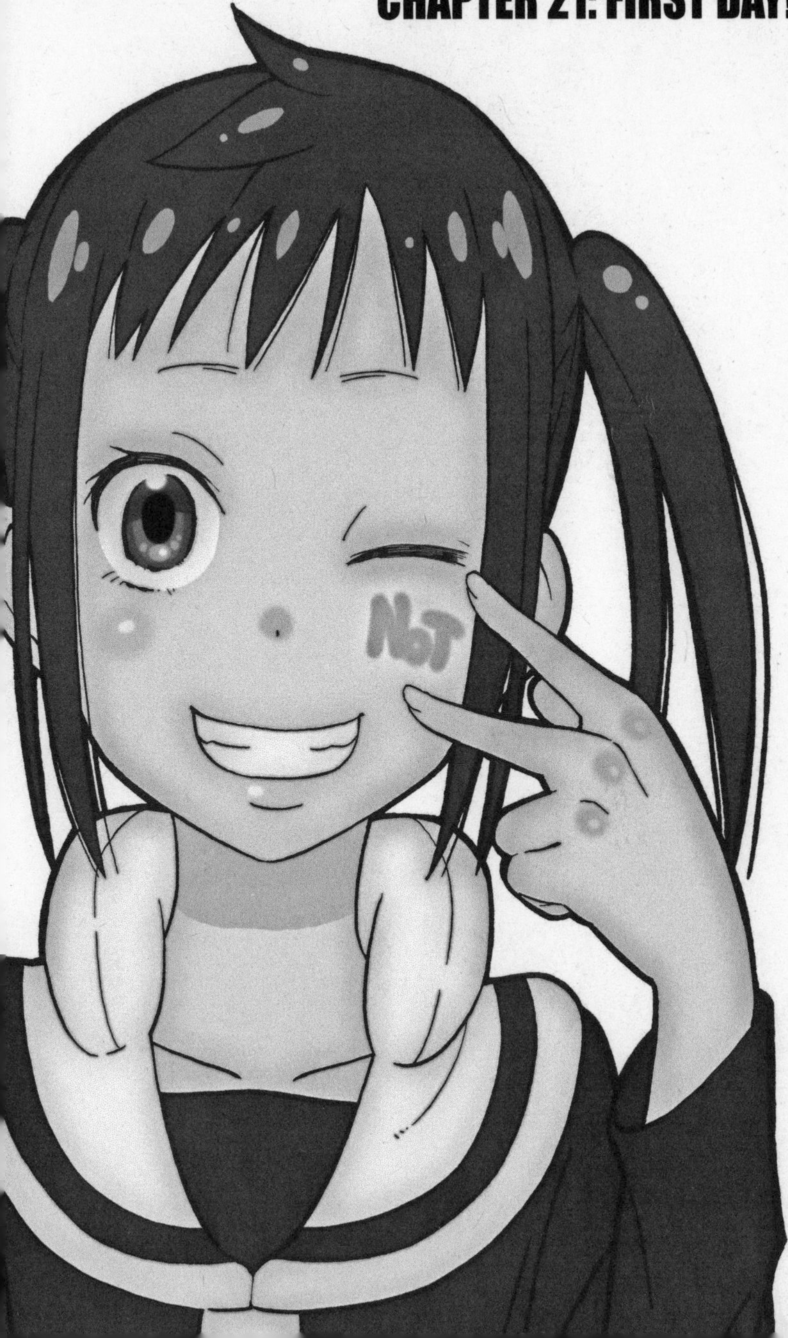
NoT

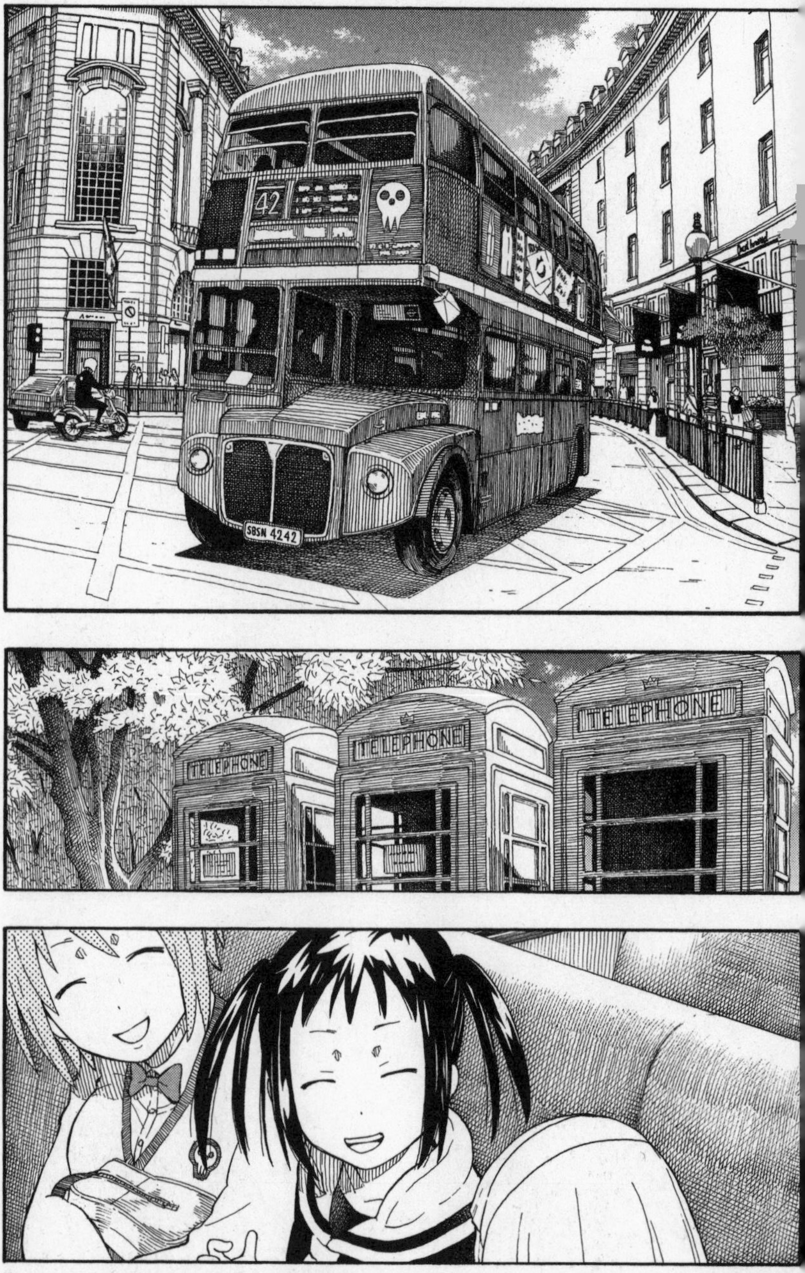
42
SBSN 4242
TELEPHONE
TELEPHONE
TELEPHONE

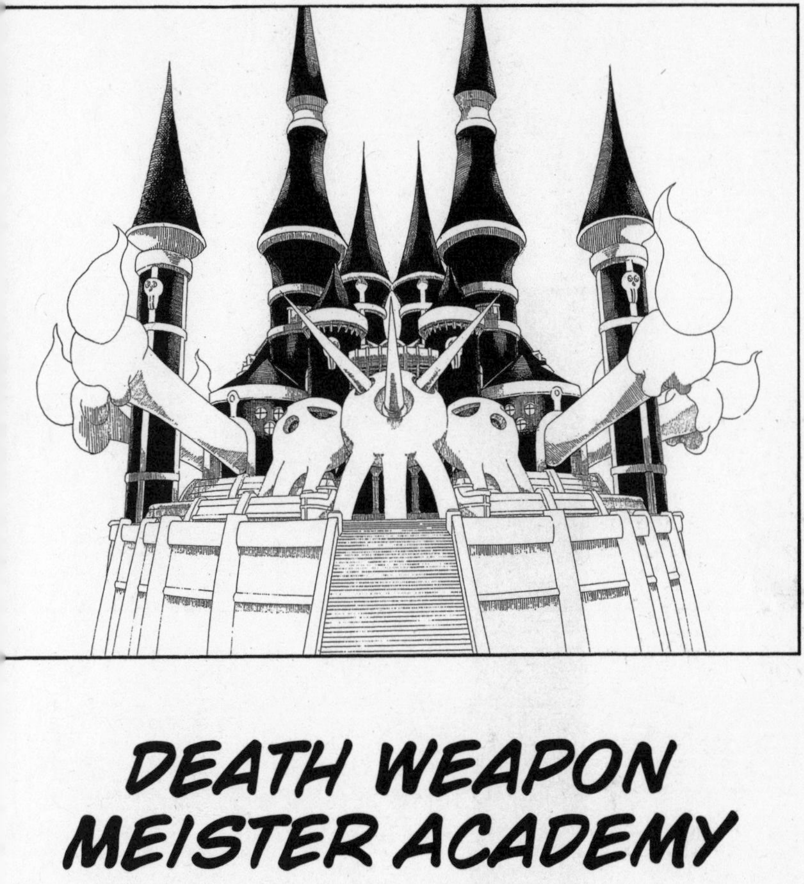

DEATH WEAPON
MEISTER ACADEMY

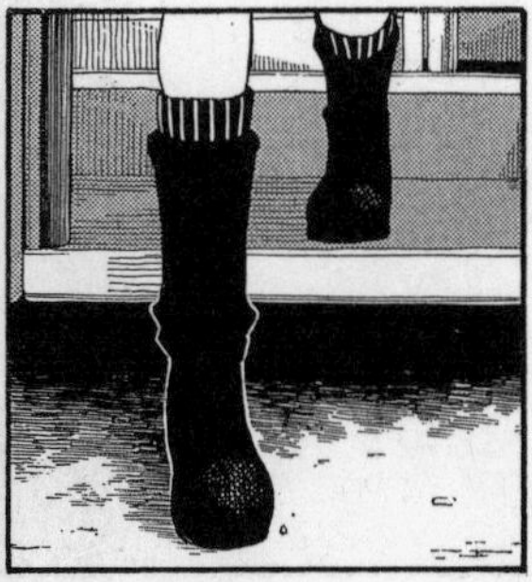

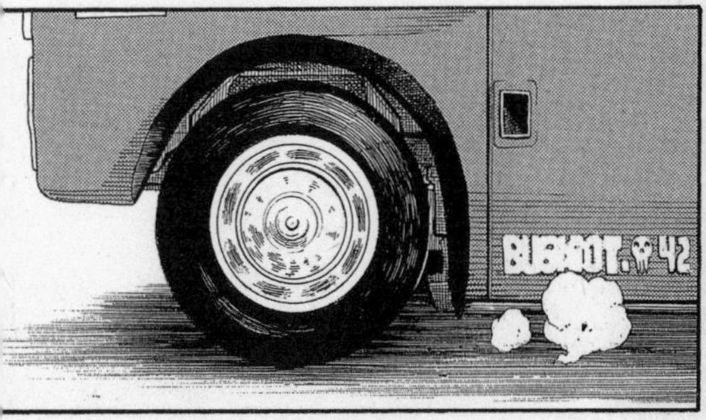

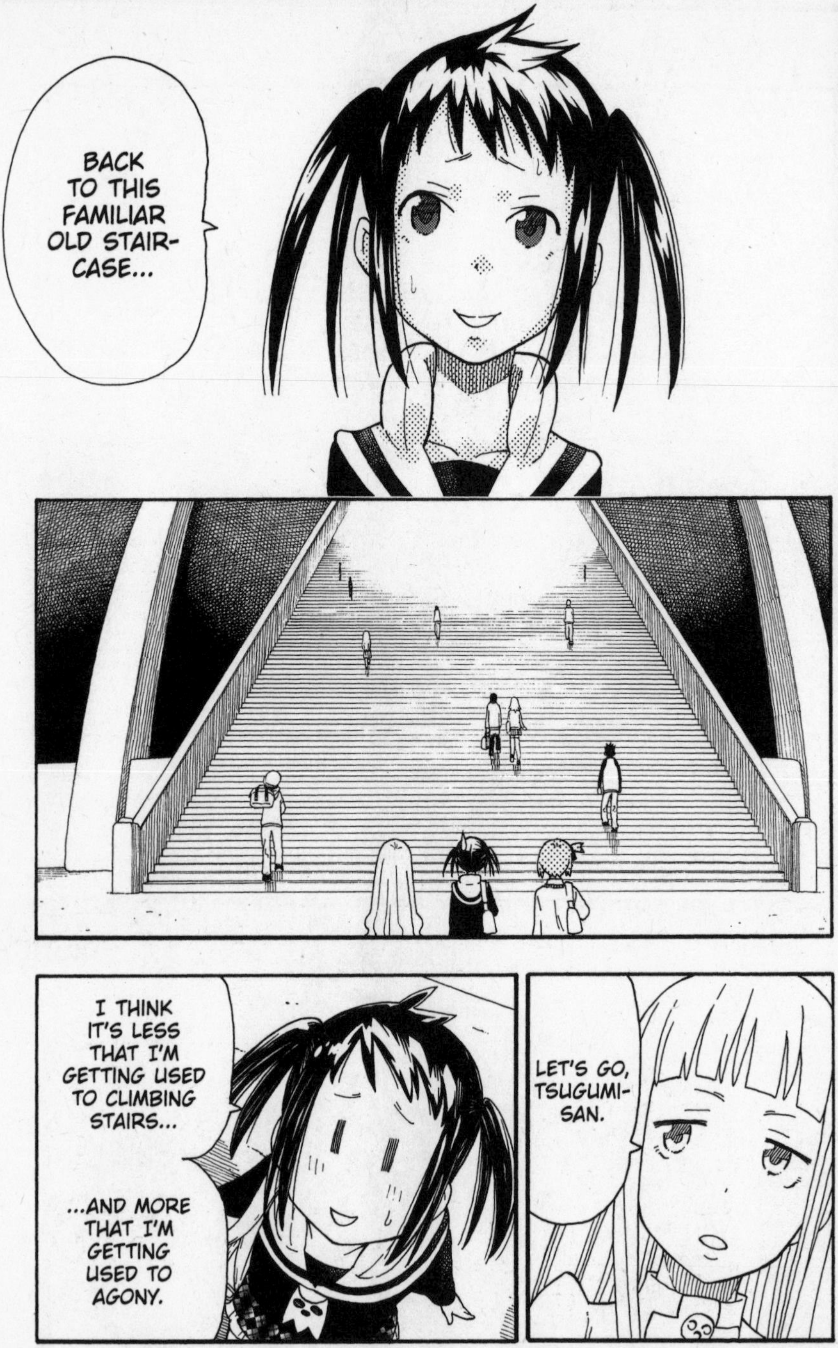
BACK TO THIS FAMILIAR OLD STAIR-CASE...
LET'S GO, TSUGUMI-SAN.
I THINK IT'S LESS THAT I'M GETTING USED TO CLIMBING STAIRS...
...AND MORE THAT I'M GETTING USED TO AGONY.

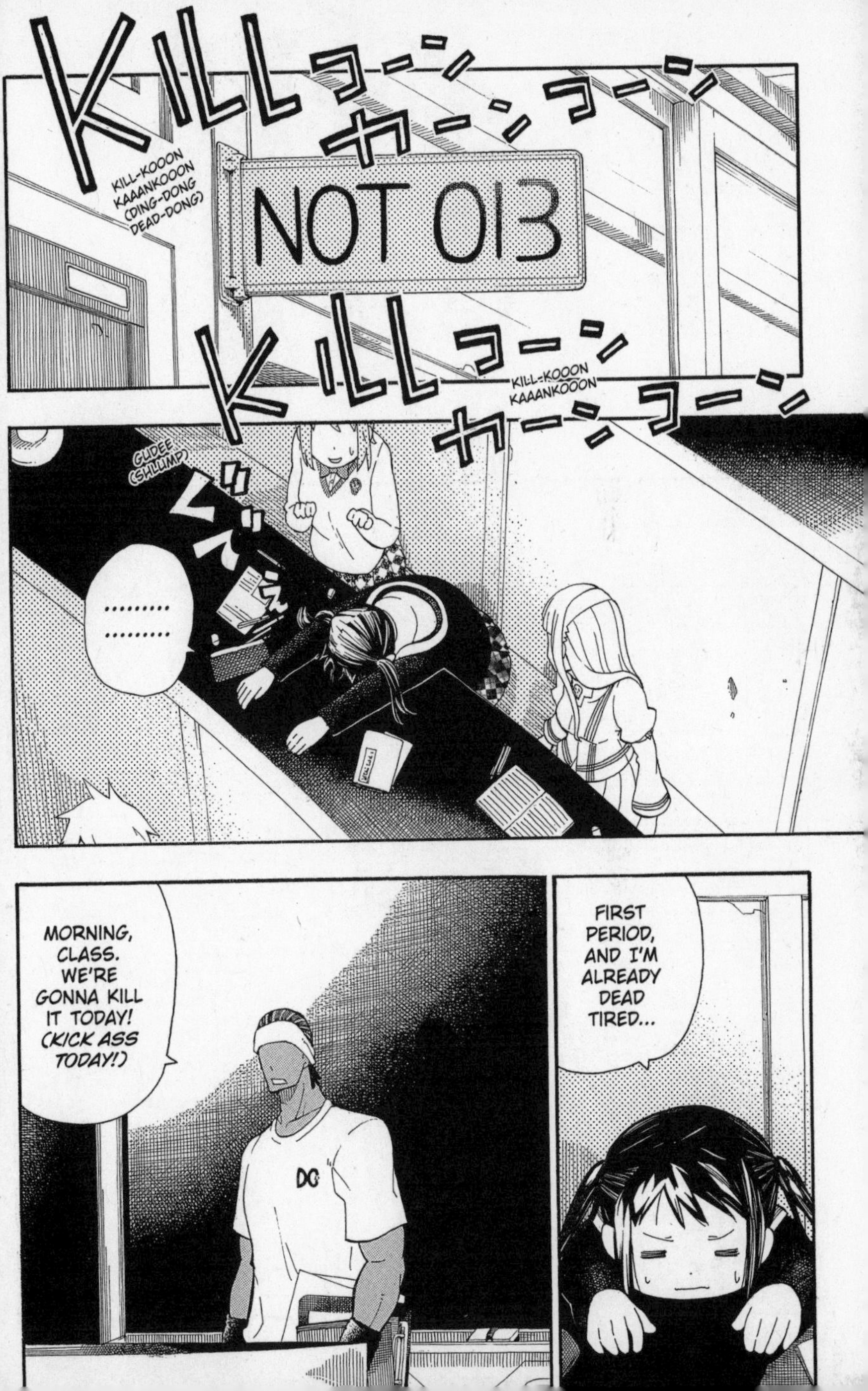
KILL
KILL-KOOON KAAANKOOON (DING-DONG DEAD-DONG)
NOT 013
KILL
KILL-KOOON KAAANKOOON
GUDEE (SHLUMP)
....
....
FIRST PERIOD, AND I'M ALREADY DEAD TIRED...
MORNING, CLASS. WE'RE GONNA KILL IT TODAY! (KICK ASS TODAY!)

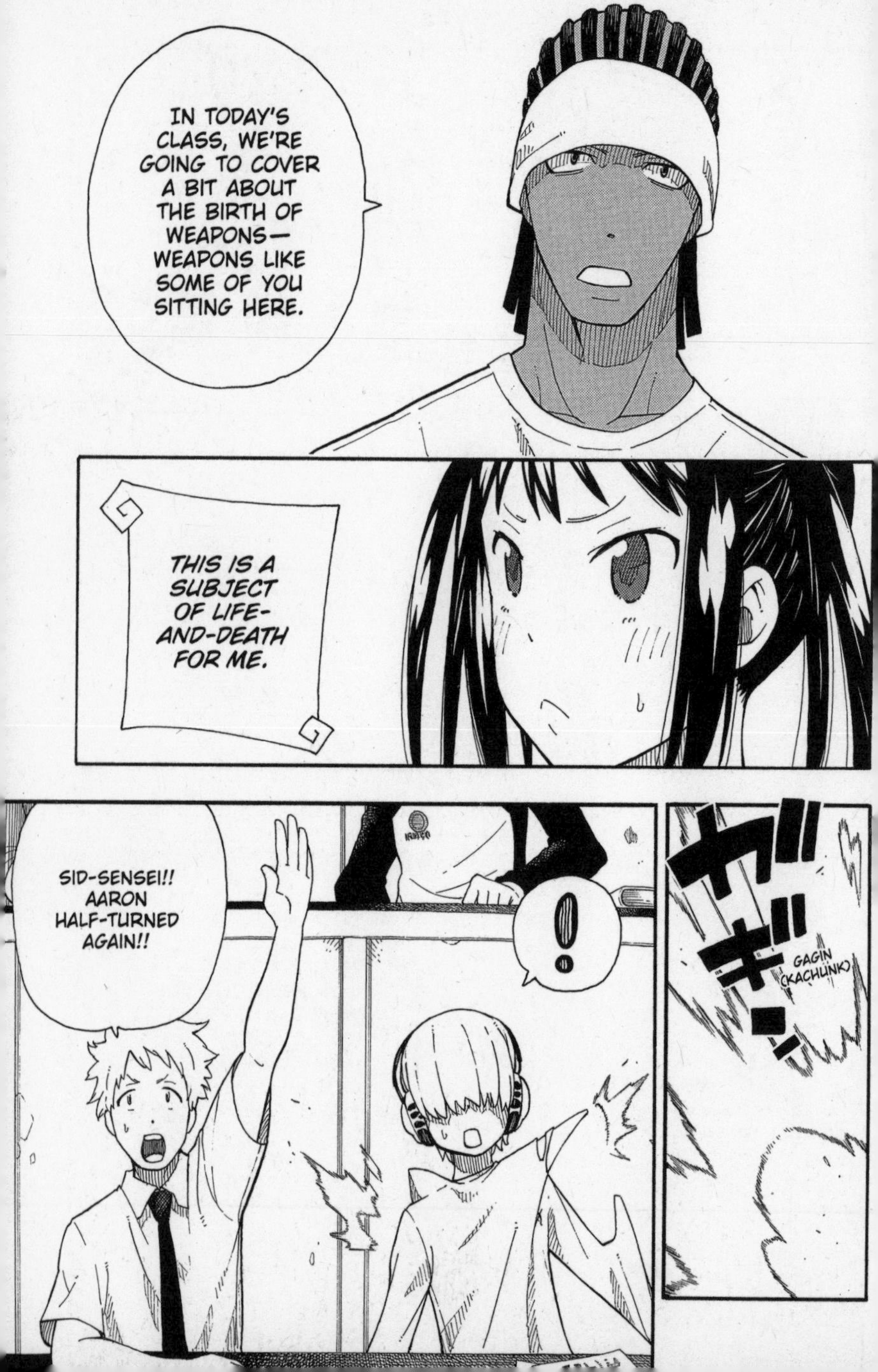
IN TODAY'S CLASS, WE'RE GOING TO COVER A BIT ABOUT THE BIRTH OF WEAPONS—WEAPONS LIKE SOME OF YOU SITTING HERE.
THIS IS A SUBJECT OF LIFE-AND-DEATH FOR ME.
GAGIN (KACHUNK)
!
SID-SENSEI!! AARON HALF-TURNED AGAIN!!

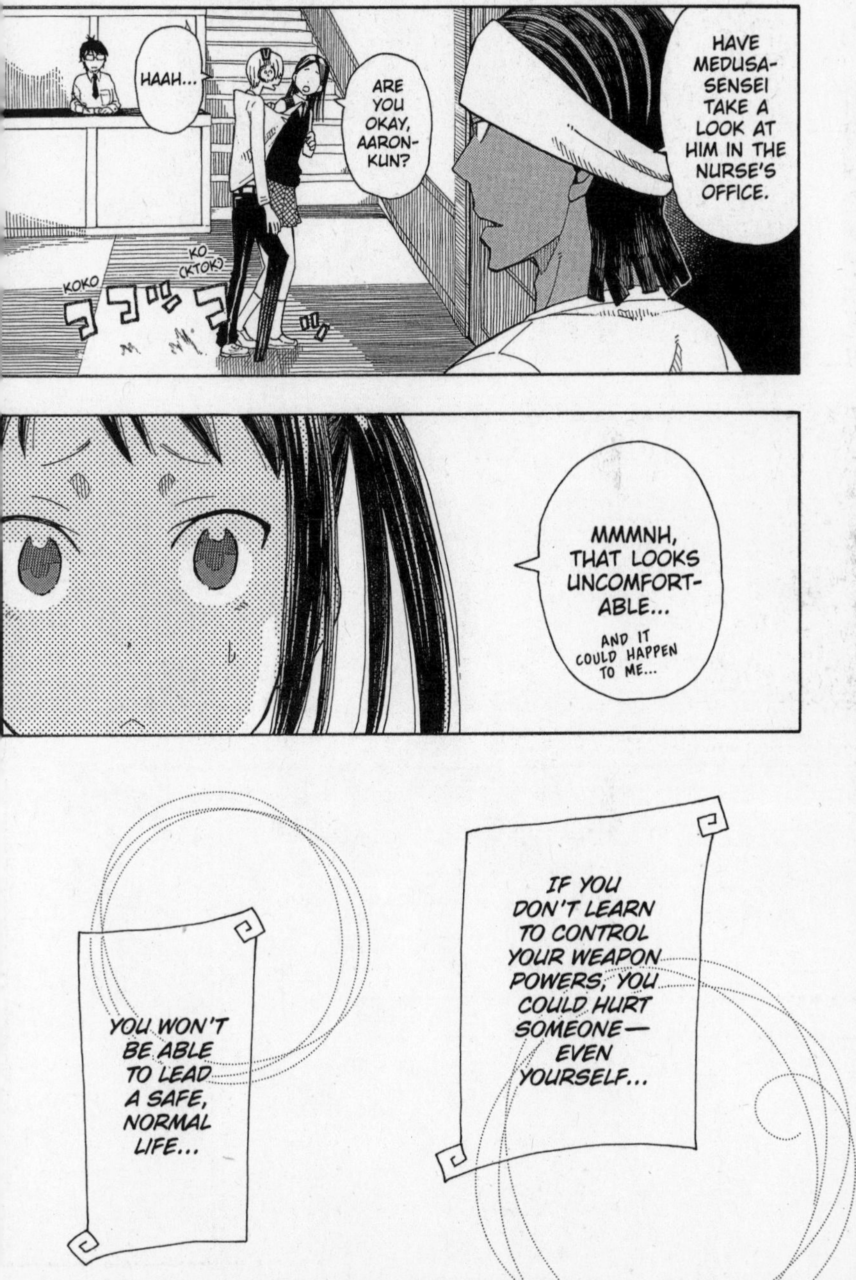
HAVE MEDUSA-SENSEI TAKE A LOOK AT HIM IN THE NURSE'S OFFICE.
ARE YOU OKAY, AARON-KUN?
HAAH...
KO (KTOK)
KOKO
MMMNH, THAT LOOKS UNCOMFORT-ABLE...
AND IT COULD HAPPEN TO ME...
IF YOU DON'T LEARN TO CONTROL YOUR WEAPON POWERS, YOU COULD HURT SOMEONE—EVEN YOURSELF...
YOU WON'T BE ABLE TO LEAD A SAFE, NORMAL LIFE...

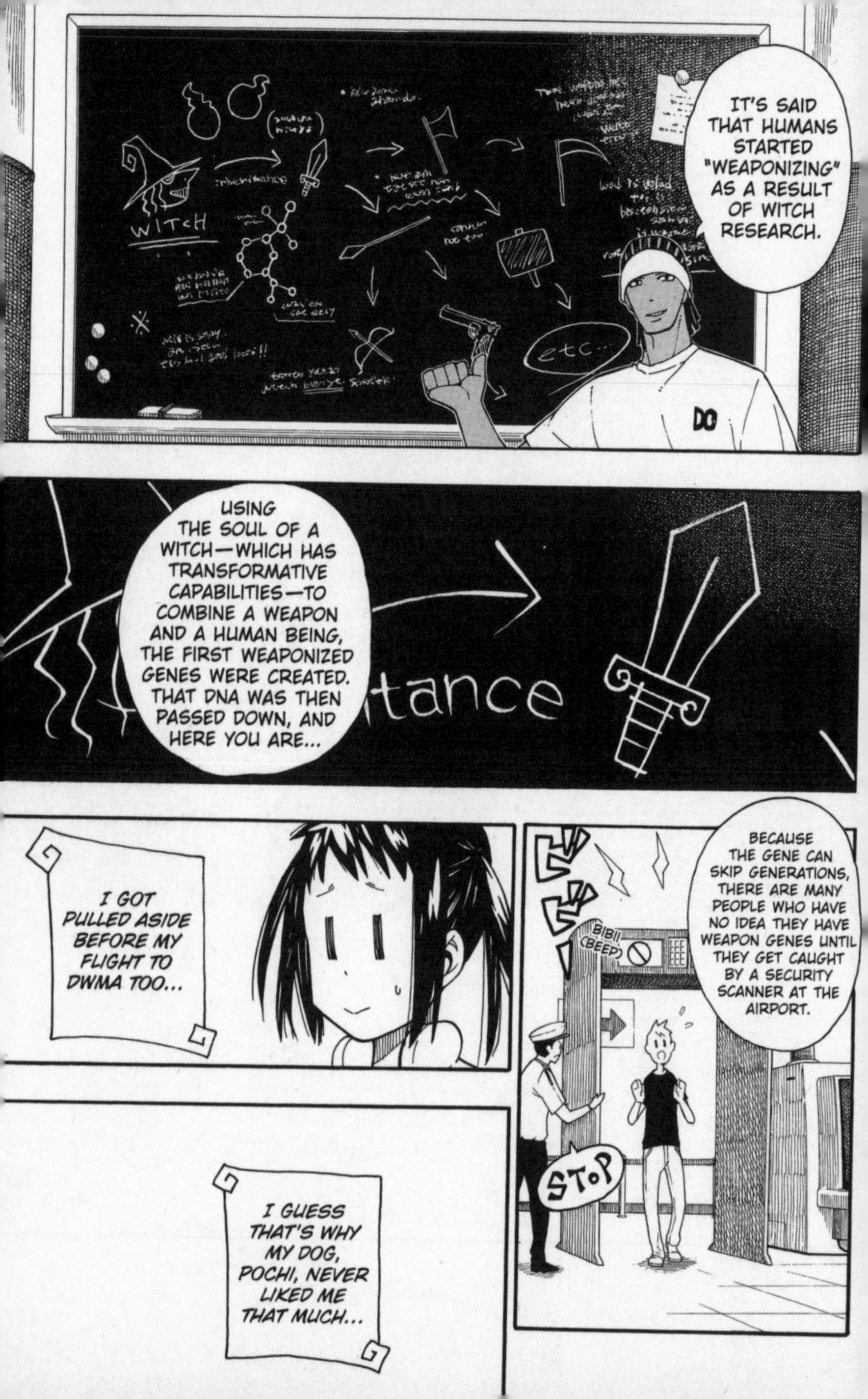
WITCH
inheritance
etc...
IT'S SAID THAT HUMANS STARTED "WEAPONIZING" AS A RESULT OF WITCH RESEARCH.
DO
USING THE SOUL OF A WITCH—WHICH HAS TRANSFORMATIVE CAPABILITIES—TO COMBINE A WEAPON AND A HUMAN BEING, THE FIRST WEAPONIZED GENES WERE CREATED. THAT DNA WAS THEN PASSED DOWN, AND HERE YOU ARE...
itance
BECAUSE THE GENE CAN SKIP GENERATIONS, THERE ARE MANY PEOPLE WHO HAVE NO IDEA THEY HAVE WEAPON GENES UNTIL THEY GET CAUGHT BY A SECURITY SCANNER AT THE AIRPORT.
BIBI! (BEEP)
STOP
I GOT PULLED ASIDE BEFORE MY FLIGHT TO DWMA TOO...
I GUESS THAT'S WHY MY DOG, POCHI, NEVER LIKED ME THAT MUCH...

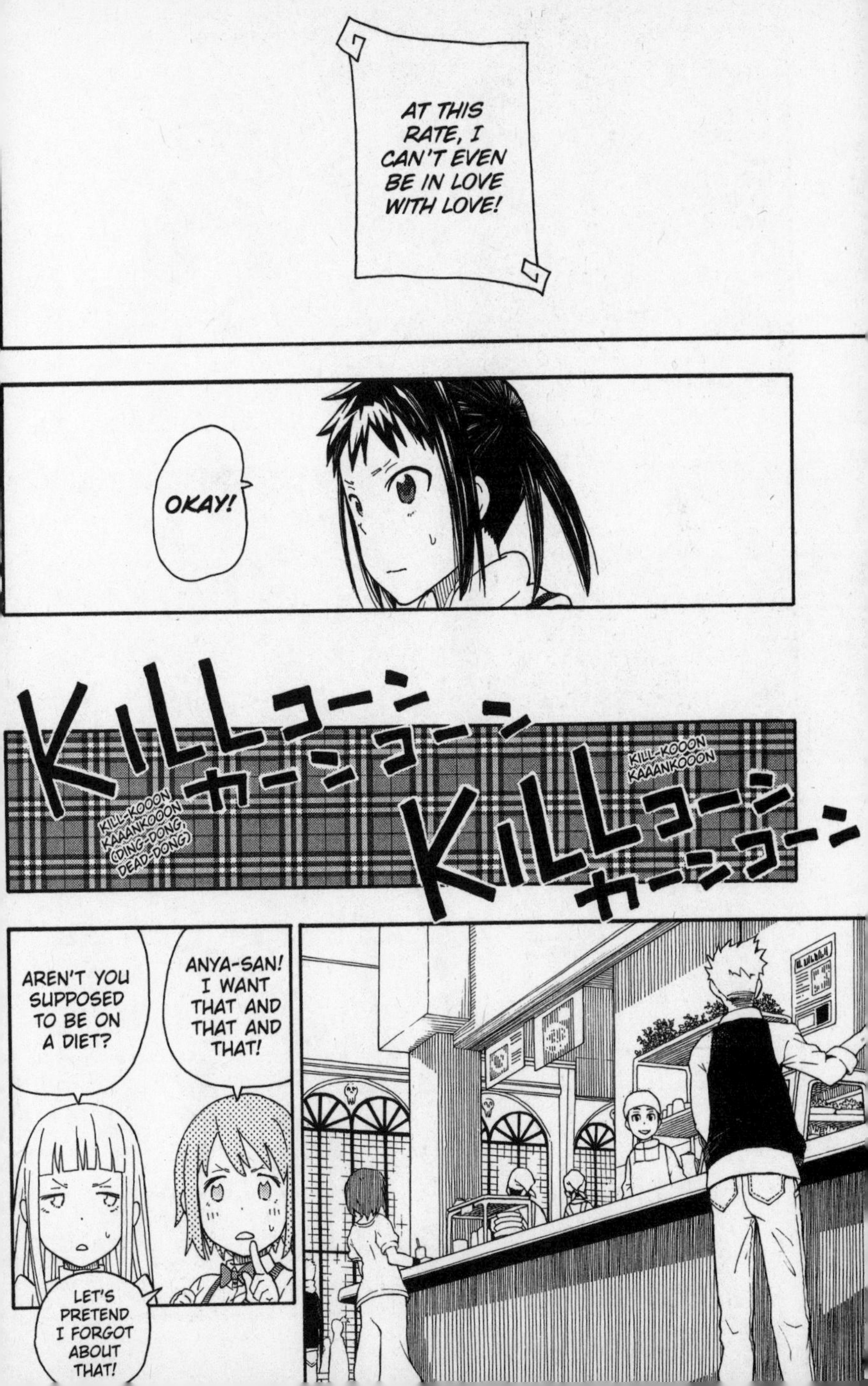

AT THIS RATE, I CAN'T EVEN BE IN LOVE WITH LOVE!
OKAY!
KILL-KOOON KAAANKOOON
KILL-KOOON KAAANKOOON (DING-DONG DEAD-DONG)
ANYA-SAN! I WANT THAT AND THAT AND THAT!
AREN'T YOU SUPPOSED TO BE ON A DIET?
LET'S PRETEND I FORGOT ABOUT THAT!

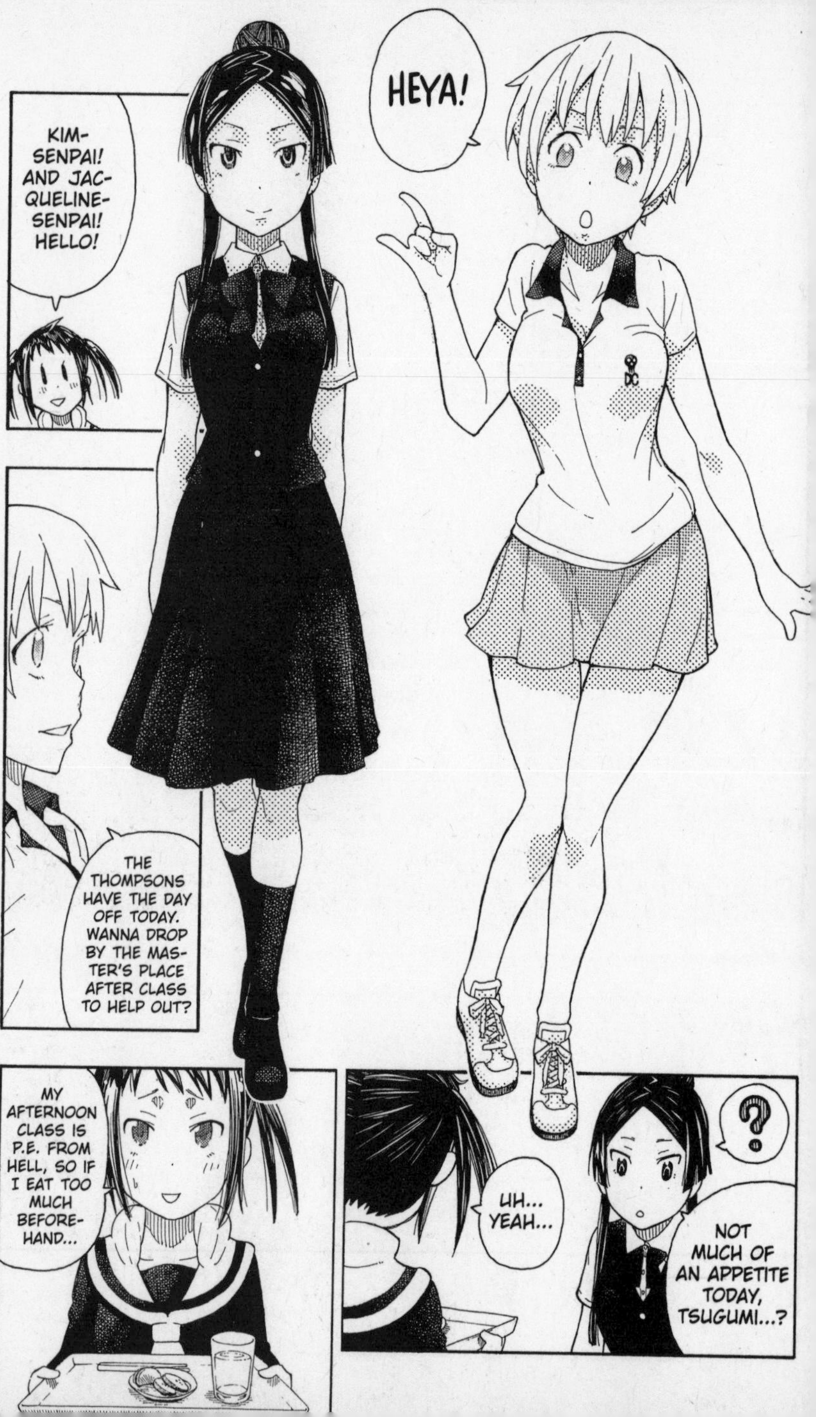
HEYA!
KIM-SENPAI! AND JACQUELINE-SENPAI! HELLO!
THE THOMPSONS HAVE THE DAY OFF TODAY. WANNA DROP BY THE MASTER'S PLACE AFTER CLASS TO HELP OUT?
?
NOT MUCH OF AN APPETITE TODAY, TSUGUMI...?
UH... YEAH...
MY AFTERNOON CLASS IS P.E. FROM HELL, SO IF I EAT TOO MUCH BEFOREHAND...

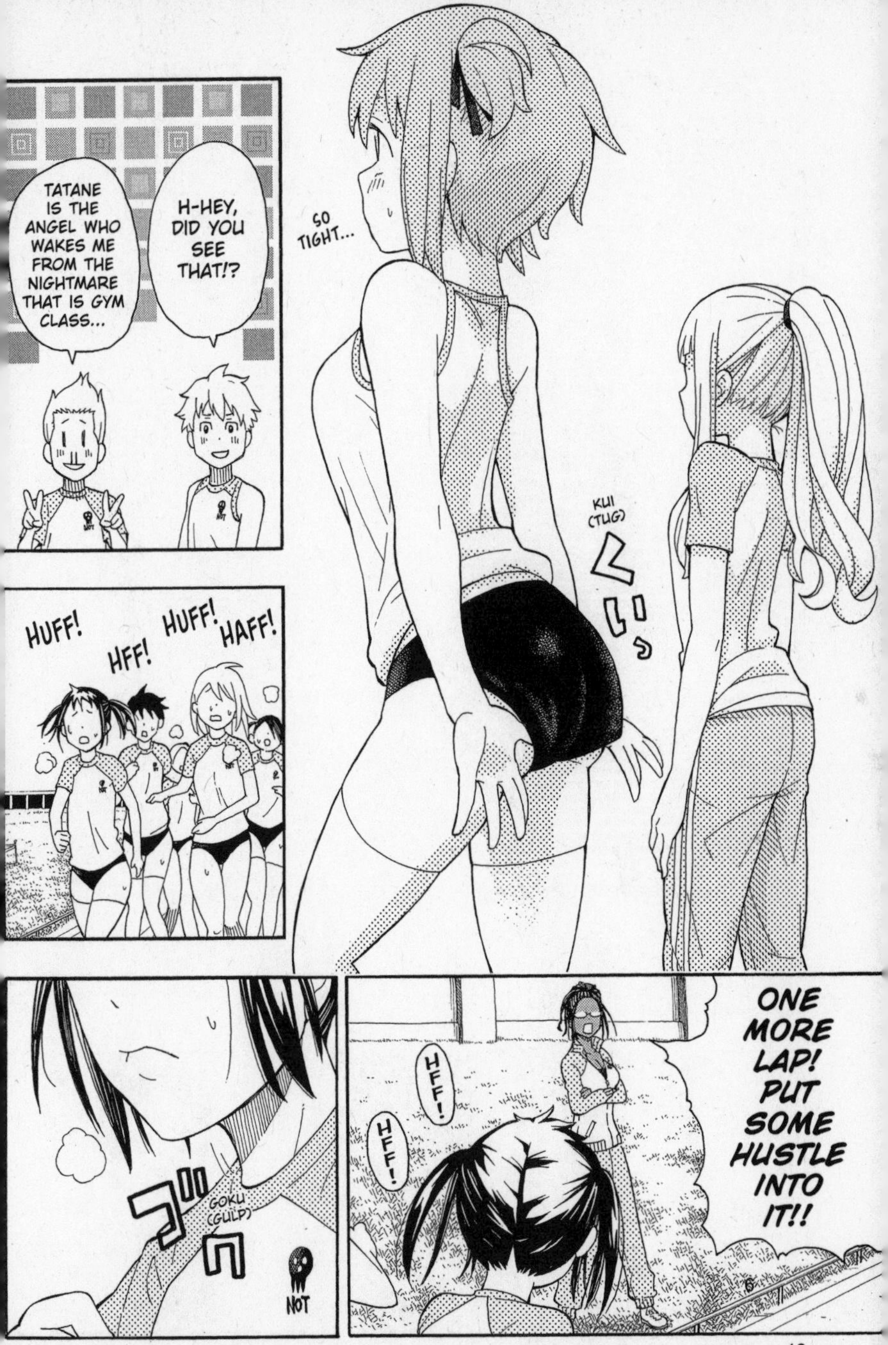
SO TIGHT...
KUI (TUG)
H-HEY, DID YOU SEE THAT!?
TATANE IS THE ANGEL WHO WAKES ME FROM THE NIGHTMARE THAT IS GYM CLASS...
HAFF!
HUFF!
HFF!
HUFF!
ONE MORE LAP! PUT SOME HUSTLE INTO IT!!
HFF!
HFF!
GOKU (GULP)

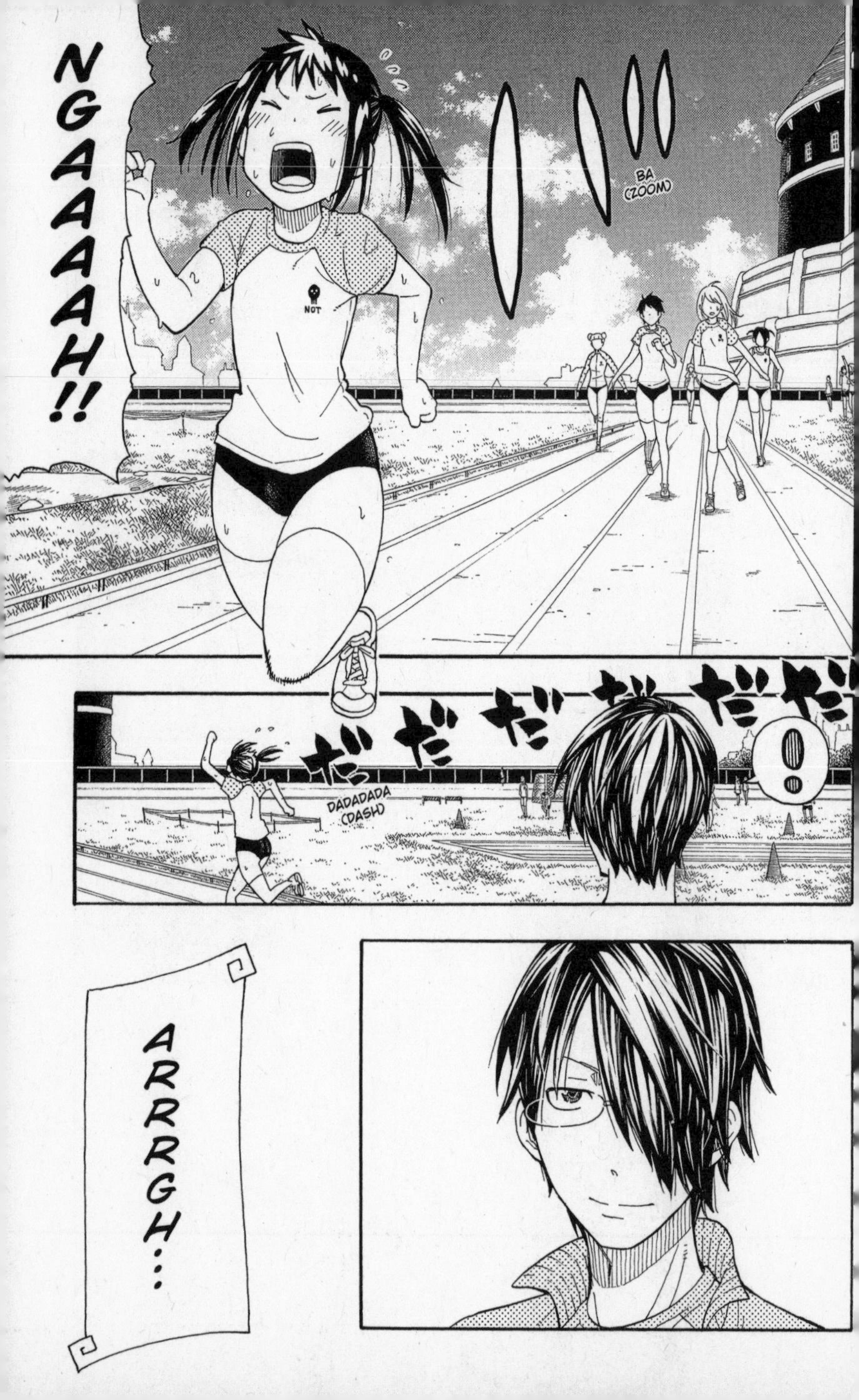
BA (ZOOM)
NGAAAAAH!!
!
DADADADA (DASH)
ARRRGH...

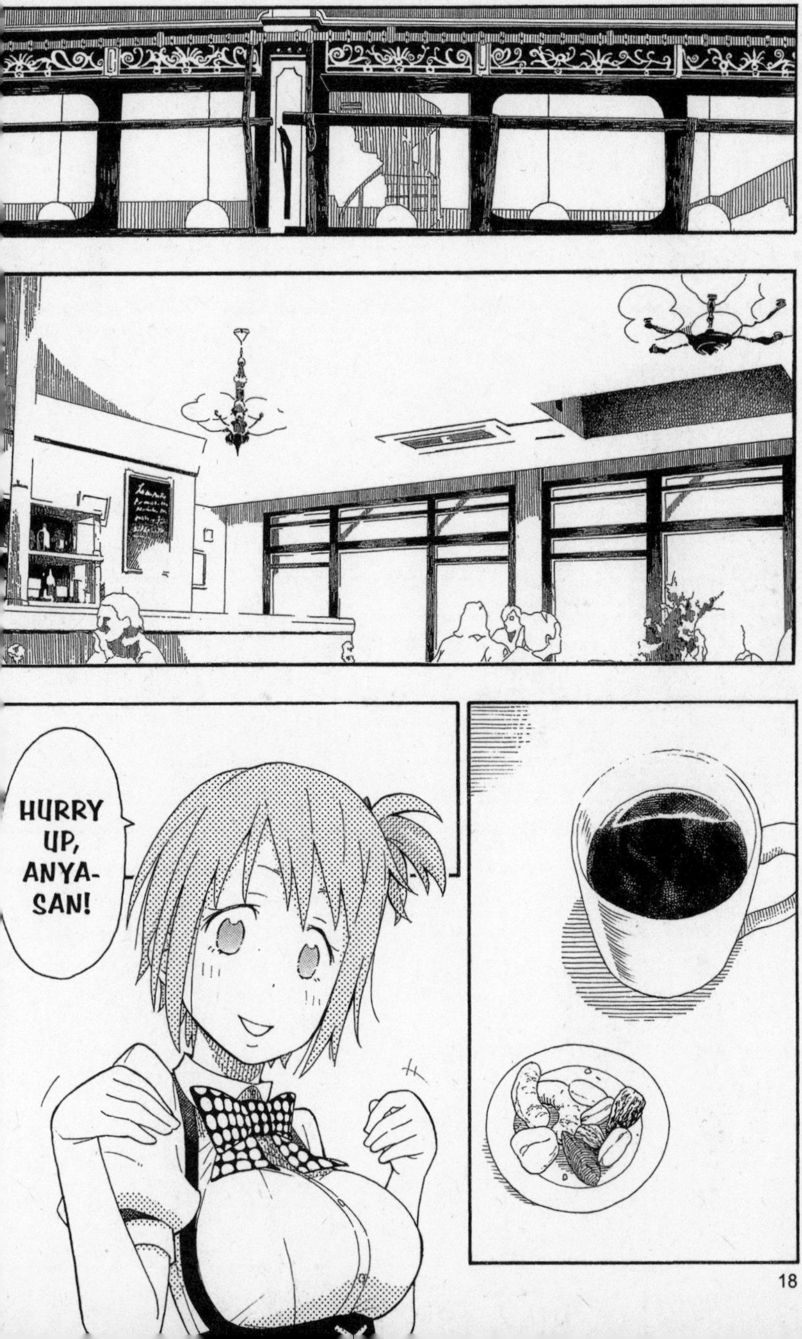
HURRY UP, ANYA-SAN!

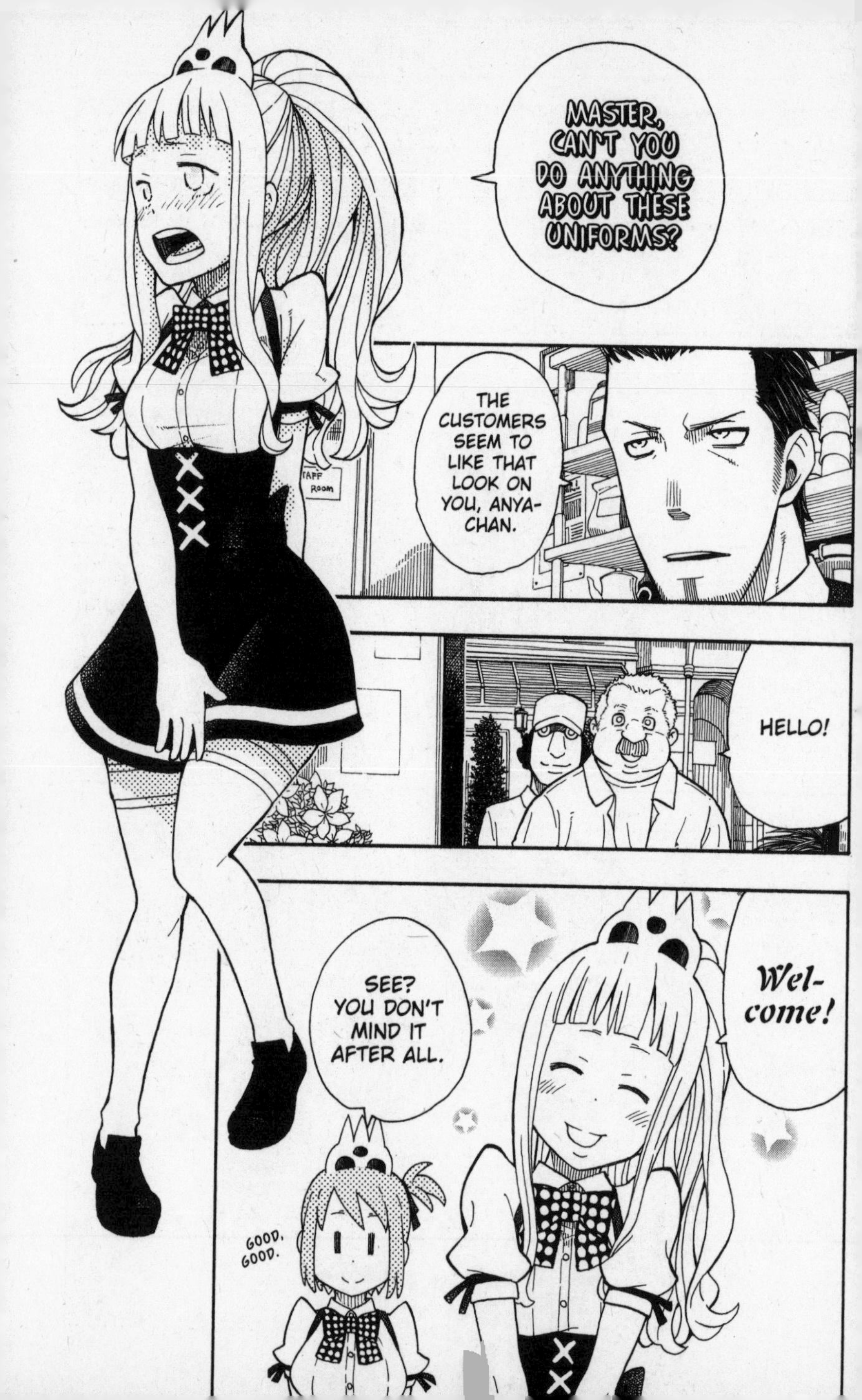
MASTER, CAN'T YOU DO ANYTHING ABOUT THESE UNIFORMS?
THE CUSTOMERS SEEM TO LIKE THAT LOOK ON YOU, ANYA-CHAN.
HELLO!
Wel-come!
SEE? YOU DON'T MIND IT AFTER ALL.
GOOD, GOOD.

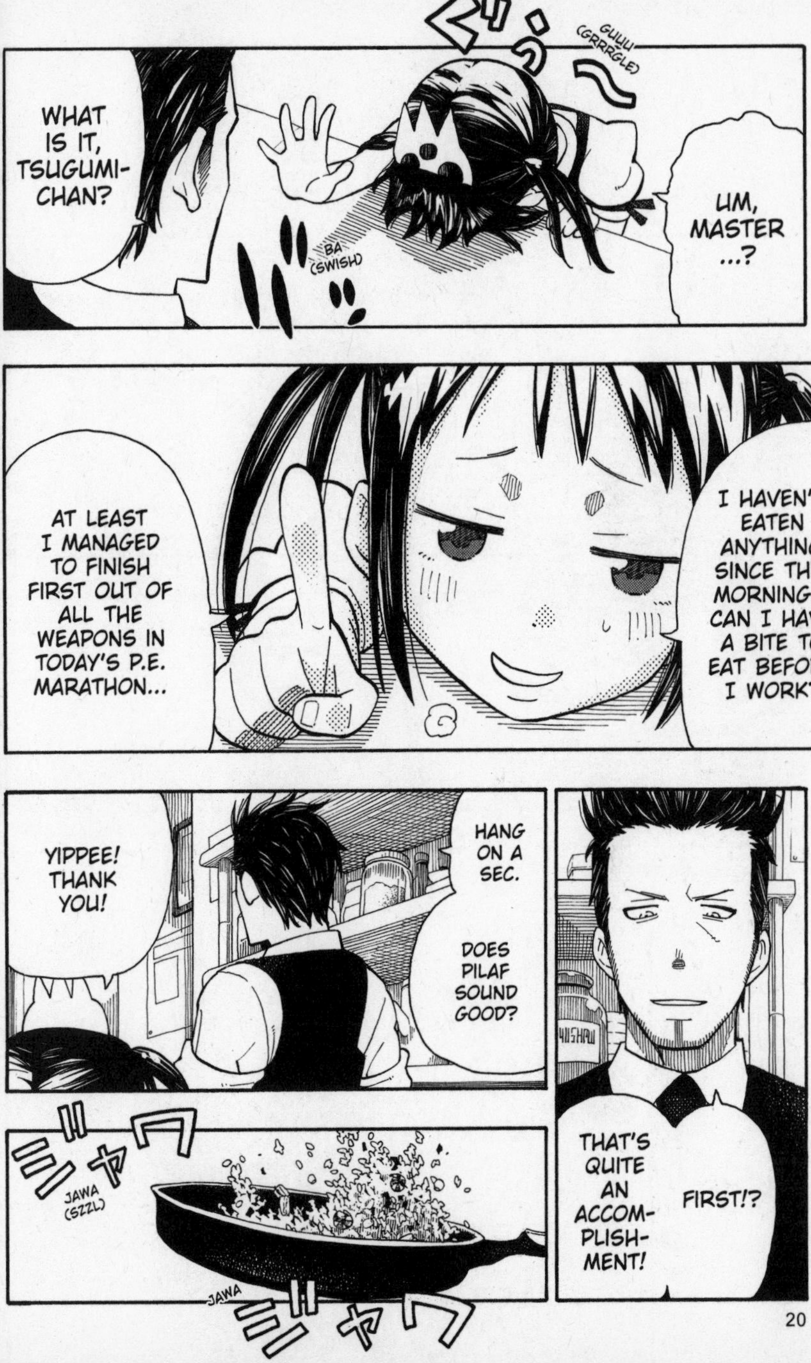
GUUU (GRRRGLE)
UM, MASTER...?
WHAT IS IT, TSUGUMI-CHAN?
BA (SWISH)
I HAVEN'T EATEN ANYTHING SINCE THIS MORNING... CAN I HAVE A BITE TO EAT BEFORE I WORK?
AT LEAST I MANAGED TO FINISH FIRST OUT OF ALL THE WEAPONS IN TODAY'S P.E. MARATHON...
FIRST!?
THAT'S QUITE AN ACCOMPLISHMENT!
HANG ON A SEC.
DOES PILAF SOUND GOOD?
YIPPEE! THANK YOU!
JAWA (SZZL)
JAWA

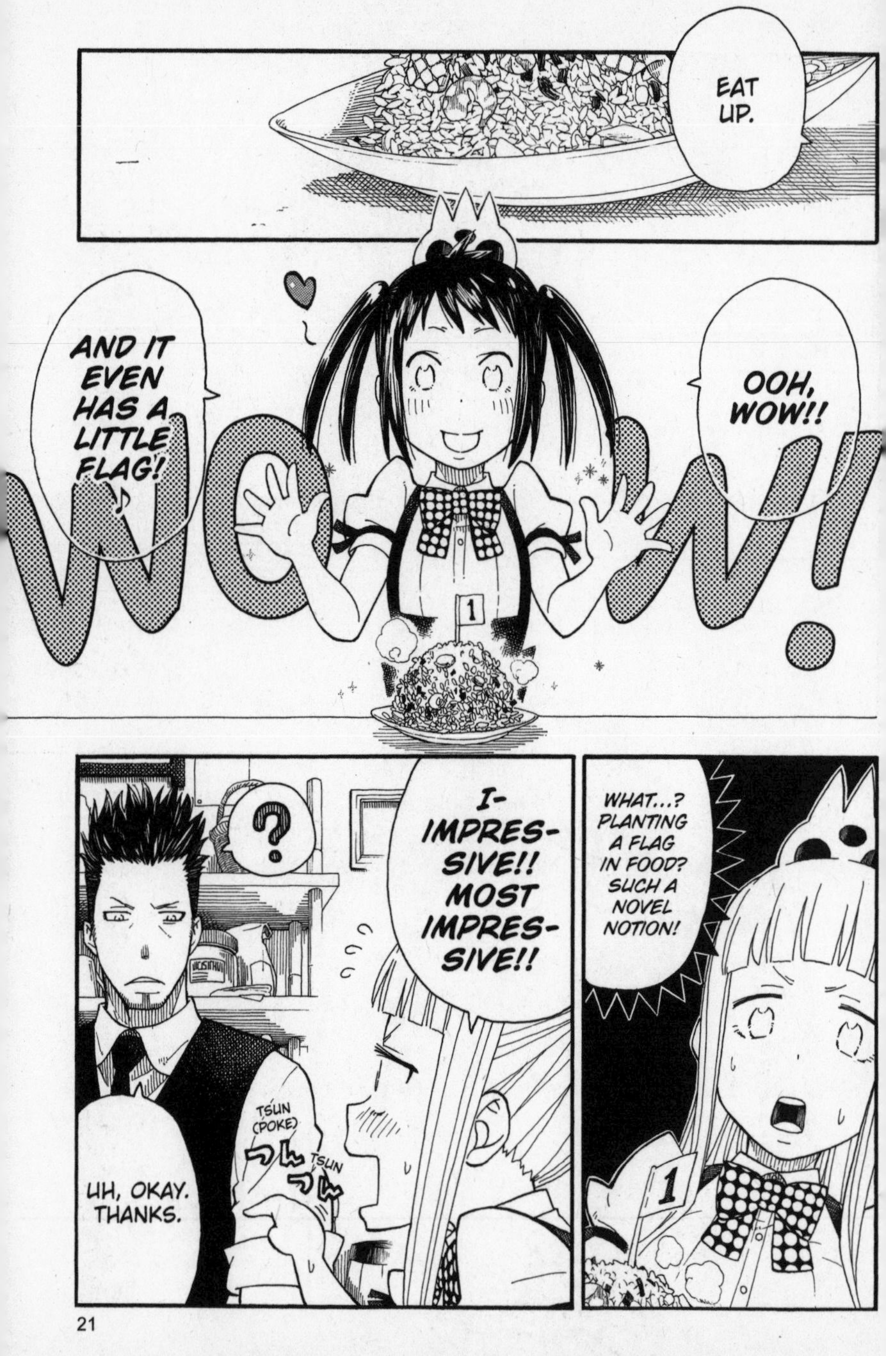
EAT UP.
OOH, WOW!!
WOW!
AND IT EVEN HAS A LITTLE FLAG! ♪
1
WHAT...? PLANTING A FLAG IN FOOD? SUCH A NOVEL NOTION!
1
I- IMPRESSIVE!! MOST IMPRESSIVE!!
?
TSUN (POKE)
TSUN
UH, OKAY. THANKS.

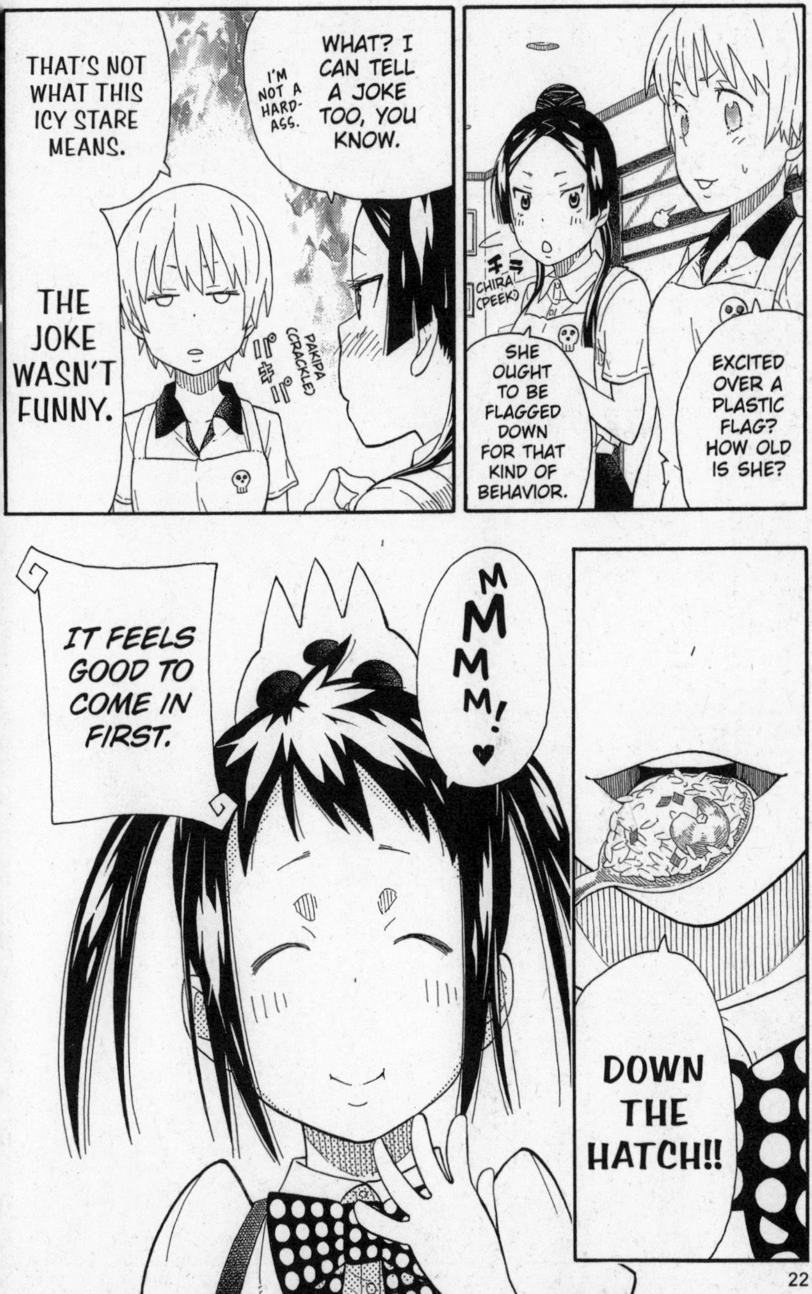
CHIRA (PEEK)
EXCITED OVER A PLASTIC FLAG? HOW OLD IS SHE?
SHE OUGHT TO BE FLAGGED DOWN FOR THAT KIND OF BEHAVIOR.
WHAT? I CAN TELL A JOKE TOO, YOU KNOW.
I'M NOT A HARD-ASS.
THAT'S NOT WHAT THIS ICY STARE MEANS.
PAKIPA (CRACKLE)
THE JOKE WASN'T FUNNY.
DOWN THE HATCH!!
MMMM! ♥
IT FEELS GOOD TO COME IN FIRST.

SOUL EATER NOT!

SOUL EATER NOT!

HAPPY LIFE

ATSUSHI OHKUBO

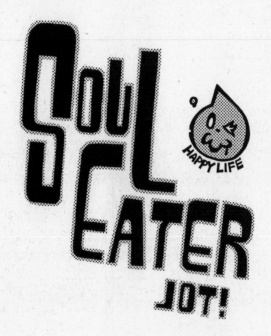

PART 7

DEMONSTRATING A JOT

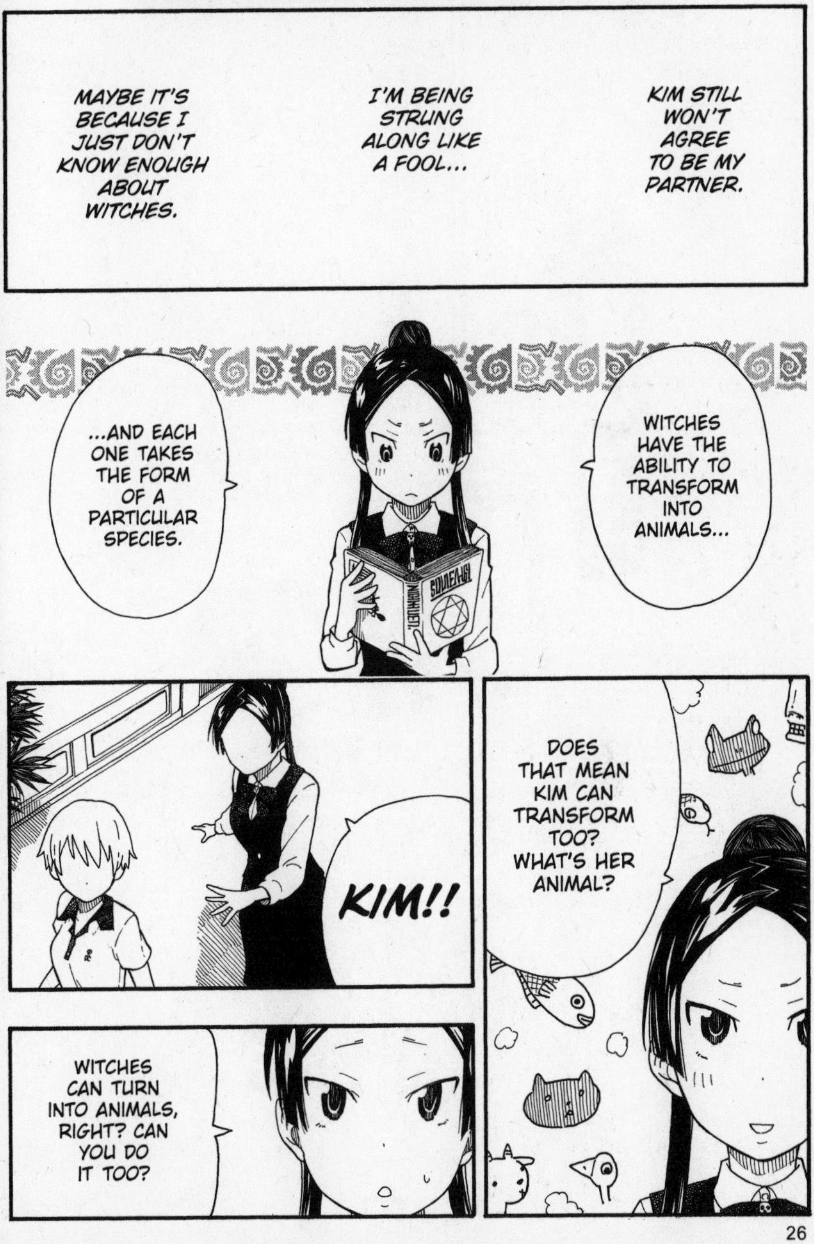
KIM STILL WON'T AGREE TO BE MY PARTNER.
I'M BEING STRUNG ALONG LIKE A FOOL...
MAYBE IT'S BECAUSE I JUST DON'T KNOW ENOUGH ABOUT WITCHES.
WITCHES HAVE THE ABILITY TO TRANSFORM INTO ANIMALS...
...AND EACH ONE TAKES THE FORM OF A PARTICULAR SPECIES.
DOES THAT MEAN KIM CAN TRANSFORM TOO? WHAT'S HER ANIMAL?
KIM!!
WITCHES CAN TURN INTO ANIMALS, RIGHT? CAN YOU DO IT TOO?

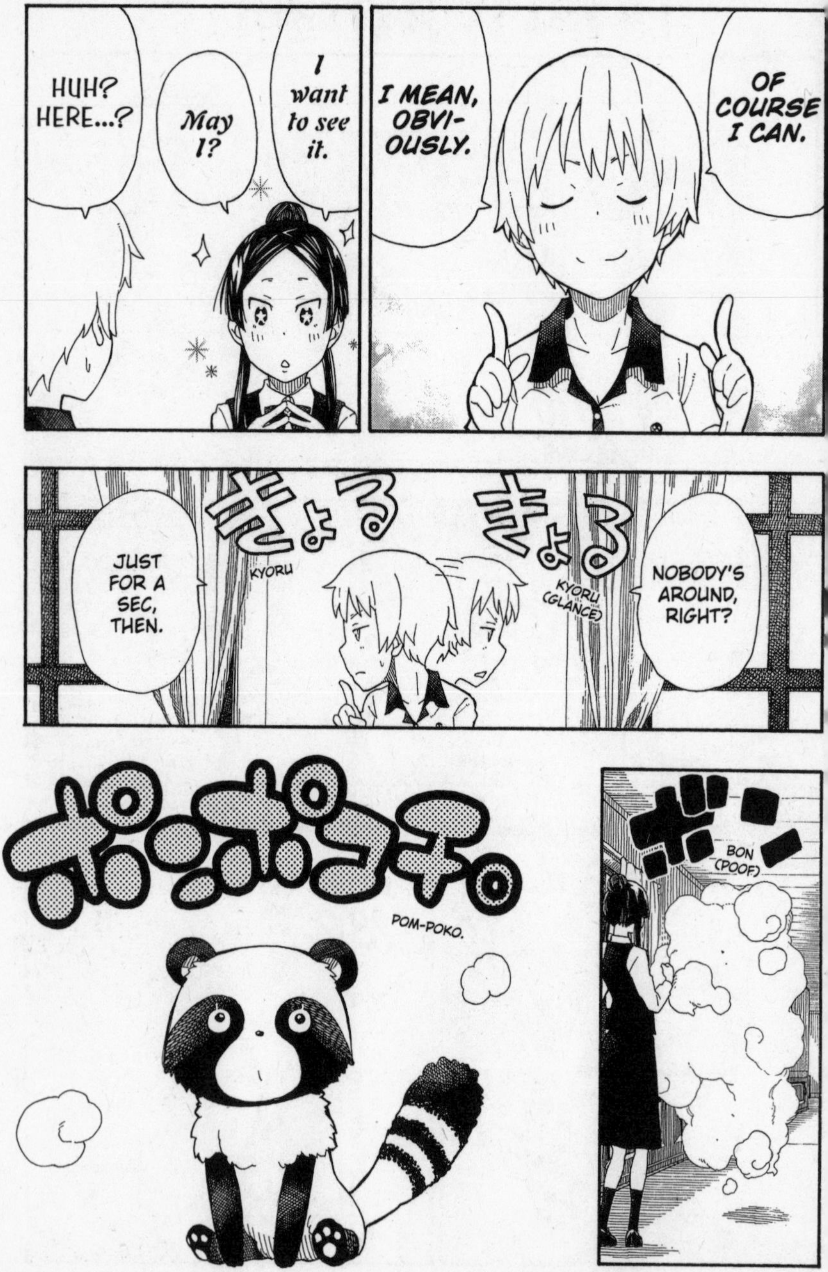
OF COURSE I CAN.
I MEAN, OBVI-OUSLY.
I want to see it.
May I?
HUH? HERE...?
NOBODY'S AROUND, RIGHT?
きょろ
KYORU (GLANCE)
きょろ
KYORU
JUST FOR A SEC, THEN.
ボン
BON (POOF)
ポンポコ。
POM-POKO.

A JOT OF REVENGE

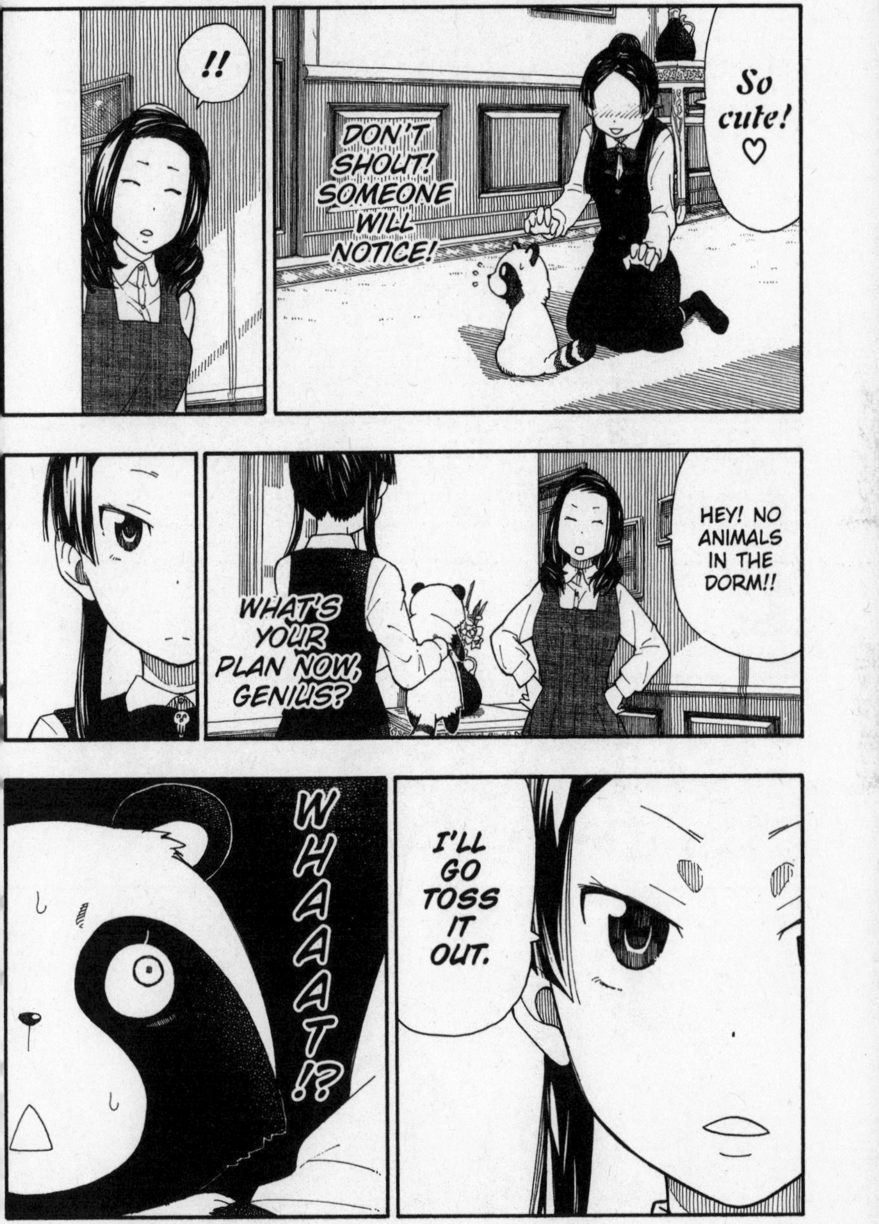
So cute! ♡
DON'T SHOUT! SOMEONE WILL NOTICE!
!!
HEY! NO ANIMALS IN THE DORM!!
WHAT'S YOUR PLAN NOW, GENIUS?
I'LL GO TOSS IT OUT.
WHAAAAT!?

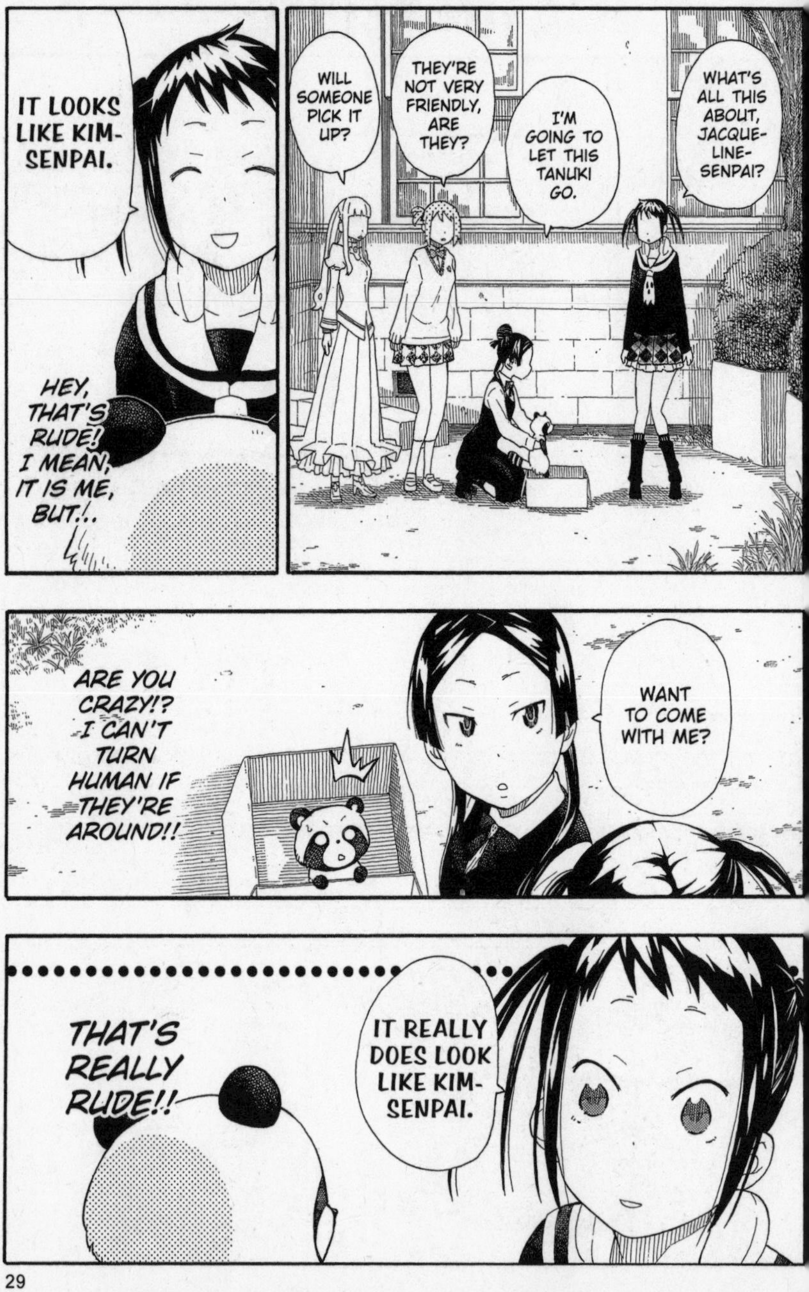
WHAT'S ALL THIS ABOUT, JACQUELINE-SENPAI?
I'M GOING TO LET THIS TANUKI GO.
THEY'RE NOT VERY FRIENDLY, ARE THEY?
WILL SOMEONE PICK IT UP?
IT LOOKS LIKE KIM-SENPAI.
HEY, THAT'S RUDE! I MEAN, IT IS ME, BUT...
WANT TO COME WITH ME?
ARE YOU CRAZY!? I CAN'T TURN HUMAN IF THEY'RE AROUND!!
IT REALLY DOES LOOK LIKE KIM-SENPAI.
THAT'S REALLY RUDE!!

A JOT BETTER

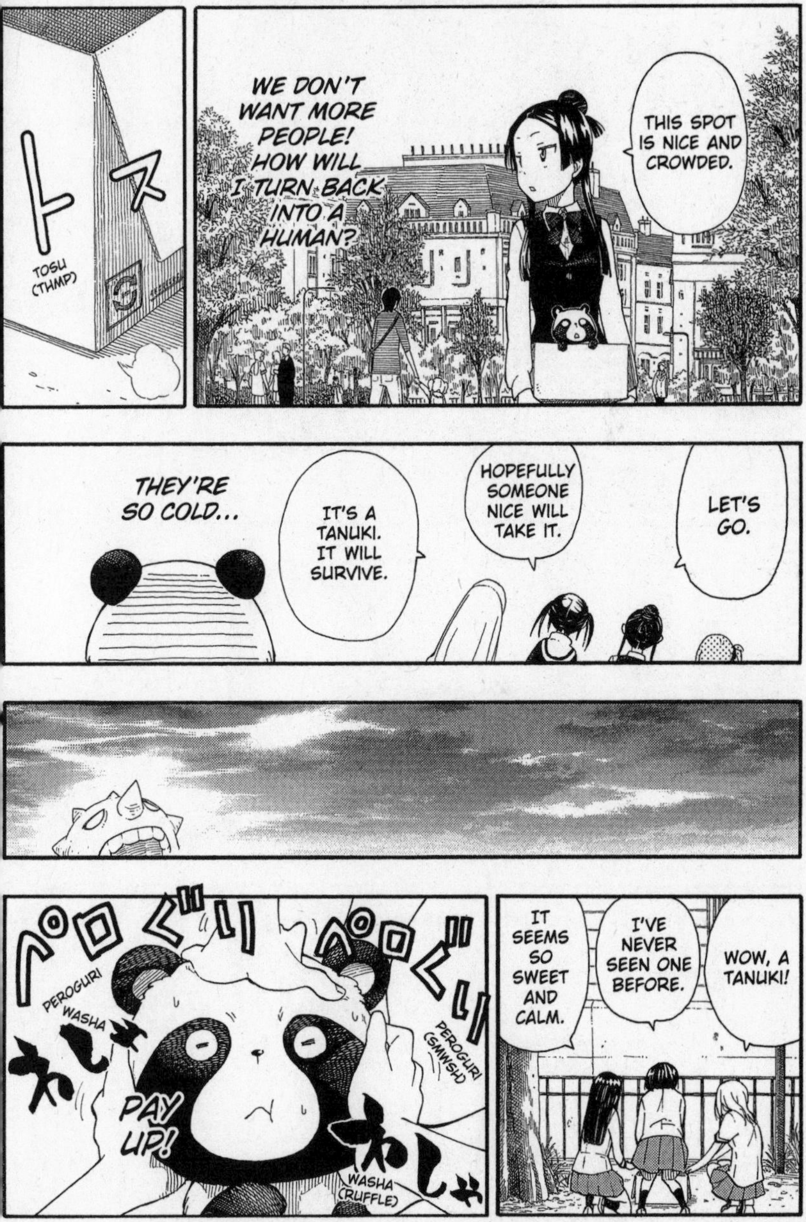
THIS SPOT IS NICE AND CROWDED.
WE DON'T WANT MORE PEOPLE! HOW WILL I TURN BACK INTO A HUMAN?
トス
TOSU (THMP)
LET'S GO.
HOPEFULLY SOMEONE NICE WILL TAKE IT.
IT'S A TANUKI. IT WILL SURVIVE.
THEY'RE SO COLD...
WOW, A TANUKI!
I'VE NEVER SEEN ONE BEFORE.
IT SEEMS SO SWEET AND CALM.
PEROGURI (SMWSH)
WASHA (RUFFLE)
PAY UP!
PEROGURI
WASHA

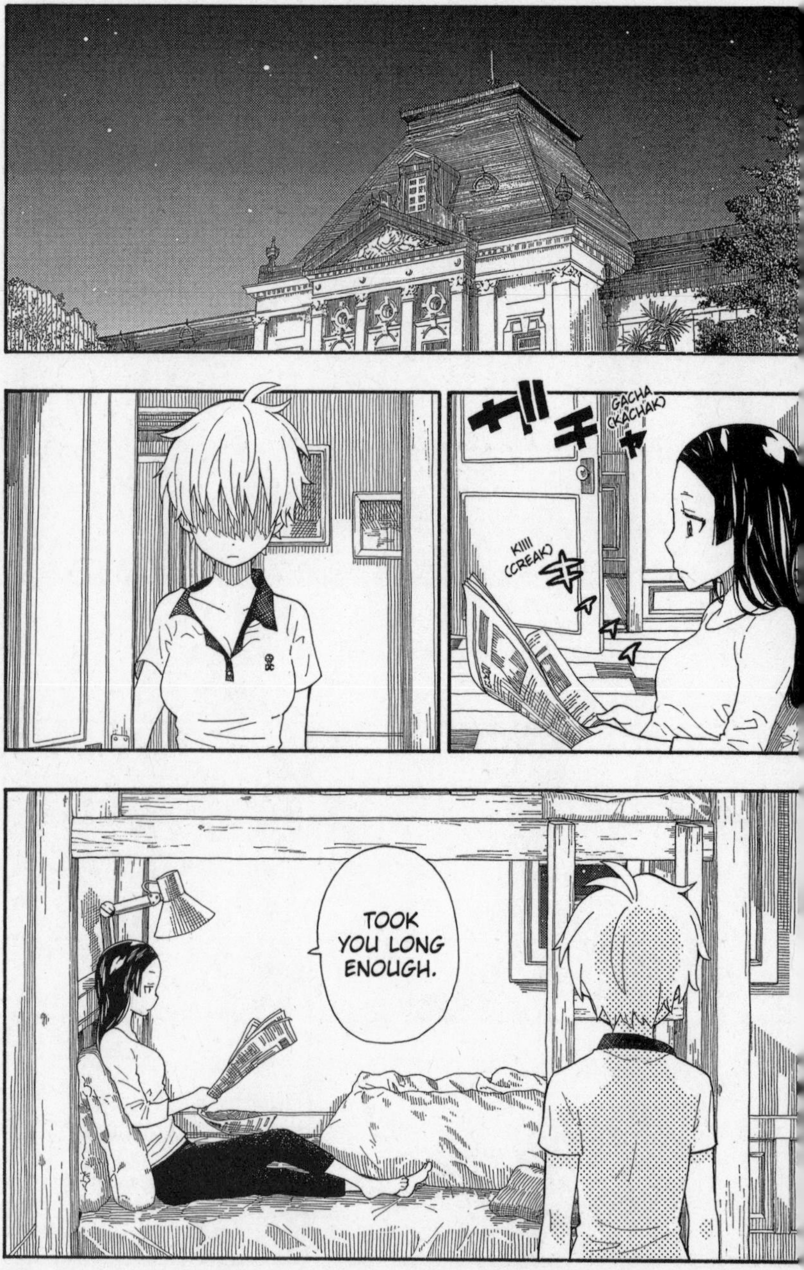
GACHA (KACHAK)
KIIII (CREAK)
TOOK YOU LONG ENOUGH.

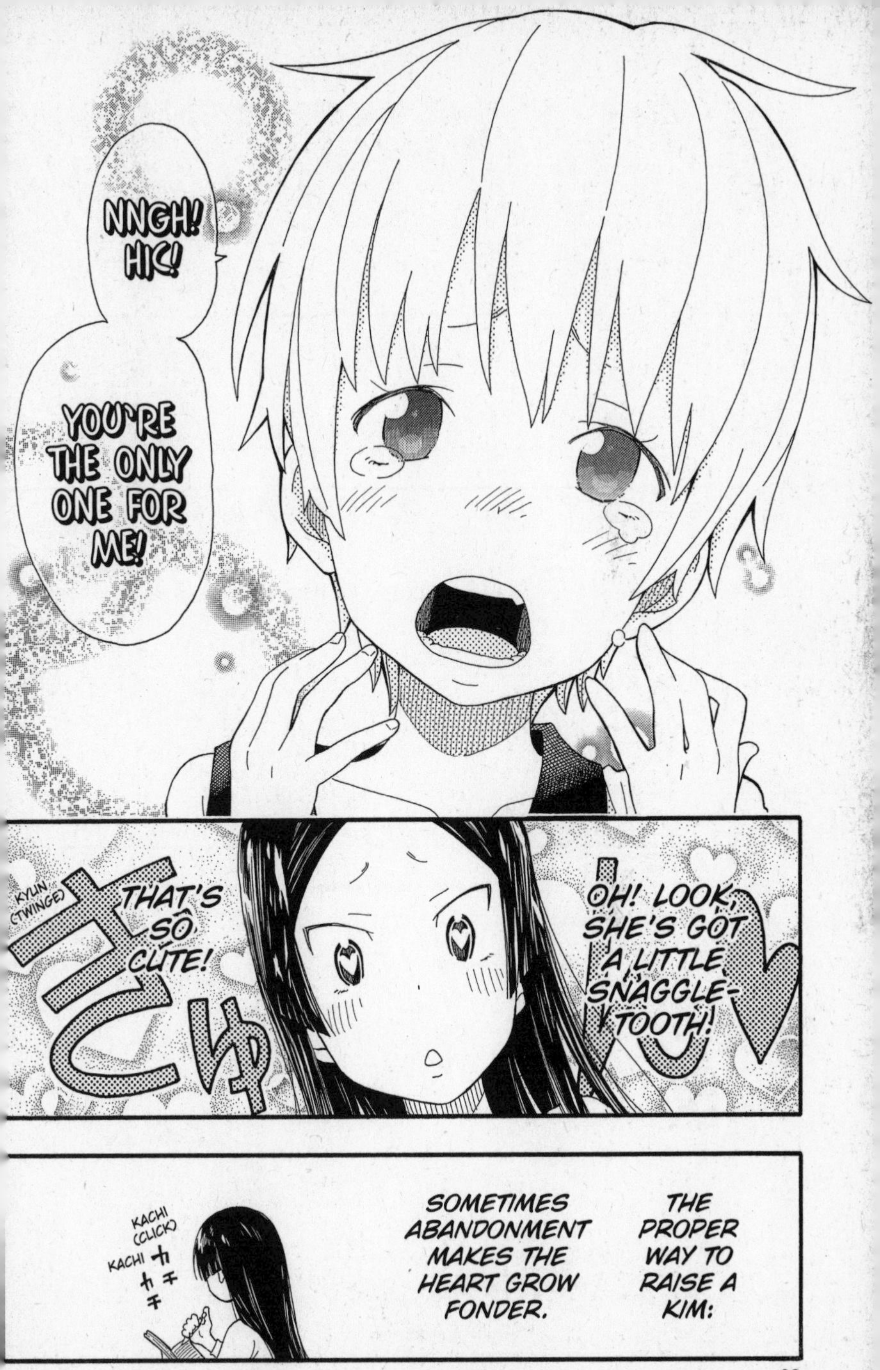
NNGH! HIC!
YOU'RE THE ONLY ONE FOR ME!
OH! LOOK, SHE'S GOT A LITTLE SNAGGLE-TOOTH!
KYUN (TWINGE)
THAT'S SO CUTE!
THE PROPER WAY TO RAISE A KIM:
SOMETIMES ABANDONMENT MAKES THE HEART GROW FONDER.
KACHI (CLICK)
KACHI

SOUL EATER NOT!

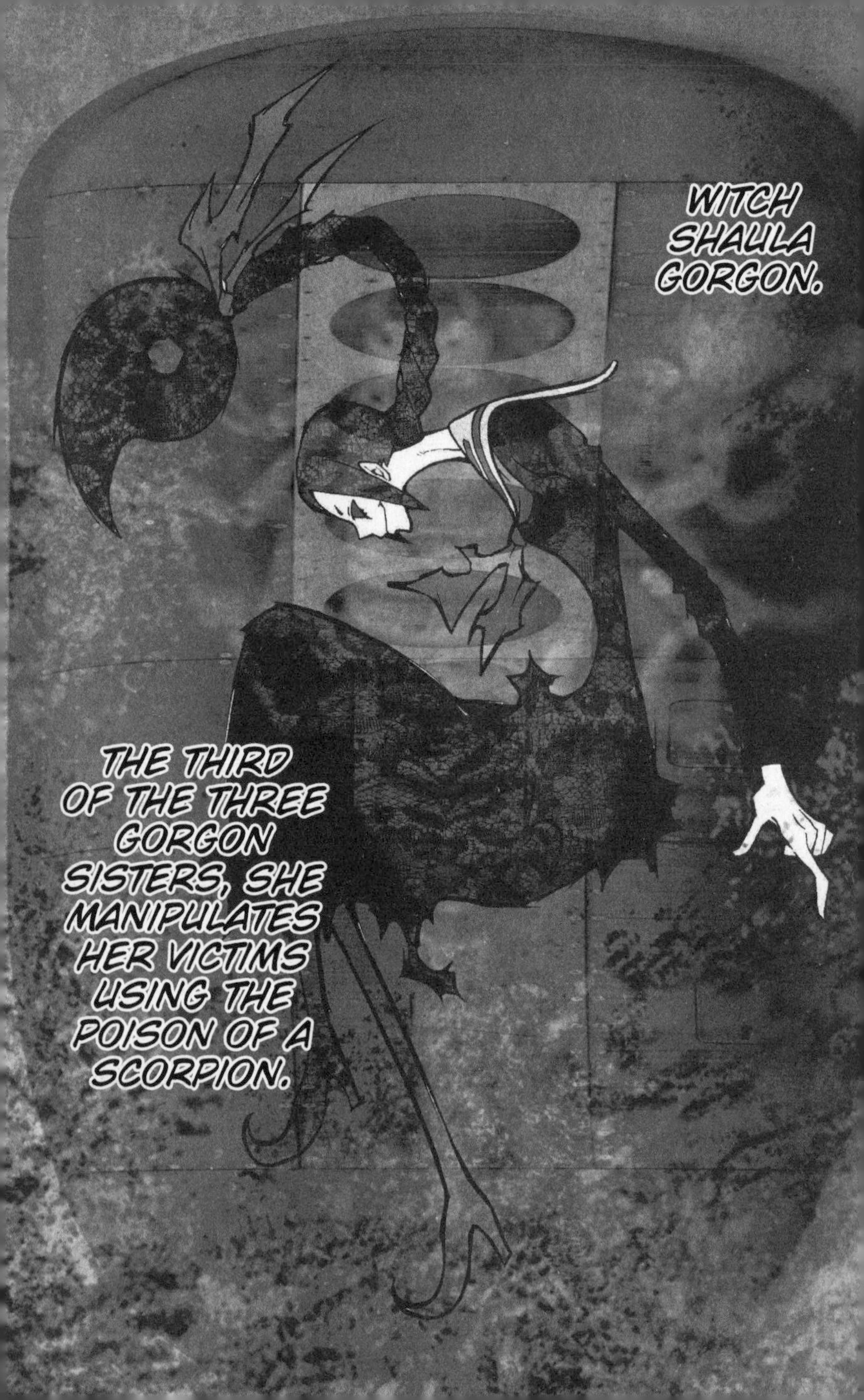
WITCH SHAULA GORGON.
THE THIRD OF THE THREE GORGON SISTERS, SHE MANIPULATES HER VICTIMS USING THE POISON OF A SCORPION.

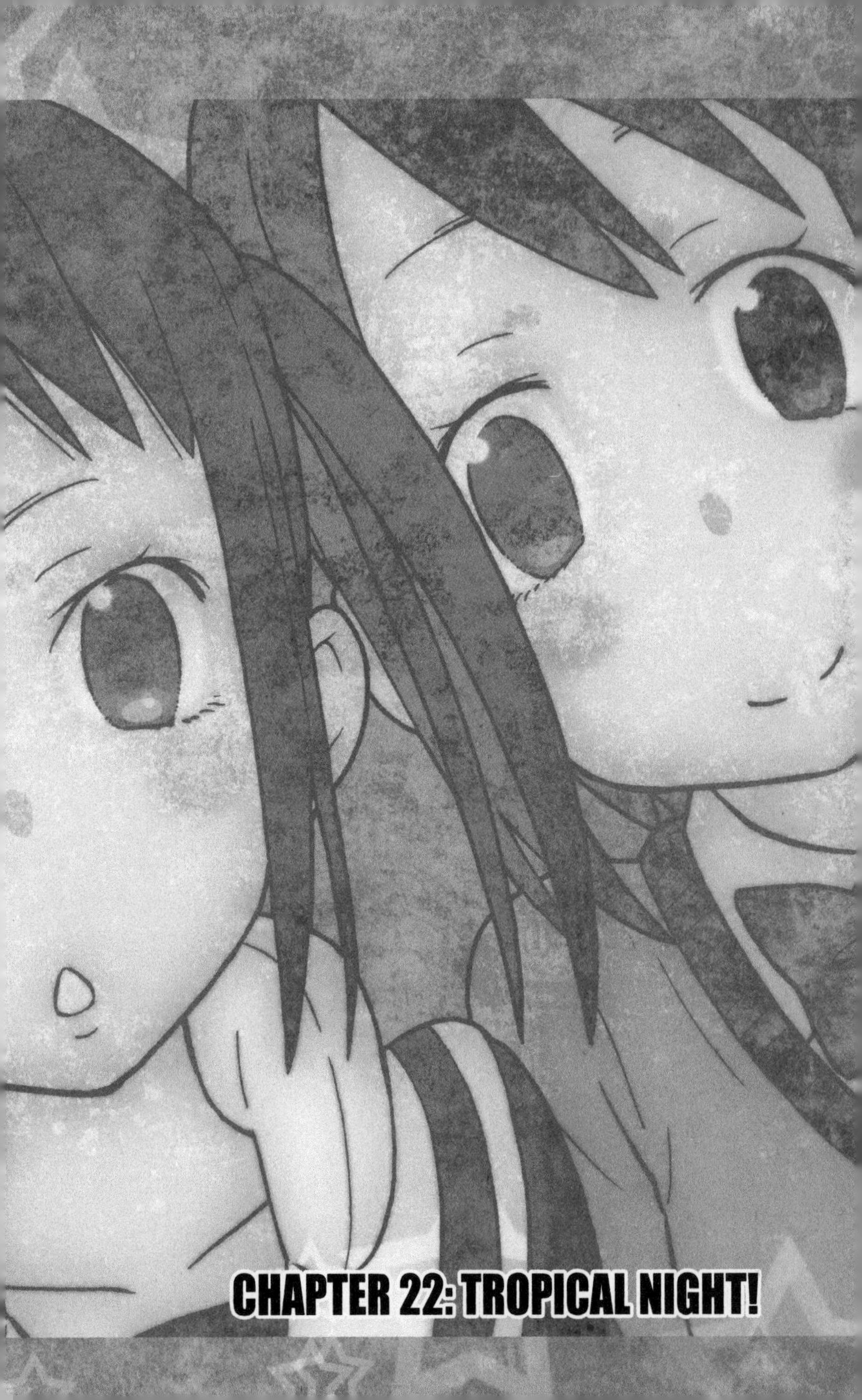

CHAPTER 22: TROPICAL NIGHT!

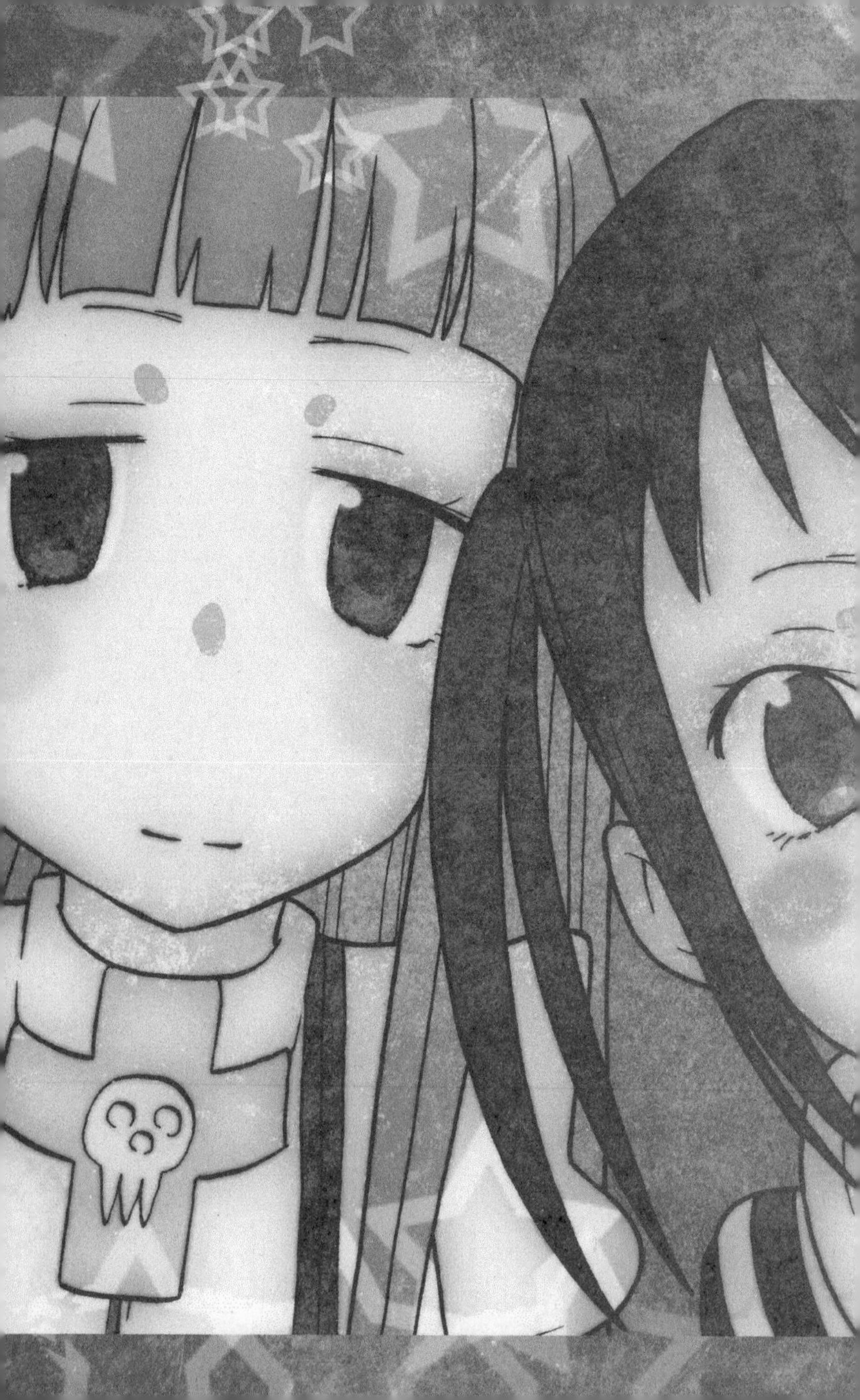

SOUL EATER NOT!

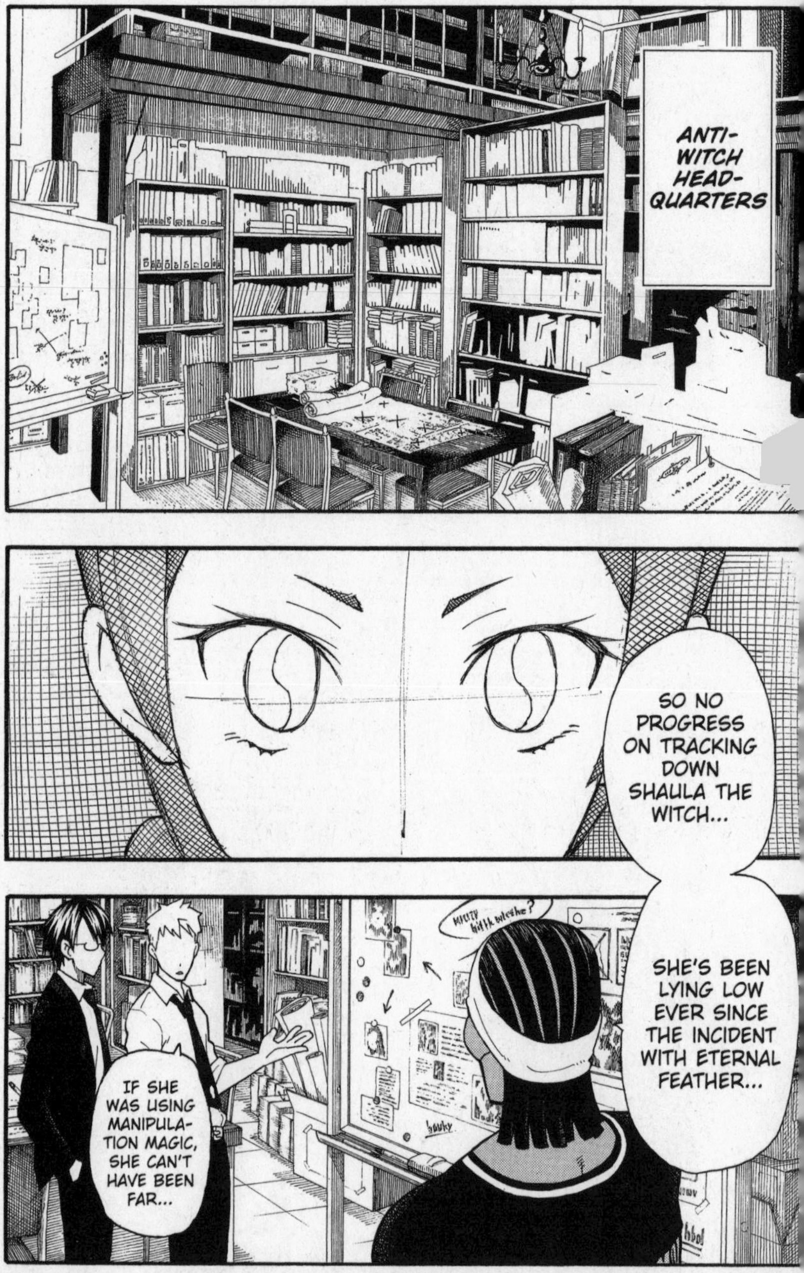
ANTI-WITCH HEAD-QUARTERS
SO NO PROGRESS ON TRACKING DOWN SHAULA THE WITCH...
SHE'S BEEN LYING LOW EVER SINCE THE INCIDENT WITH ETERNAL FEATHER...
IF SHE WAS USING MANIPULATION MAGIC, SHE CAN'T HAVE BEEN FAR...

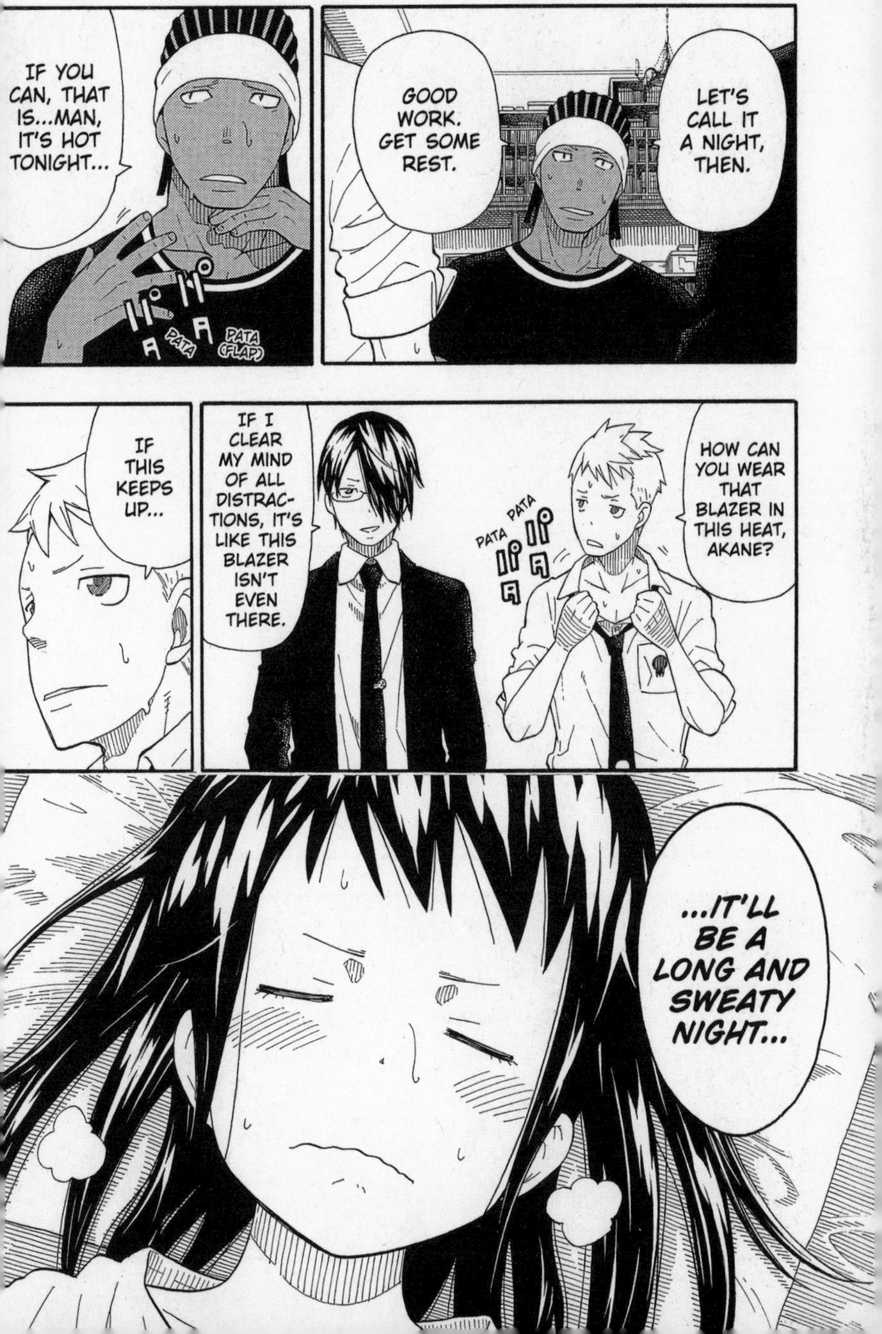
LET'S CALL IT A NIGHT, THEN.
GOOD WORK. GET SOME REST.
IF YOU CAN, THAT IS...MAN, IT'S HOT TONIGHT...
PATA (FLAP)
PATA
HOW CAN YOU WEAR THAT BLAZER IN THIS HEAT, AKANE?
PATA PATA
IF I CLEAR MY MIND OF ALL DISTRACTIONS, IT'S LIKE THIS BLAZER ISN'T EVEN THERE.
IF THIS KEEPS UP...
...IT'LL BE A LONG AND SWEATY NIGHT...

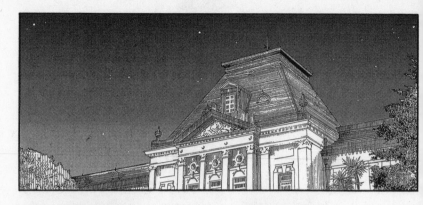

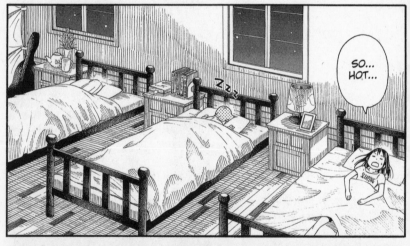

SO...
HOT...

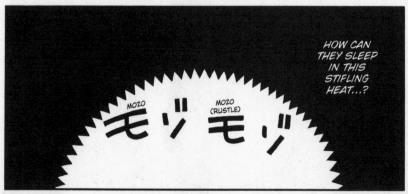

HOW CAN
THEY SLEEP
IN THIS
STIFLING
HEAT...?

MOZO MOZO
(RUSTLE)

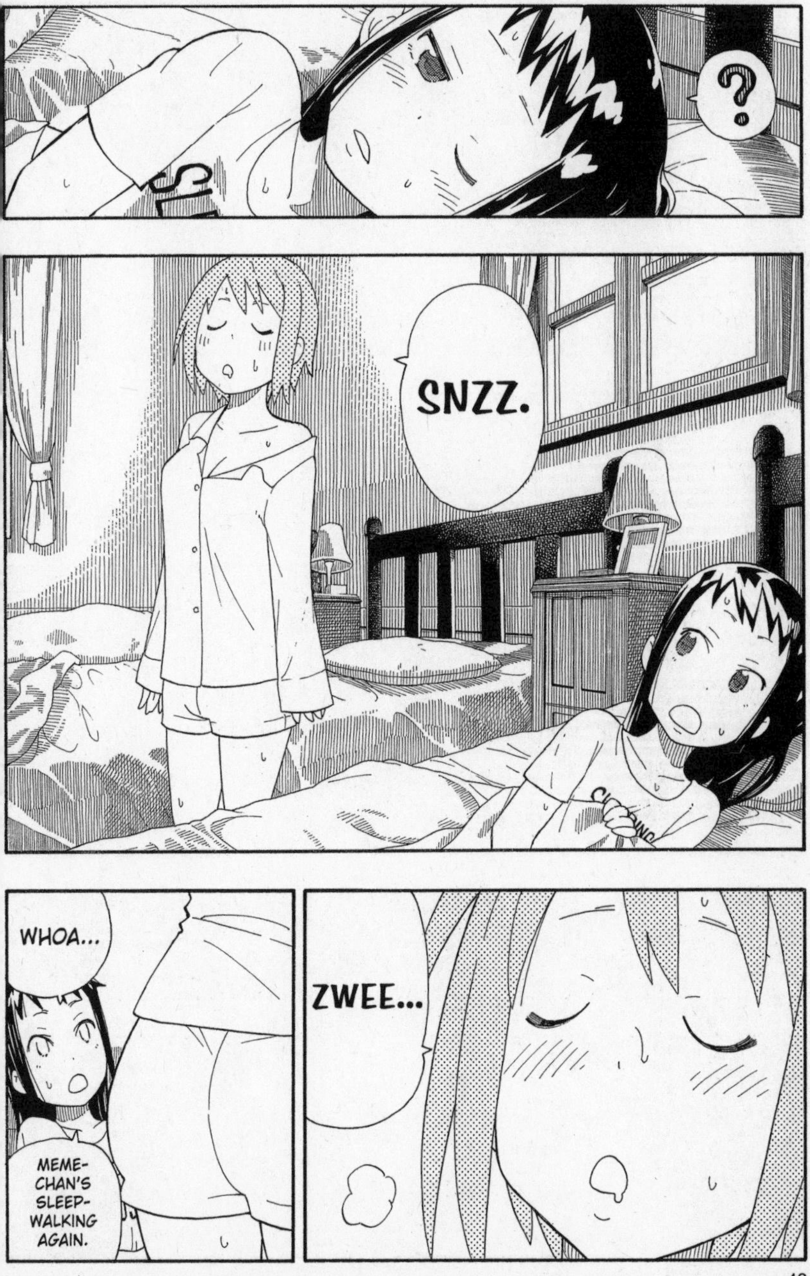
?
SNZZ.
ZWEE...
WHOA...
MEME-CHAN'S SLEEP-WALKING AGAIN.

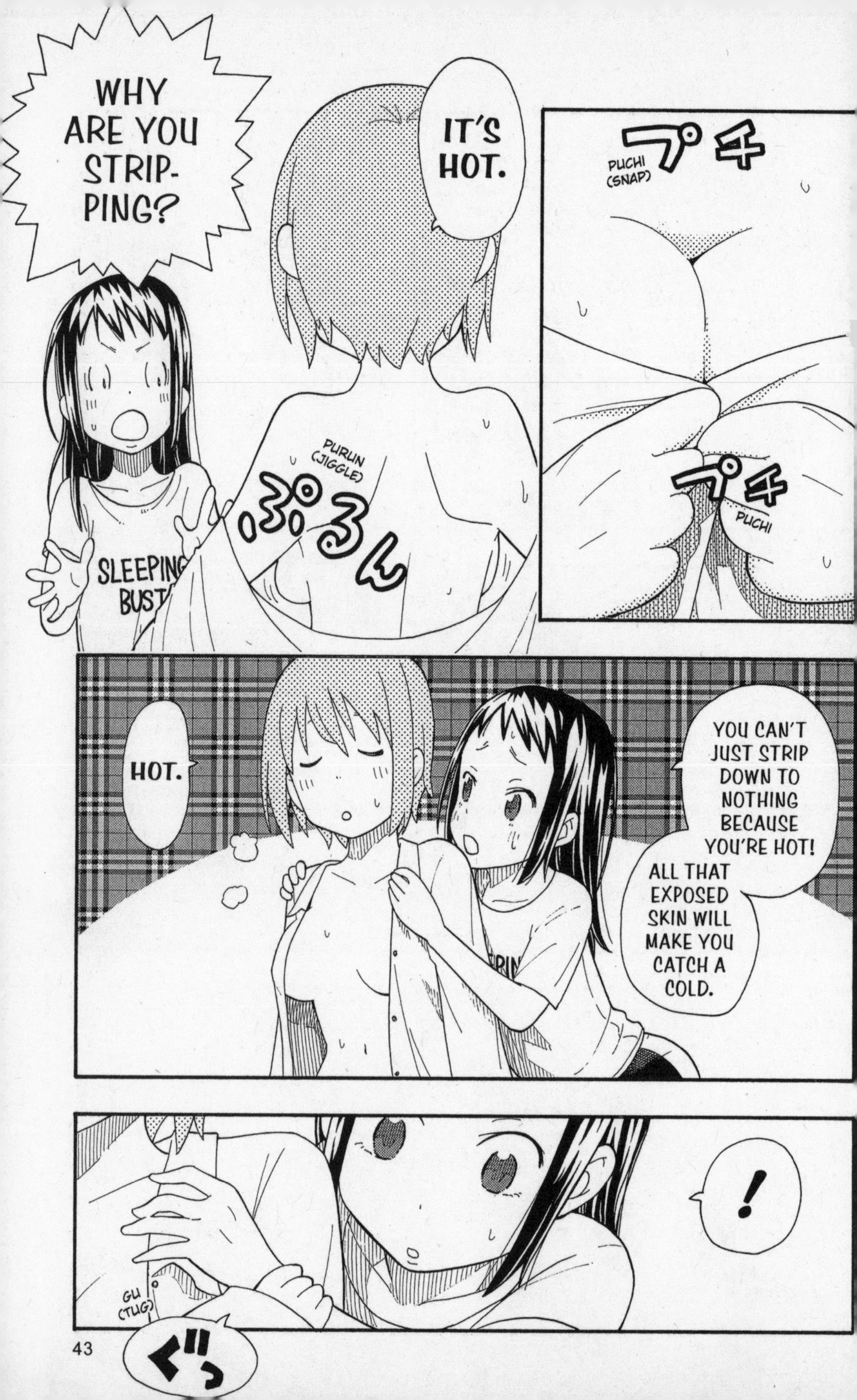

PUCHI (SNAP)
プチ
プチ
PUCHI
WHY ARE YOU STRIP-PING?
IT'S HOT.
PURUN (JIGGLE)
ぷるん
SLEEPING BUST
YOU CAN'T JUST STRIP DOWN TO NOTHING BECAUSE YOU'RE HOT!
ALL THAT EXPOSED SKIN WILL MAKE YOU CATCH A COLD.
HOT.
!
GU (TUG)
ぐッ

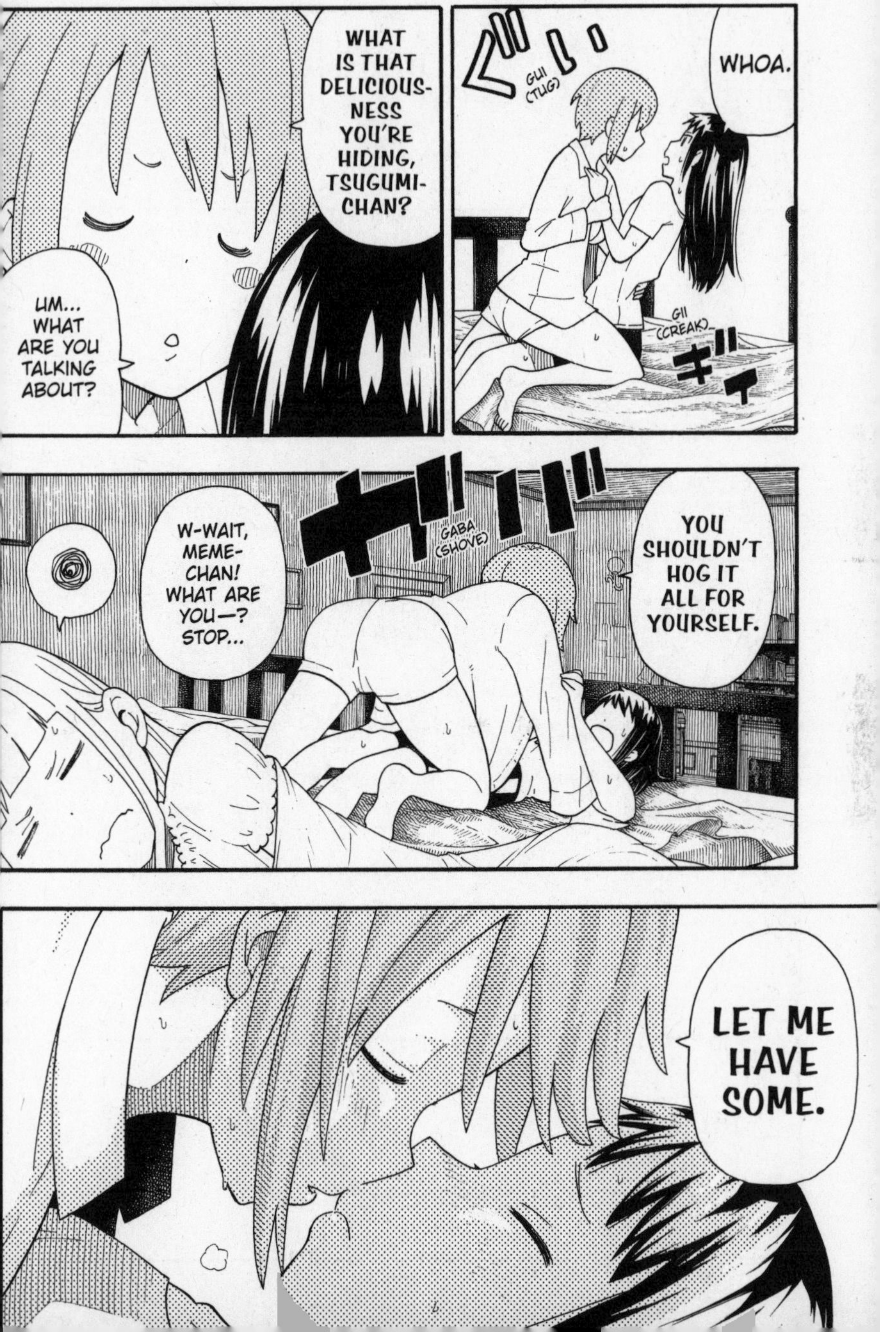
WHOA.
GUI (TUG)
GII (CREAK)
WHAT IS THAT DELICIOUSNESS YOU'RE HIDING, TSUGUMI-CHAN?
UM... WHAT ARE YOU TALKING ABOUT?
YOU SHOULDN'T HOG IT ALL FOR YOURSELF.
GABA (SHOVE)
W-WAIT, MEME-CHAN! WHAT ARE YOU—? STOP...
LET ME HAVE SOME.

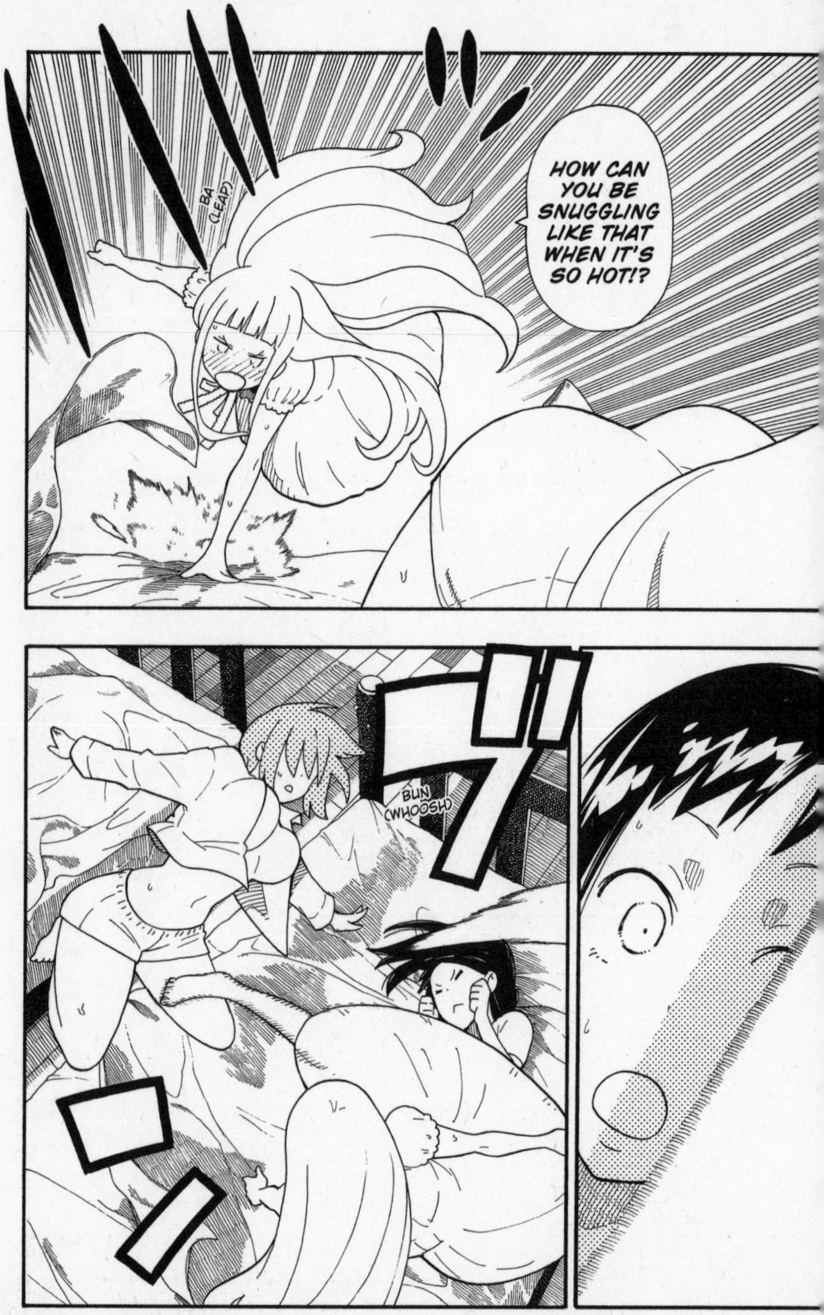
HOW CAN YOU BE SNUGGLING LIKE THAT WHEN IT'S SO HOT!?
BA (LEAP)
BUN (WHOOSH)

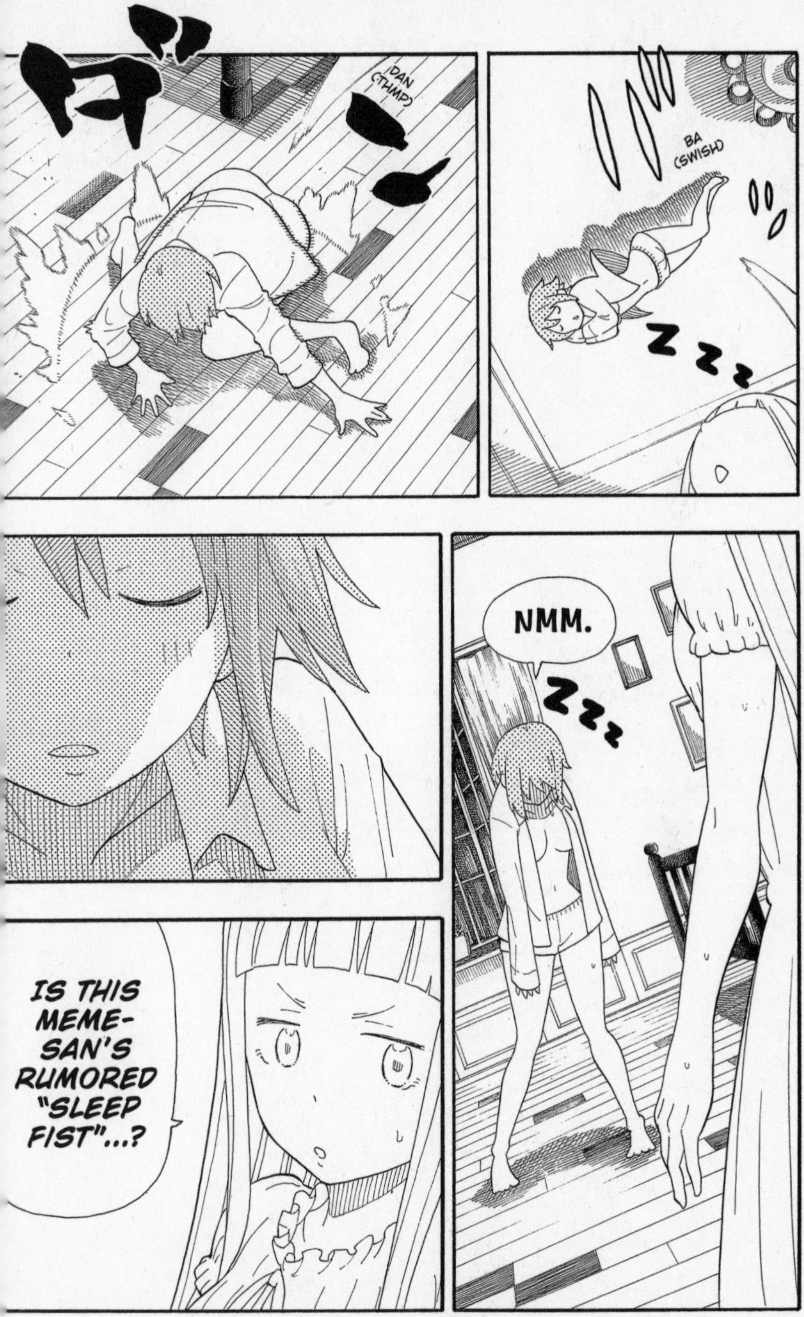
BA (SWISH)
Z Z Z
DAN (THMP)
NMM.
Z Z Z
IS THIS MEME-SAN'S RUMORED "SLEEP FIST"...?

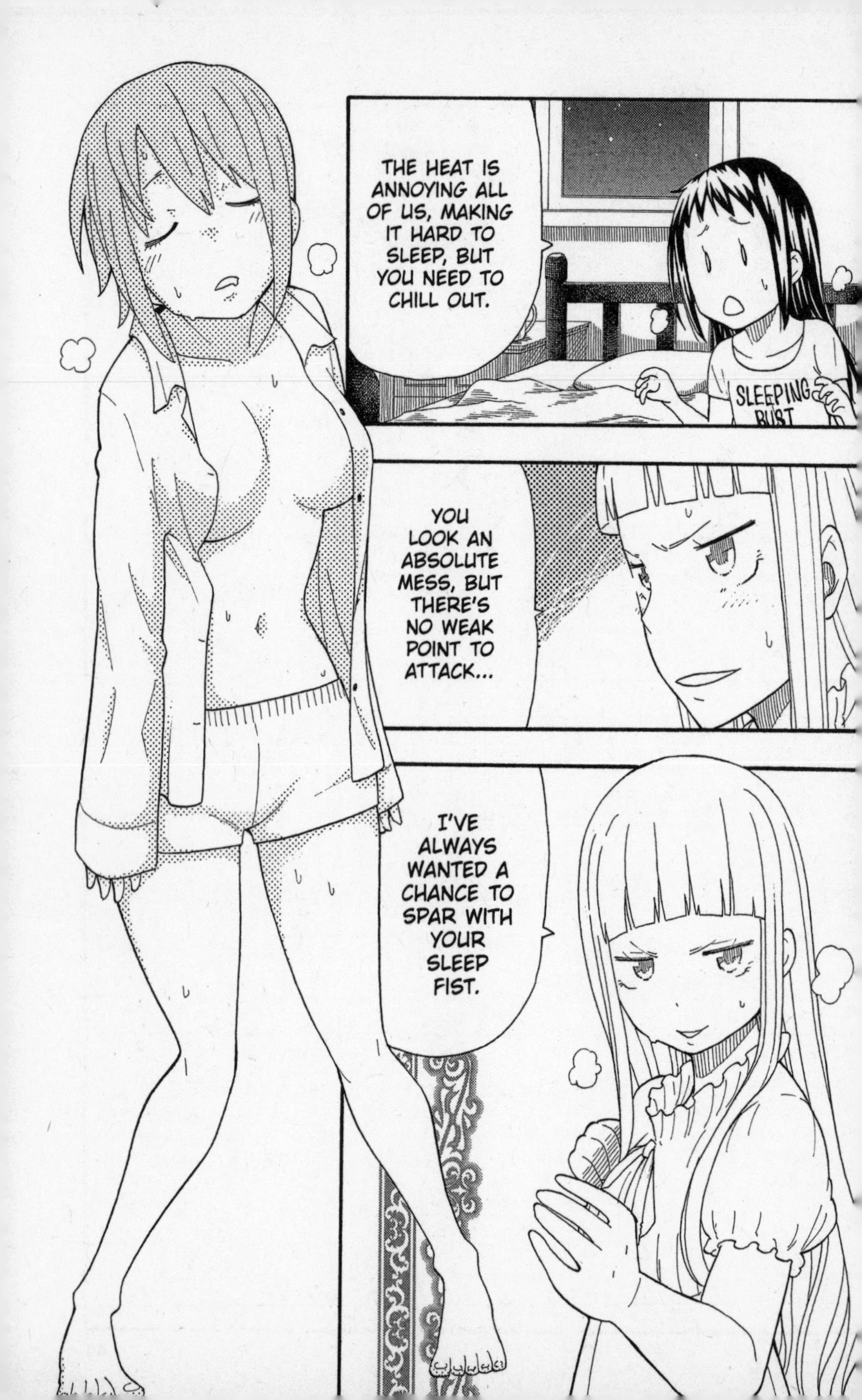
THE HEAT IS ANNOYING ALL OF US, MAKING IT HARD TO SLEEP, BUT YOU NEED TO CHILL OUT.
SLEEPING BUST
YOU LOOK AN ABSOLUTE MESS, BUT THERE'S NO WEAK POINT TO ATTACK...
I'VE ALWAYS WANTED A CHANCE TO SPAR WITH YOUR SLEEP FIST.

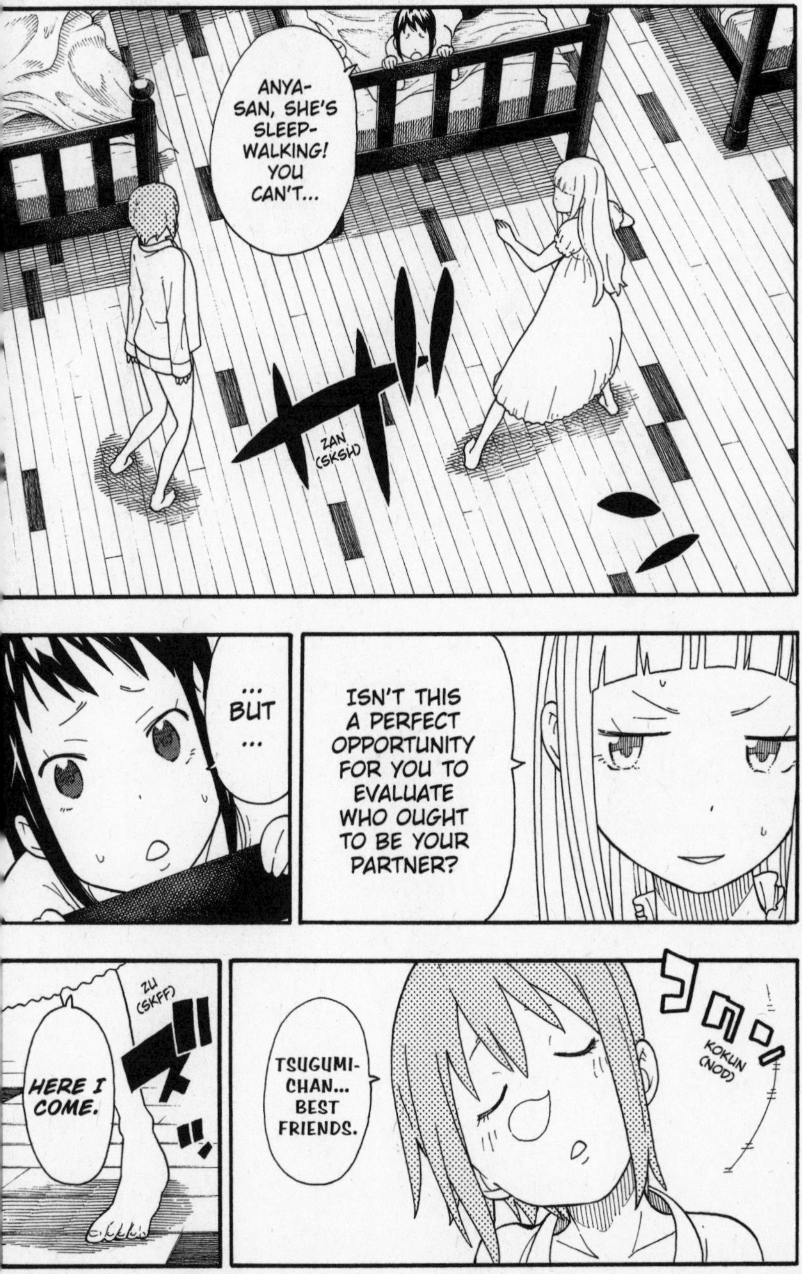
ANYA-SAN, SHE'S SLEEP-WALKING! YOU CAN'T...
ZAN (SKSH)
ISN'T THIS A PERFECT OPPORTUNITY FOR YOU TO EVALUATE WHO OUGHT TO BE YOUR PARTNER?
... BUT ...
KOKUN (NOD)
TSUGUMI-CHAN... BEST FRIENDS.
ZU (SKFF)
HERE I COME.

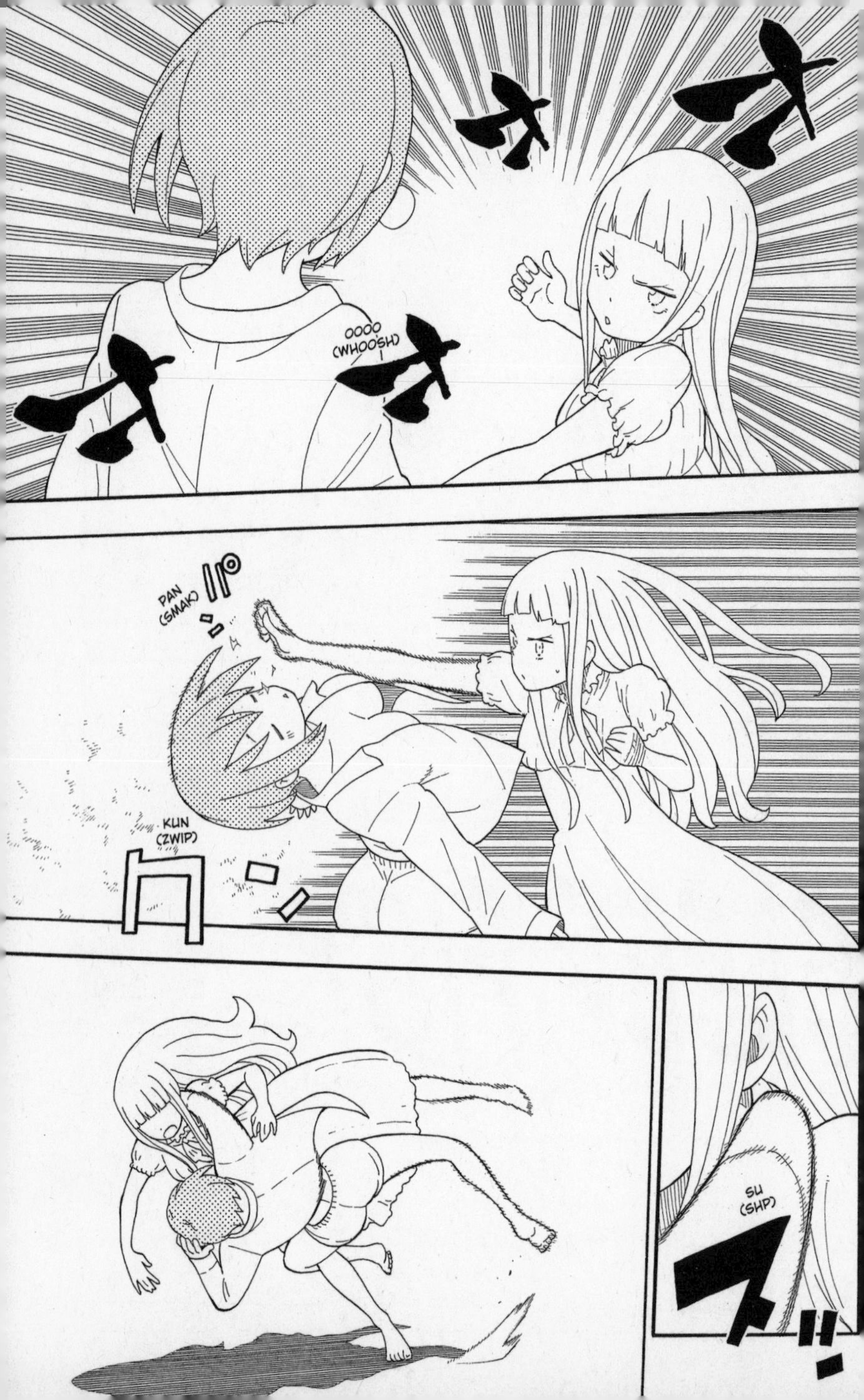
OOOO (WHOOSH)
PAN (SMAK)
KUN (ZWIP)
SU (SHP)

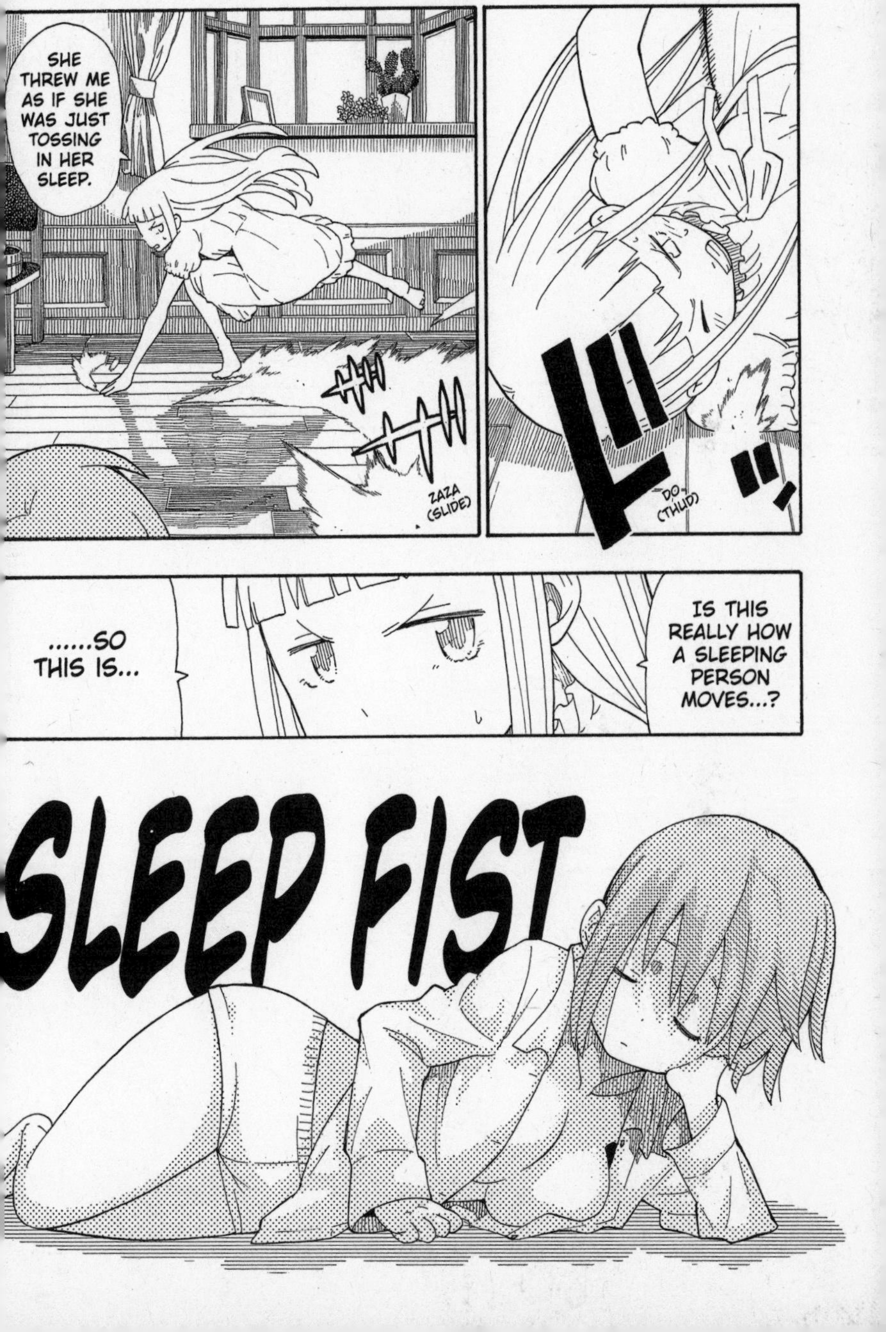
DO- (THUD)
SHE THREW ME AS IF SHE WAS JUST TOSSING IN HER SLEEP.
ZAZA (SLIDE)
IS THIS REALLY HOW A SLEEPING PERSON MOVES...?
......SO THIS IS...
SLEEP FIST

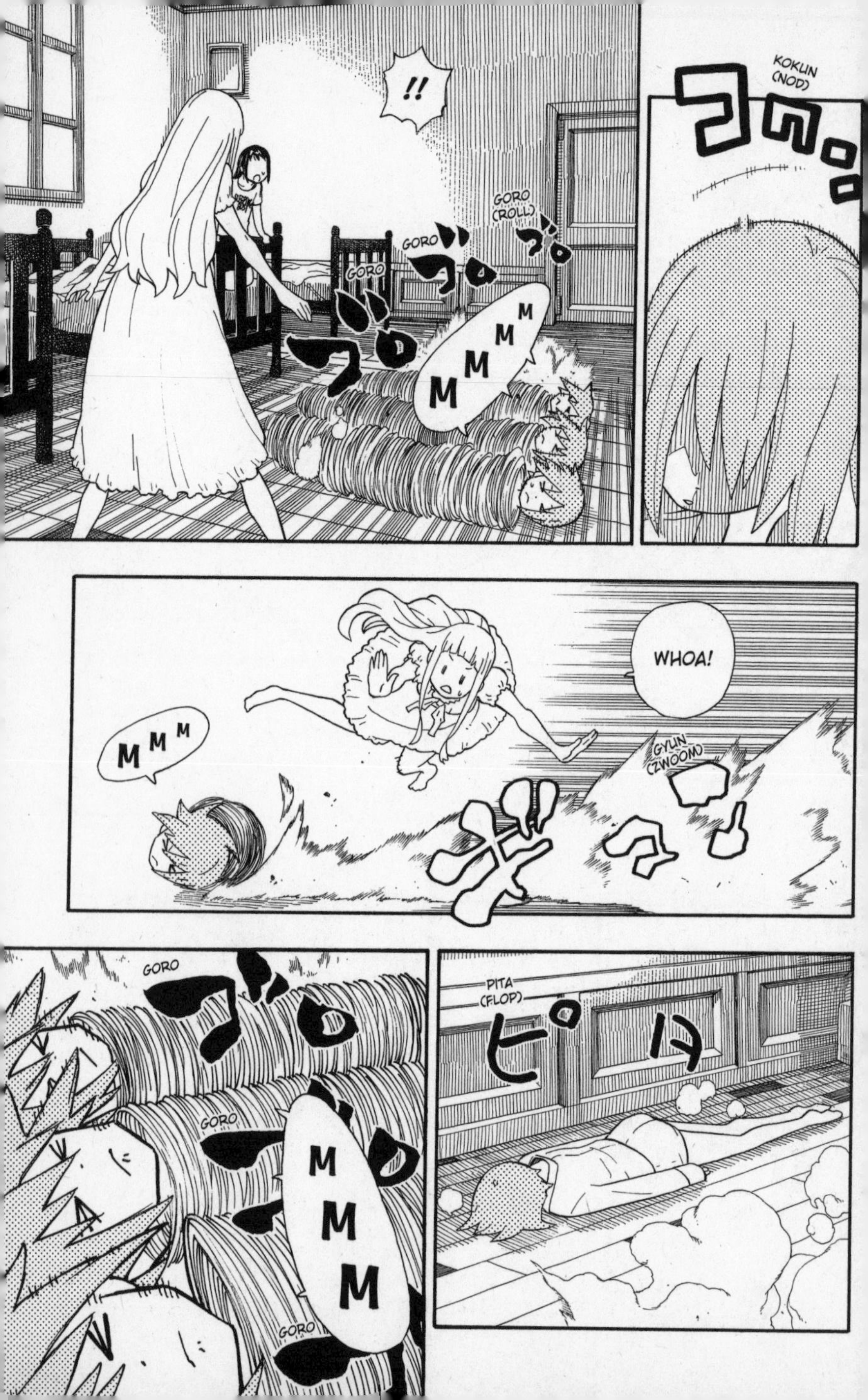
KOKUN (NOD)
!!
GORO (ROLL)
GORO
MMMM
GORO
WHOA!
GYLIN (ZWOOM)
MMM
PITA (FLOP)
GORO
GORO
MMM
GORO

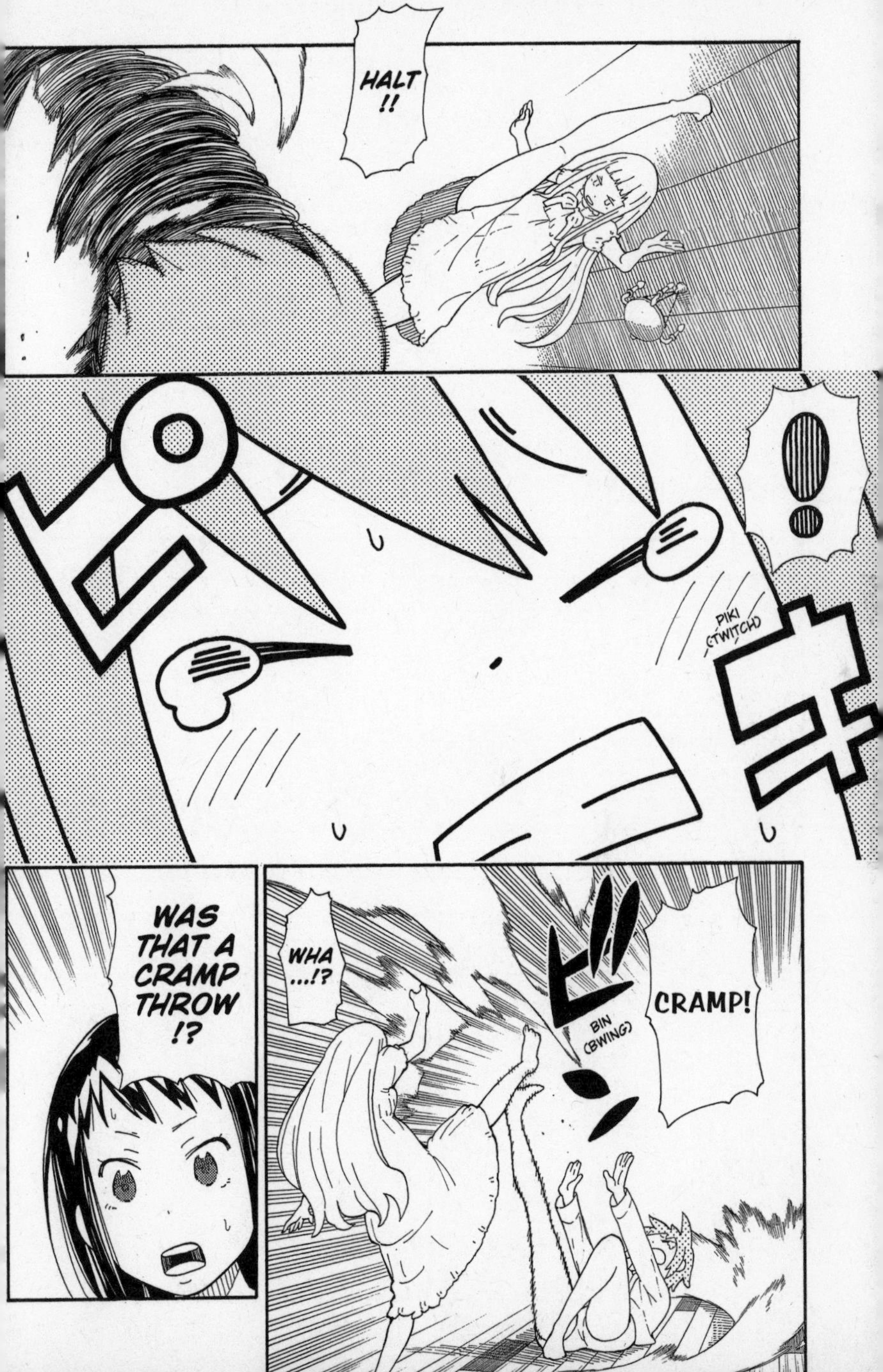
HALT !!
!!
PIKI (TWITCH)
CRAMP!
BIN (BWING)
WHA ...!?
WAS THAT A CRAMP THROW !?

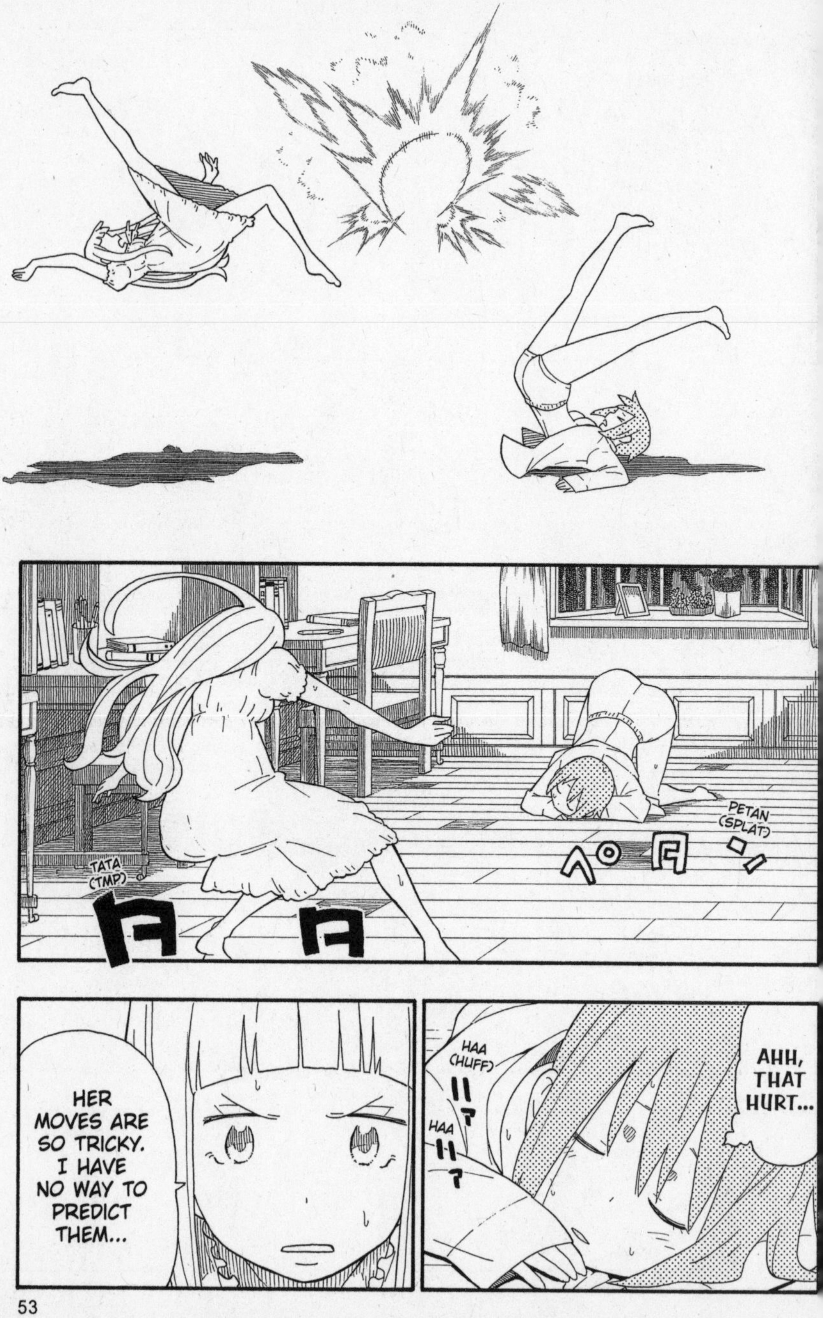
PETAN (SPLAT)
TATA (TMP)
AHH, THAT HURT...
HAA (HUFF)
HAA
HER MOVES ARE SO TRICKY. I HAVE NO WAY TO PREDICT THEM...

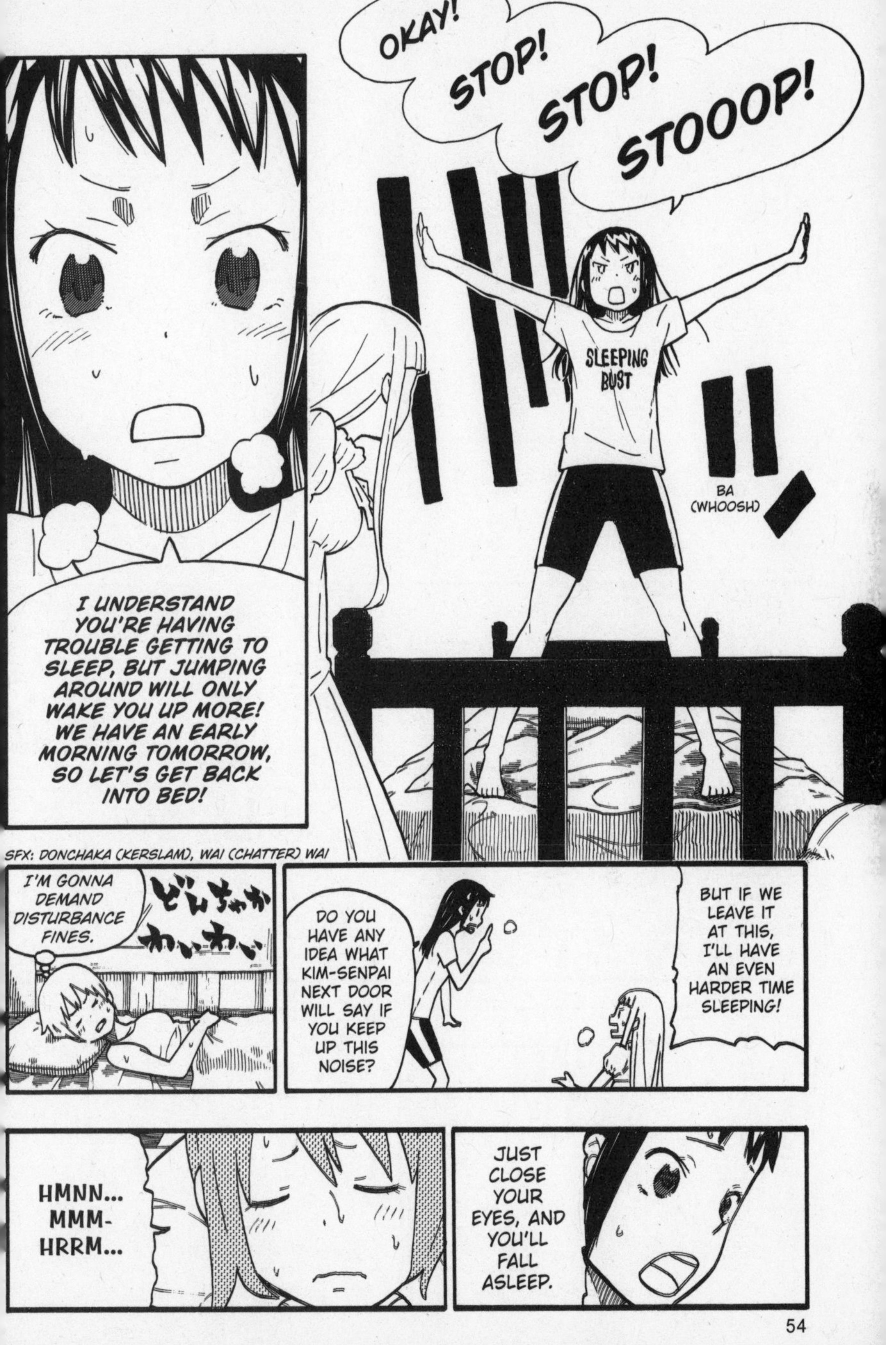
OKAY! STOP! STOP! STOOOP!
SLEEPING BUST
BA (WHOOSH)
I UNDERSTAND YOU'RE HAVING TROUBLE GETTING TO SLEEP, BUT JUMPING AROUND WILL ONLY WAKE YOU UP MORE! WE HAVE AN EARLY MORNING TOMORROW, SO LET'S GET BACK INTO BED!
SFX: DONCHAKA (KERSLAM), WAI (CHATTER) WAI
BUT IF WE LEAVE IT AT THIS, I'LL HAVE AN EVEN HARDER TIME SLEEPING!
DO YOU HAVE ANY IDEA WHAT KIM-SENPAI NEXT DOOR WILL SAY IF YOU KEEP UP THIS NOISE?
I'M GONNA DEMAND DISTURBANCE FINES.
どんちゃか
わいわい
JUST CLOSE YOUR EYES, AND YOU'LL FALL ASLEEP.
HMNN... MMM-HRRM...

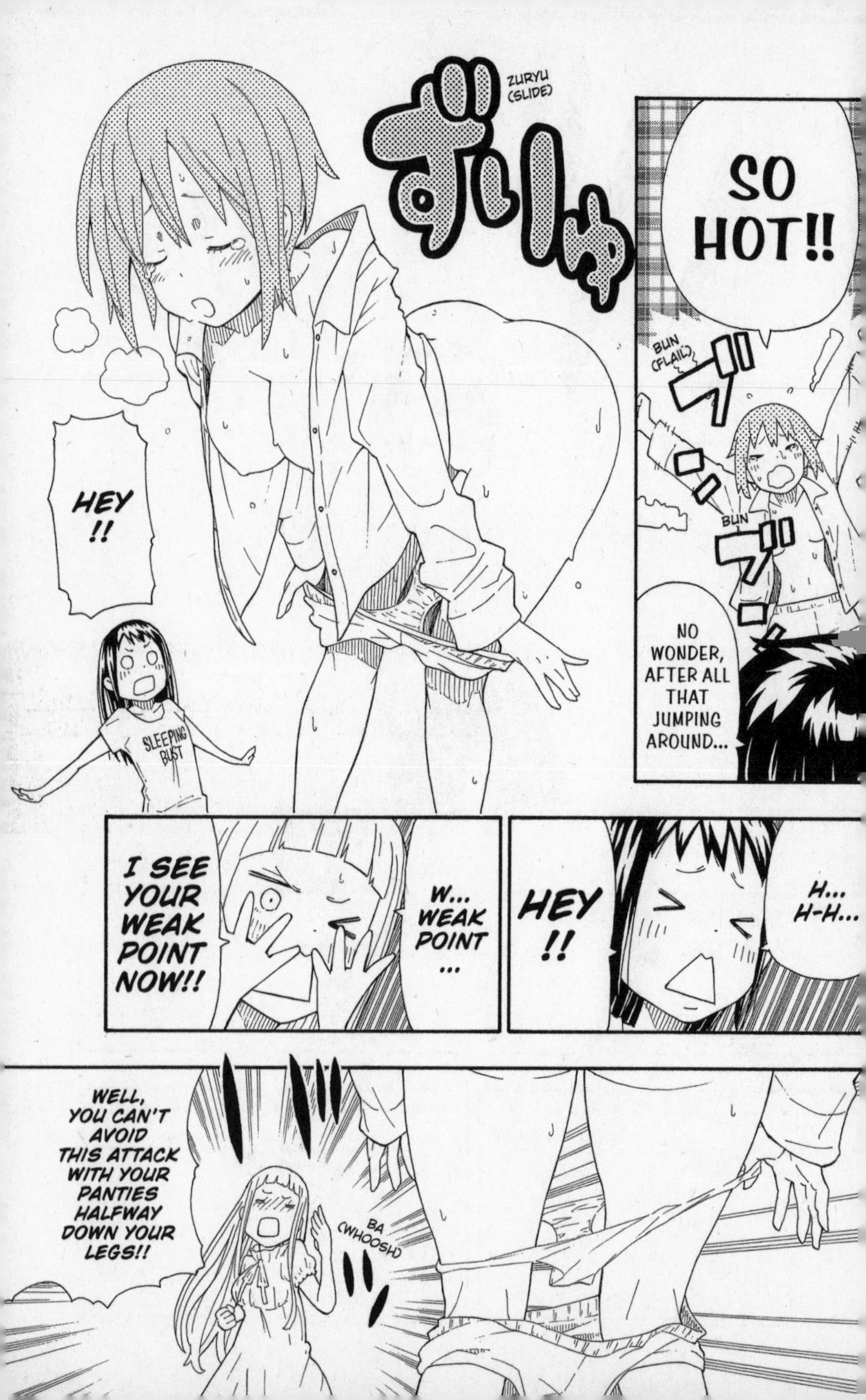
SO HOT!!
BUN (FLAIL)
BUN
NO WONDER, AFTER ALL THAT JUMPING AROUND...
ZURYU (SLIDE)
HEY!!
SLEEPING BUST
H... H-H...
HEY!!
W... WEAK POINT...
I SEE YOUR WEAK POINT NOW!!
WELL, YOU CAN'T AVOID THIS ATTACK WITH YOUR PANTIES HALFWAY DOWN YOUR LEGS!!
BA (WHOOSH)

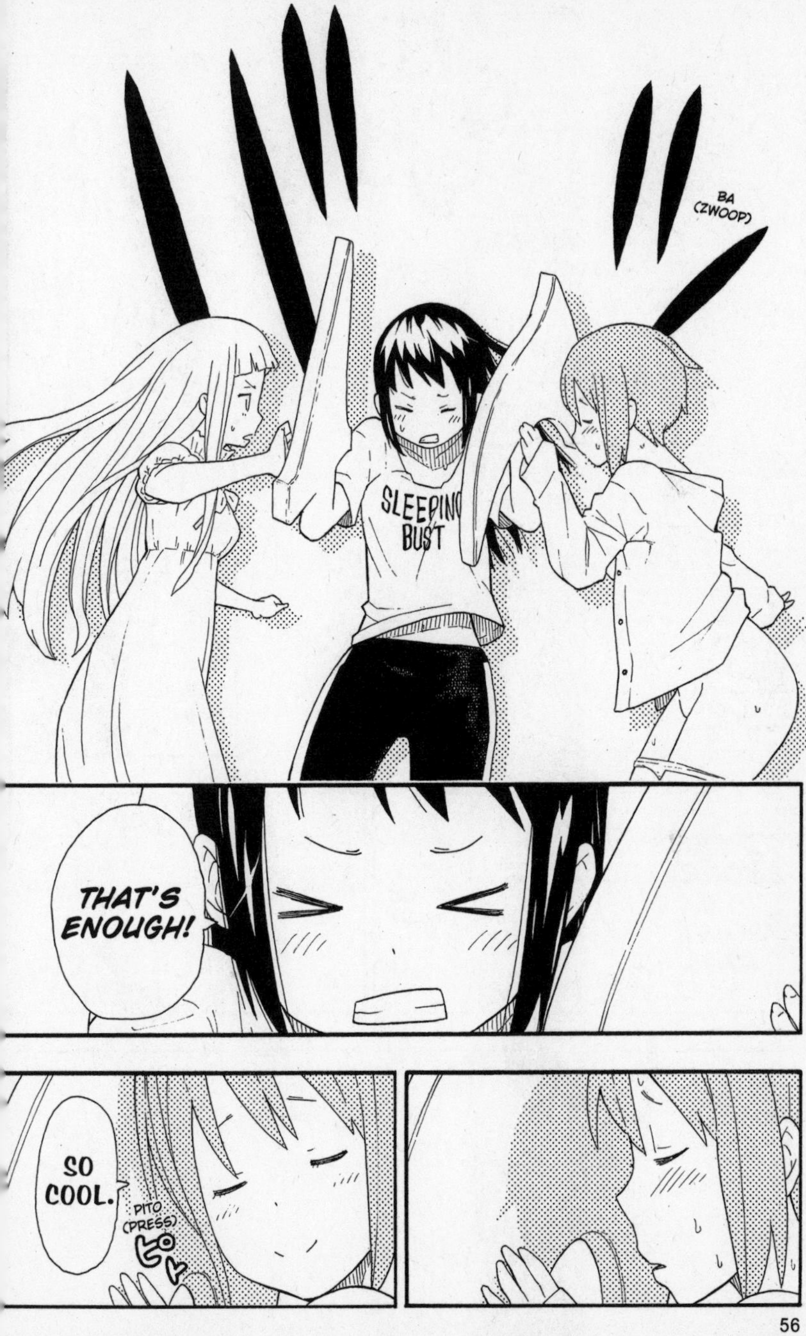
BA (ZWOOP)
SLEEPING BUST
THAT'S ENOUGH!
SO COOL.
PITO (PRESS)

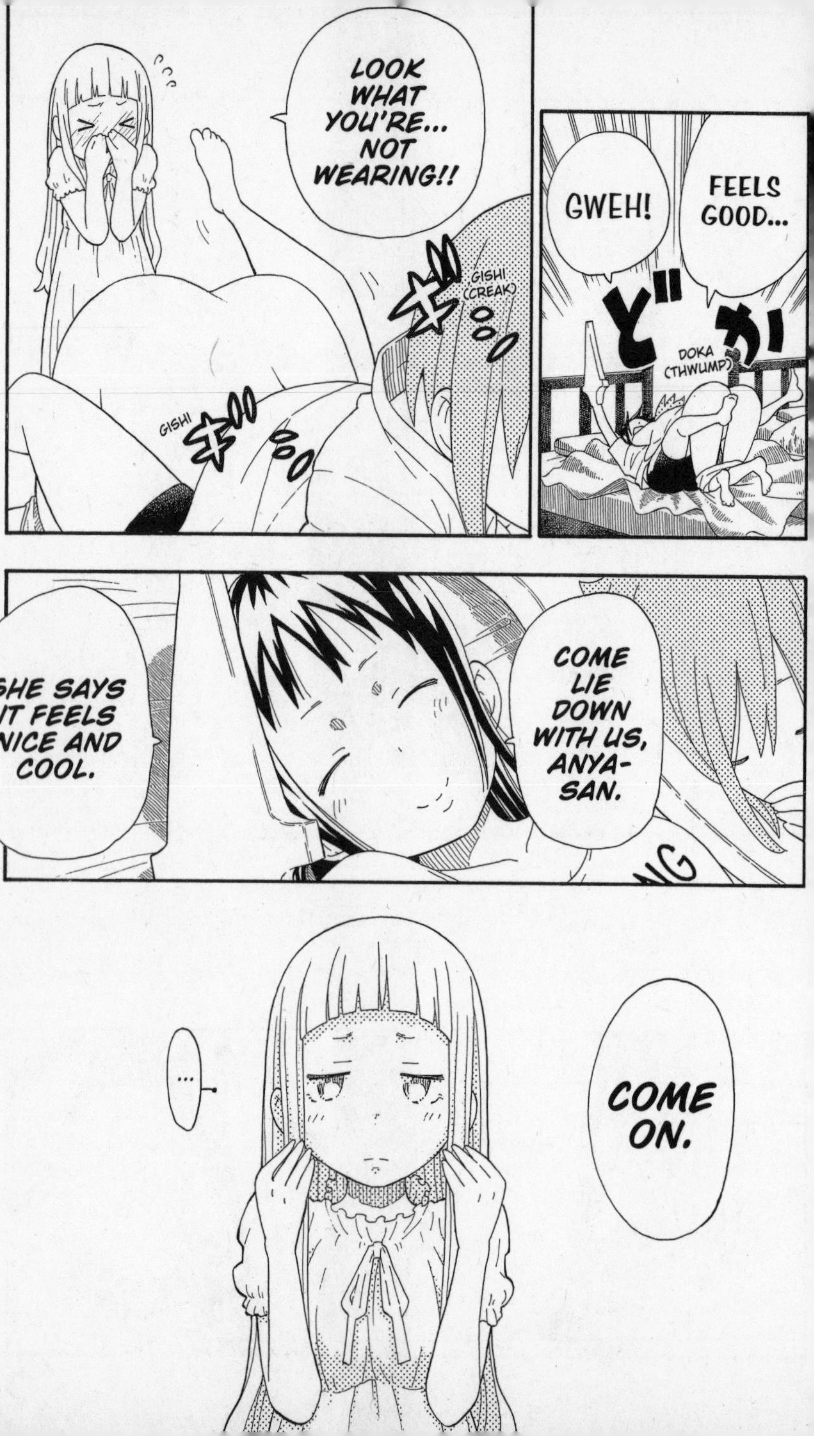
FEELS GOOD...
GWEH!
DOKA (THWUMP)
LOOK WHAT YOU'RE... NOT WEARING!!
GISHI (CREAK)
GISHI
COME LIE DOWN WITH US, ANYA-SAN.
SHE SAYS IT FEELS NICE AND COOL.
COME ON.
...

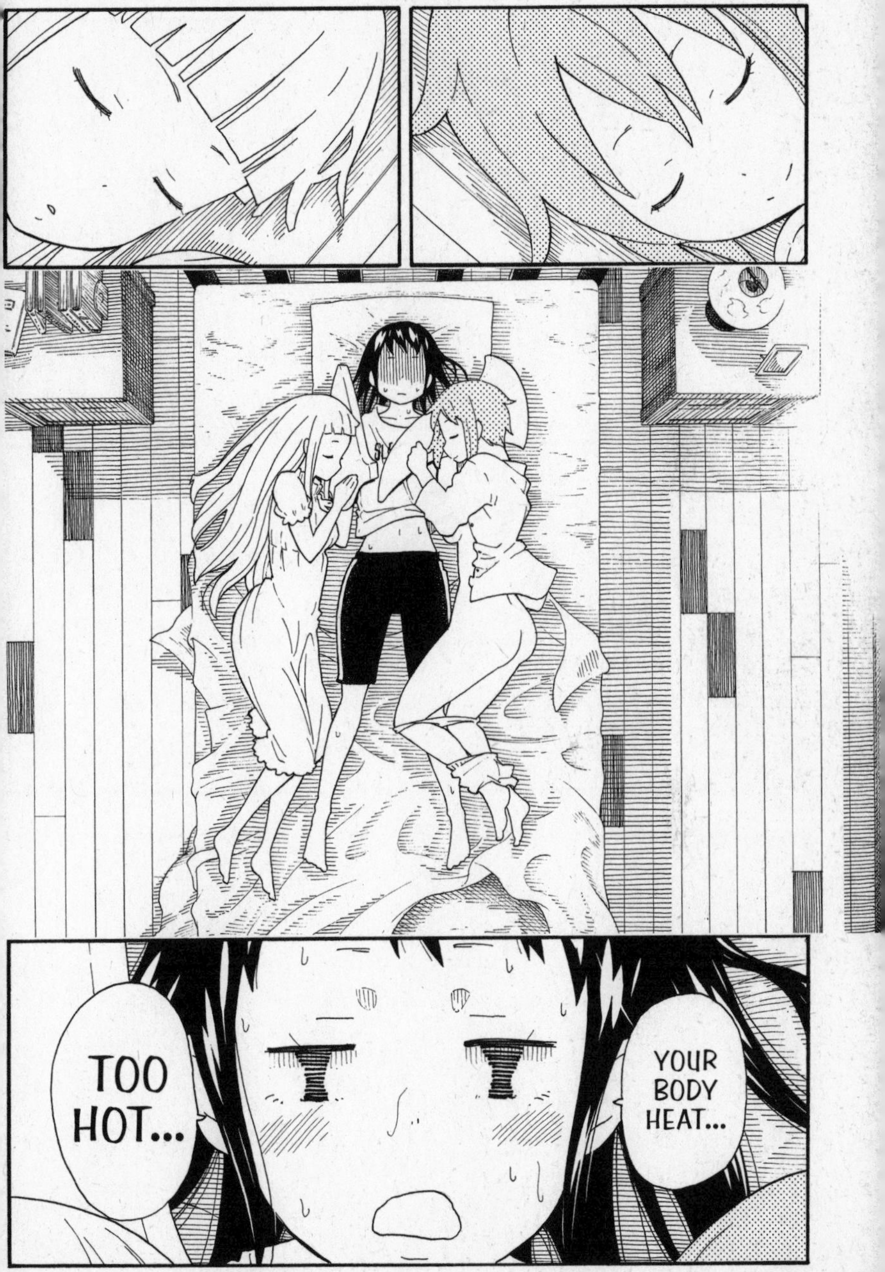
YOUR BODY HEAT...
TOO HOT...

SOUL EATER NOT!

SOUL EATER NOT

ATSUSHI OHKUBO

PART 8

A JOT CHAOTIC

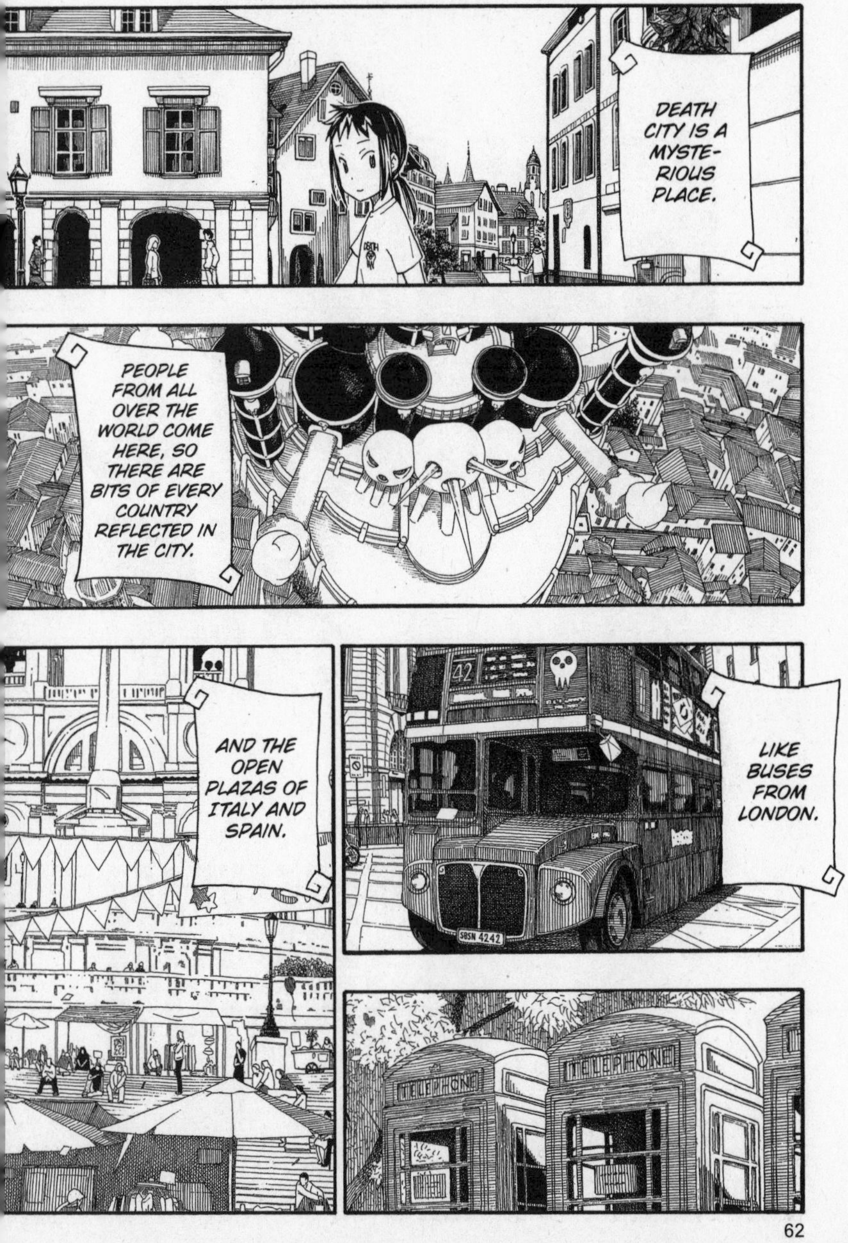
DEATH CITY IS A MYSTERIOUS PLACE.
PEOPLE FROM ALL OVER THE WORLD COME HERE, SO THERE ARE BITS OF EVERY COUNTRY REFLECTED IN THE CITY.
42
LIKE BUSES FROM LONDON.
SBSN 4242
TELEPHONE
TELEPHONE
AND THE OPEN PLAZAS OF ITALY AND SPAIN.

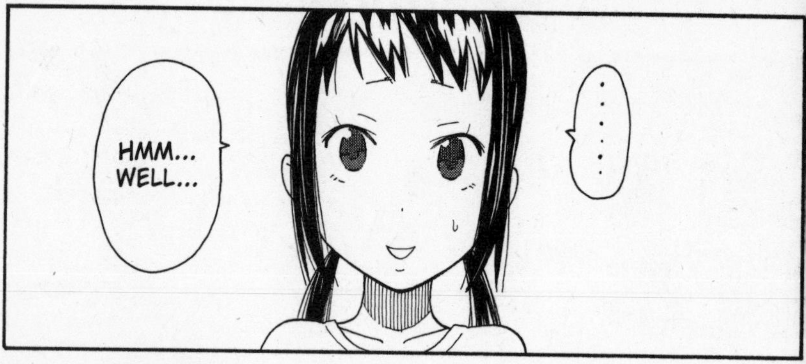
......
HMM... WELL...

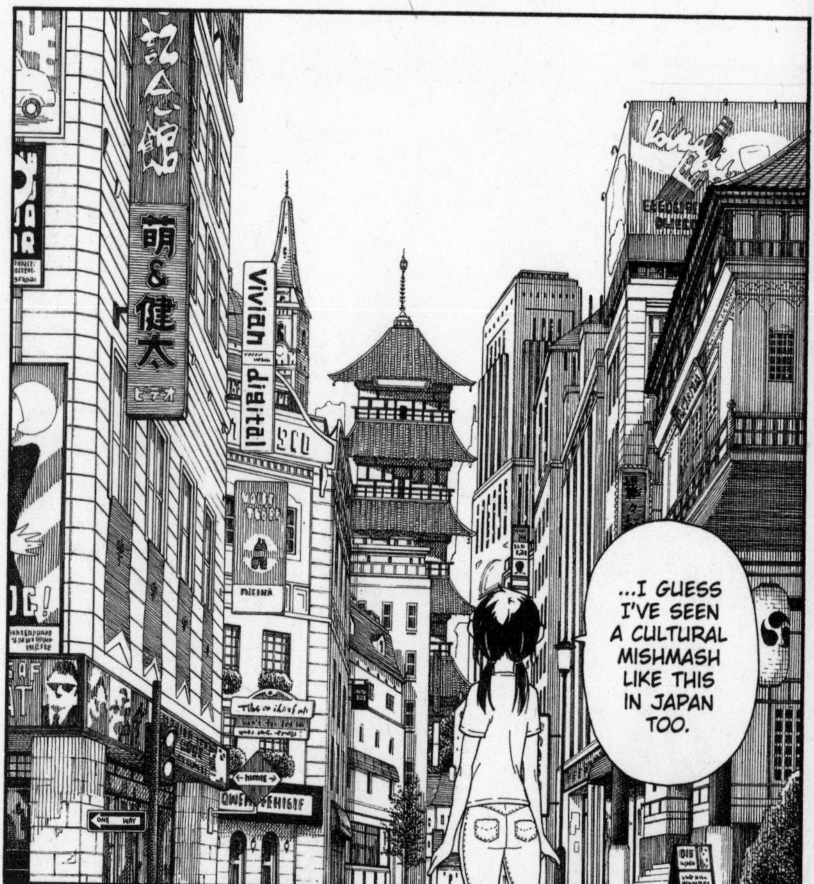
...I GUESS I'VE SEEN A CULTURAL MISHMASH LIKE THIS IN JAPAN TOO.
記念館
萌&健太
ビデオ
vivian digital
ONE WAY

A JOT POINTLESS

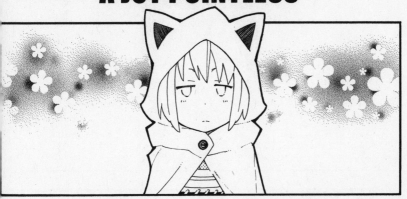

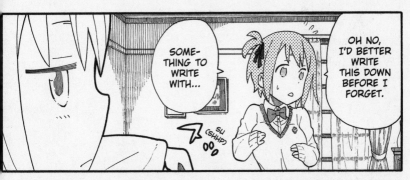

SOMETHING TO WRITE WITH...

OH NO, I'D BETTER WRITE THIS DOWN BEFORE I FORGET.

SLI (SHHP)

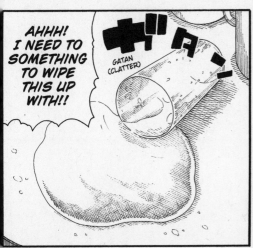

AHHH! I NEED TO SOMETHING TO WIPE THIS UP WITH!!

GATAN (CLATTER)

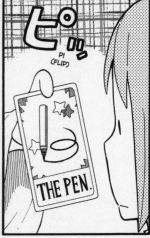

PI (FLIP)

THE PEN.

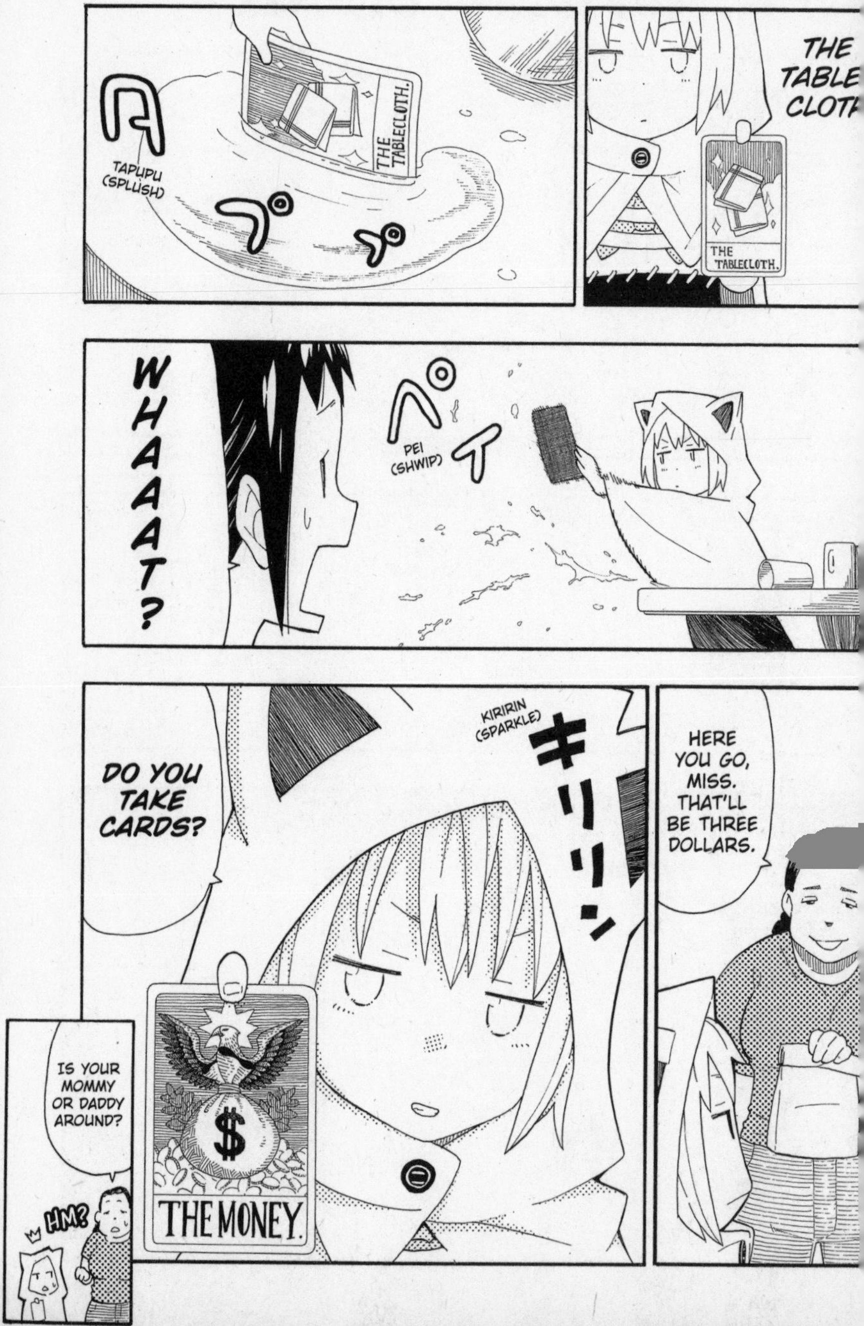

THE TABLE CLOT
THE TABLECLOTH.
THE TABLECLOTH.
TAPUPU (SPLUSH)
PEI (SHWIP)
WHAAAAT?
HERE YOU GO, MISS. THAT'LL BE THREE DOLLARS.
KIRIRIN (SPARKLE)
DO YOU TAKE CARDS?
THE MONEY.
IS YOUR MOMMY OR DADDY AROUND?
HM?

A JOT A LOT POINTLESS

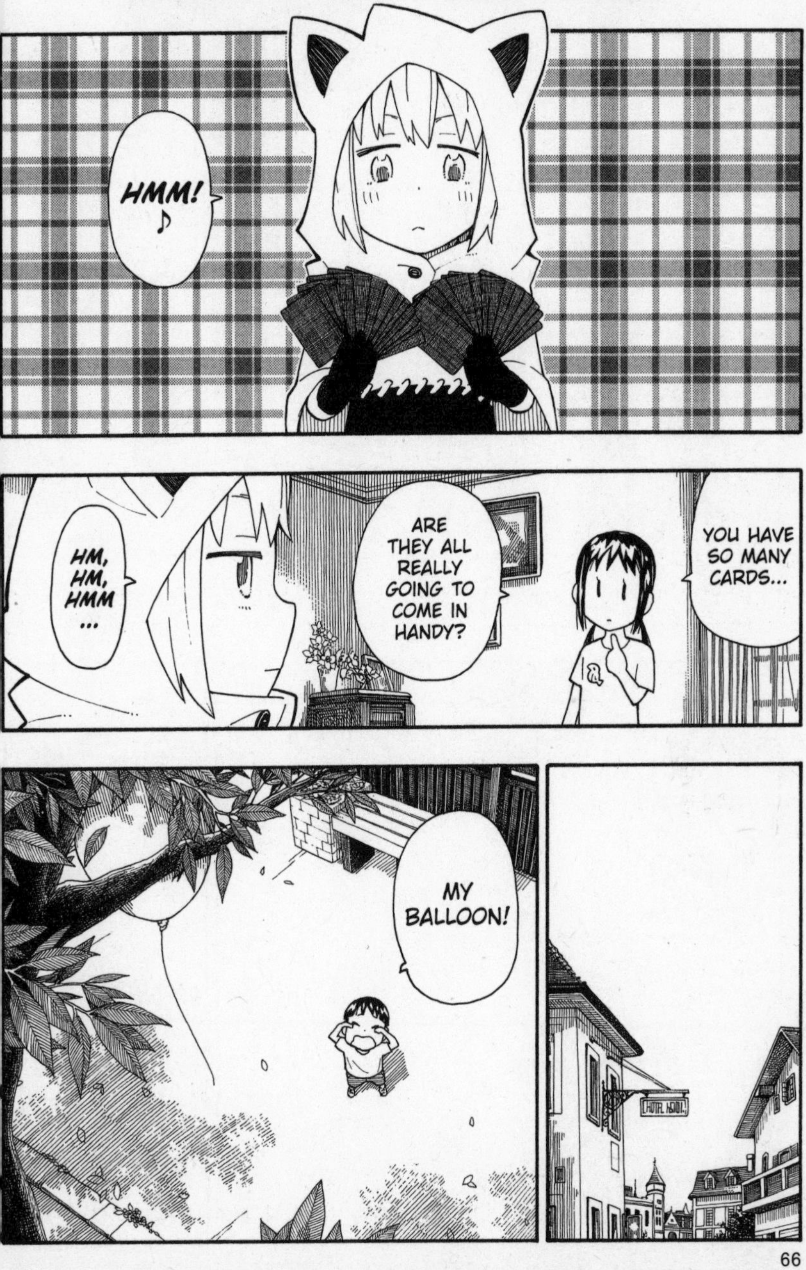
HMM! ♪
YOU HAVE SO MANY CARDS...
ARE THEY ALL REALLY GOING TO COME IN HANDY?
HM, HM, HMM ...
MY BALLOON!

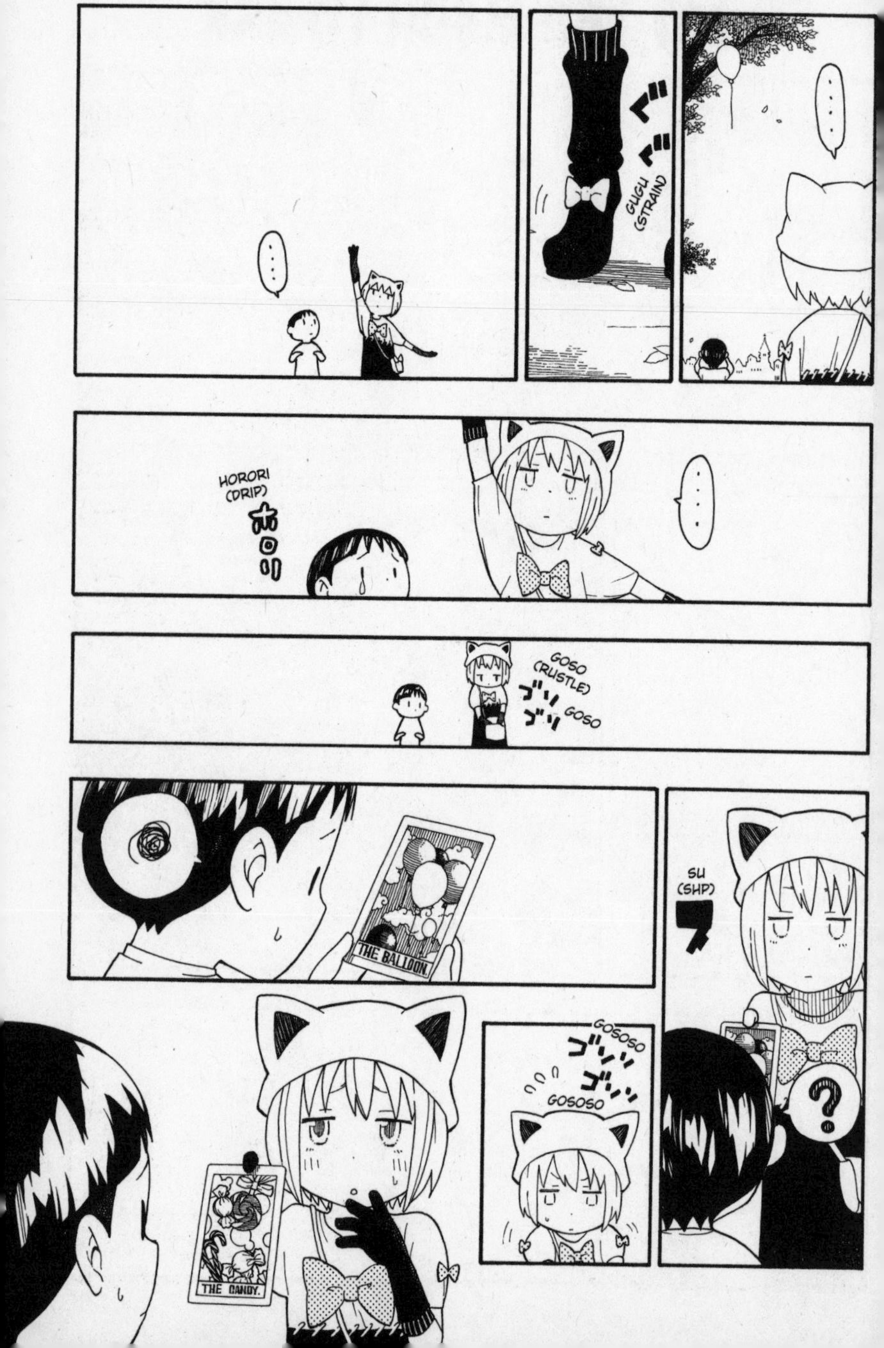

...
GUGU (STRAIN)
...
...
HORORI (DRIP)
ホロリ
GOSO (RUSTLE)
ゴソ ゴソ
GOSO
SU (SHP)
?
THE BALLOON.
GOSOSO
ゴソソ ゴソソ
GOSOSO
THE CANDY.

A JOT TOO MUCH TO ASK

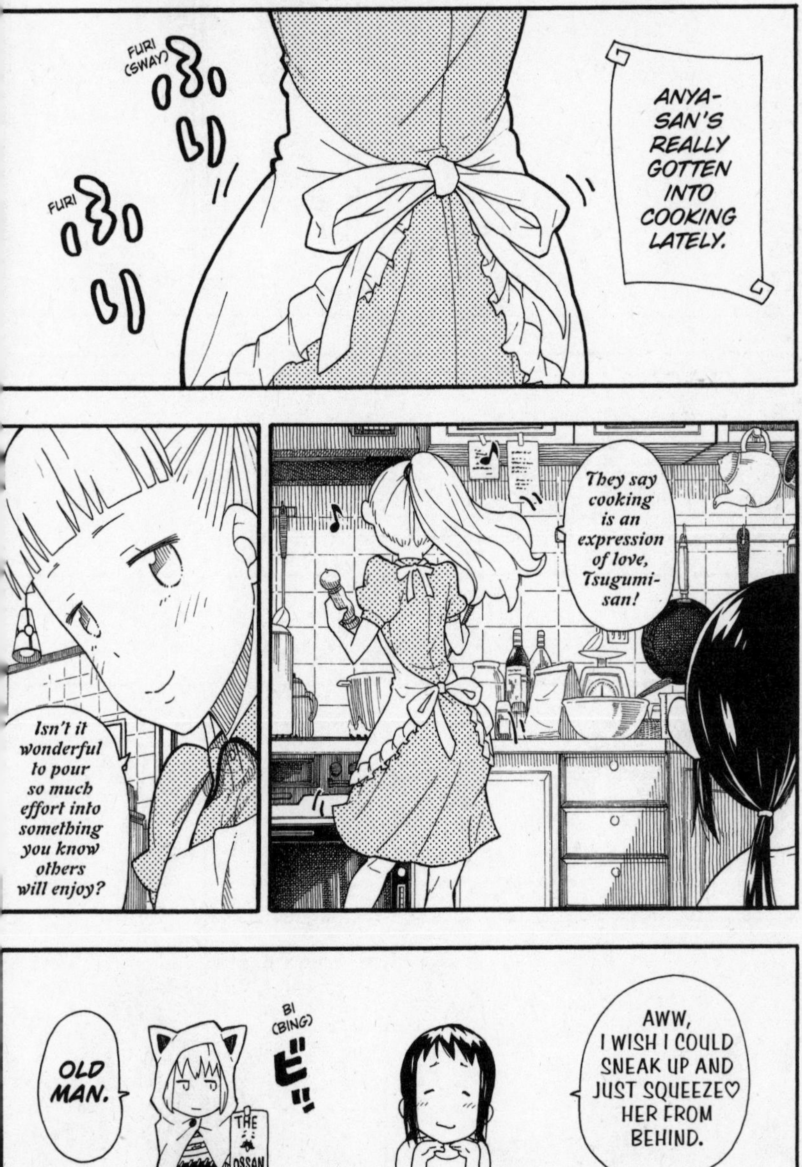
ANYA-SAN'S REALLY GOTTEN INTO COOKING LATELY.
FURI (SWAY)
FURI
They say cooking is an expression of love, Tsugumi-san!
Isn't it wonderful to pour so much effort into something you know others will enjoy?
AWW, I WISH I COULD SNEAK UP AND JUST SQUEEZE♡ HER FROM BEHIND.
BI (BING)
OLD MAN.
THE OSSAN

OSSAN: OLD MAN

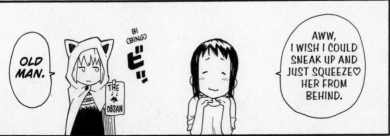

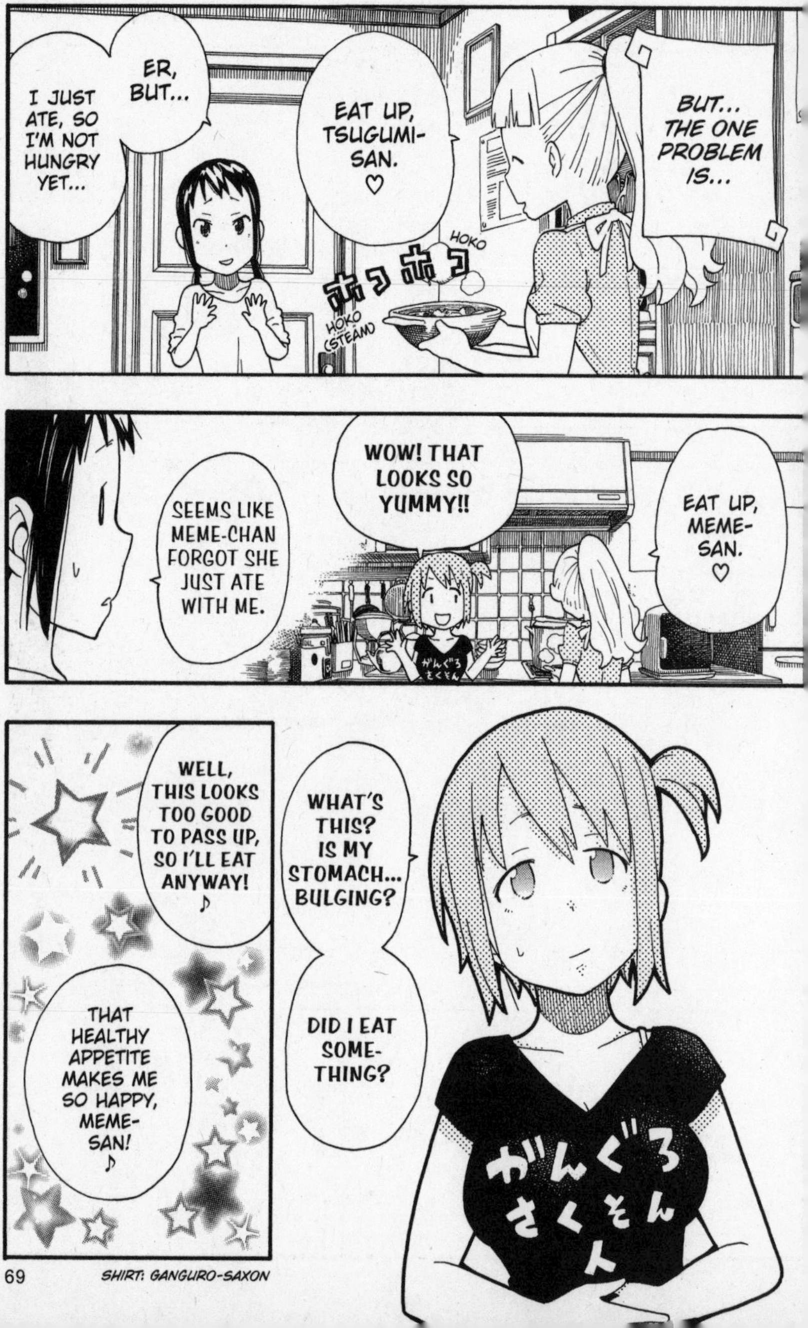
BUT... THE ONE PROBLEM IS...
EAT UP, TSUGUMI-SAN. ♡
HOKO
HOKO (STEAM)
ER, BUT...
I JUST ATE, SO I'M NOT HUNGRY YET...
EAT UP, MEME-SAN. ♡
WOW! THAT LOOKS SO YUMMY!!
SEEMS LIKE MEME-CHAN FORGOT SHE JUST ATE WITH ME.
WHAT'S THIS? IS MY STOMACH... BULGING?
DID I EAT SOME-THING?
がんぐろさくそん
WELL, THIS LOOKS TOO GOOD TO PASS UP, SO I'LL EAT ANYWAY! ♪
THAT HEALTHY APPETITE MAKES ME SO HAPPY, MEME-SAN! ♪

SHIRT: GANGURO-SAXON

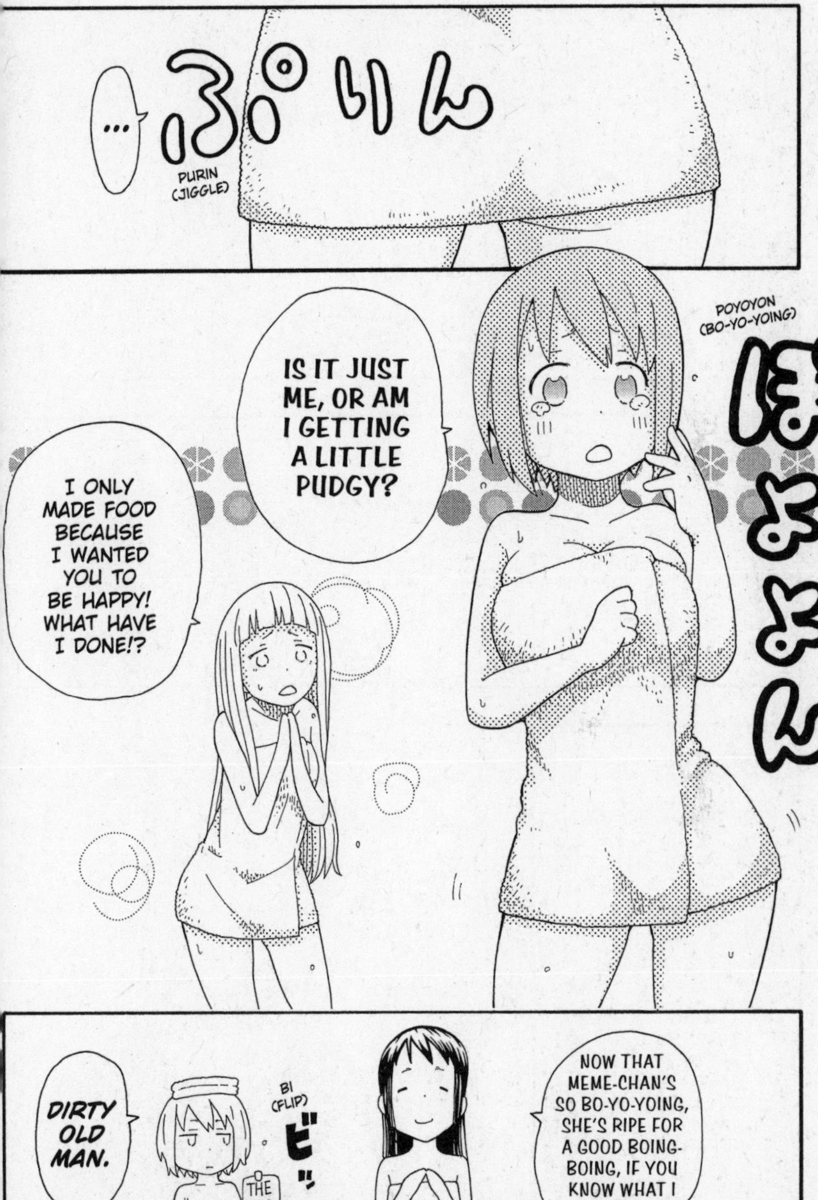
ぷりん
PURIN (JIGGLE)
...
ぽよよん
POYOYON (BO-YO-YOING)
IS IT JUST ME, OR AM I GETTING A LITTLE PUDGY?
I ONLY MADE FOOD BECAUSE I WANTED YOU TO BE HAPPY! WHAT HAVE I DONE!?
NOW THAT MEME-CHAN'S SO BO-YO-YOING, SHE'S RIPE FOR A GOOD BOING-BOING, IF YOU KNOW WHAT I MEAN.
BI (FLIP)
ビッ
THE ERO JIJI
DIRTY OLD MAN.

ERO JIJI: DIRTY OLD MAN

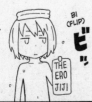

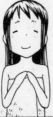

SOUL EATER NOT!

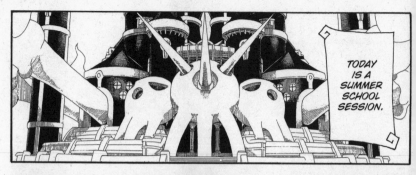

TODAY IS A SUMMER SCHOOL SESSION.

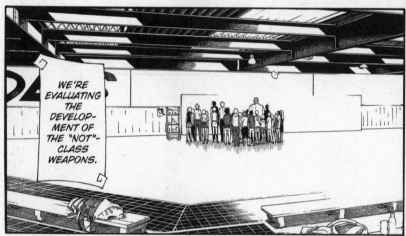

WE'RE EVALUATING THE DEVELOPMENT OF THE "NOT"-CLASS WEAPONS.

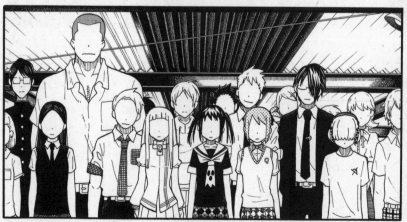

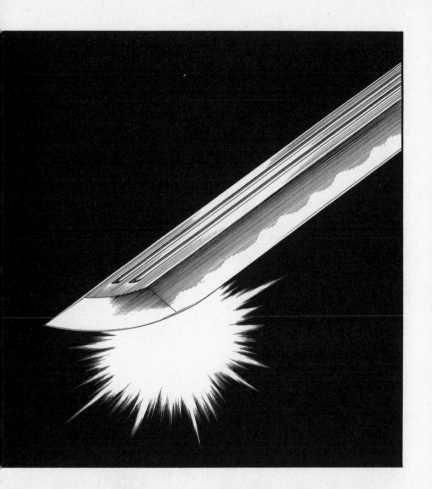

SOUL EATER NOT!

CHAPTER 23: BLADE!

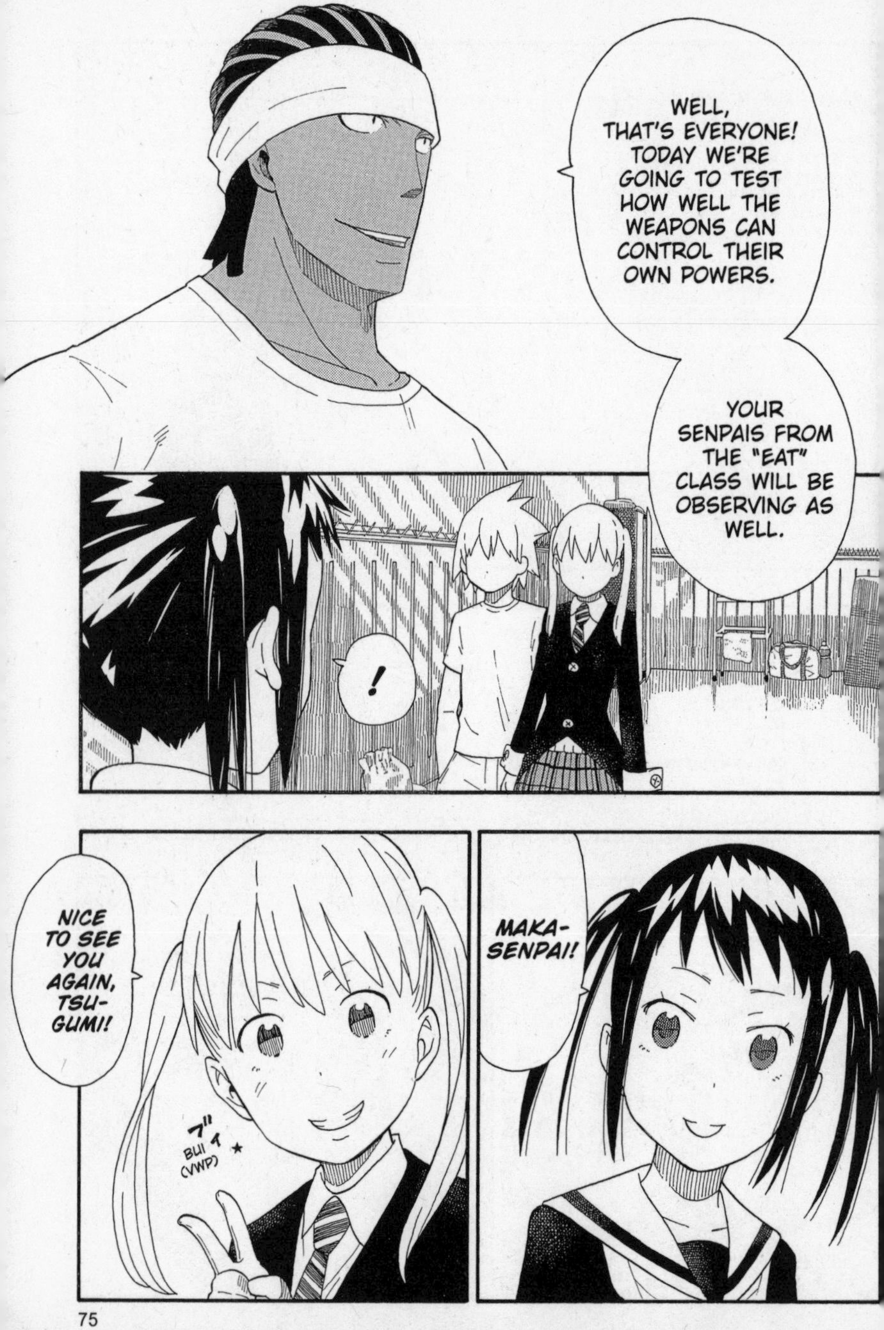
WELL, THAT'S EVERYONE! TODAY WE'RE GOING TO TEST HOW WELL THE WEAPONS CAN CONTROL THEIR OWN POWERS.
YOUR SENPAIS FROM THE "EAT" CLASS WILL BE OBSERVING AS WELL.
!
MAKA-SENPAI!
NICE TO SEE YOU AGAIN, TSUGUMI!
ブイ
BUI (VWP) ★

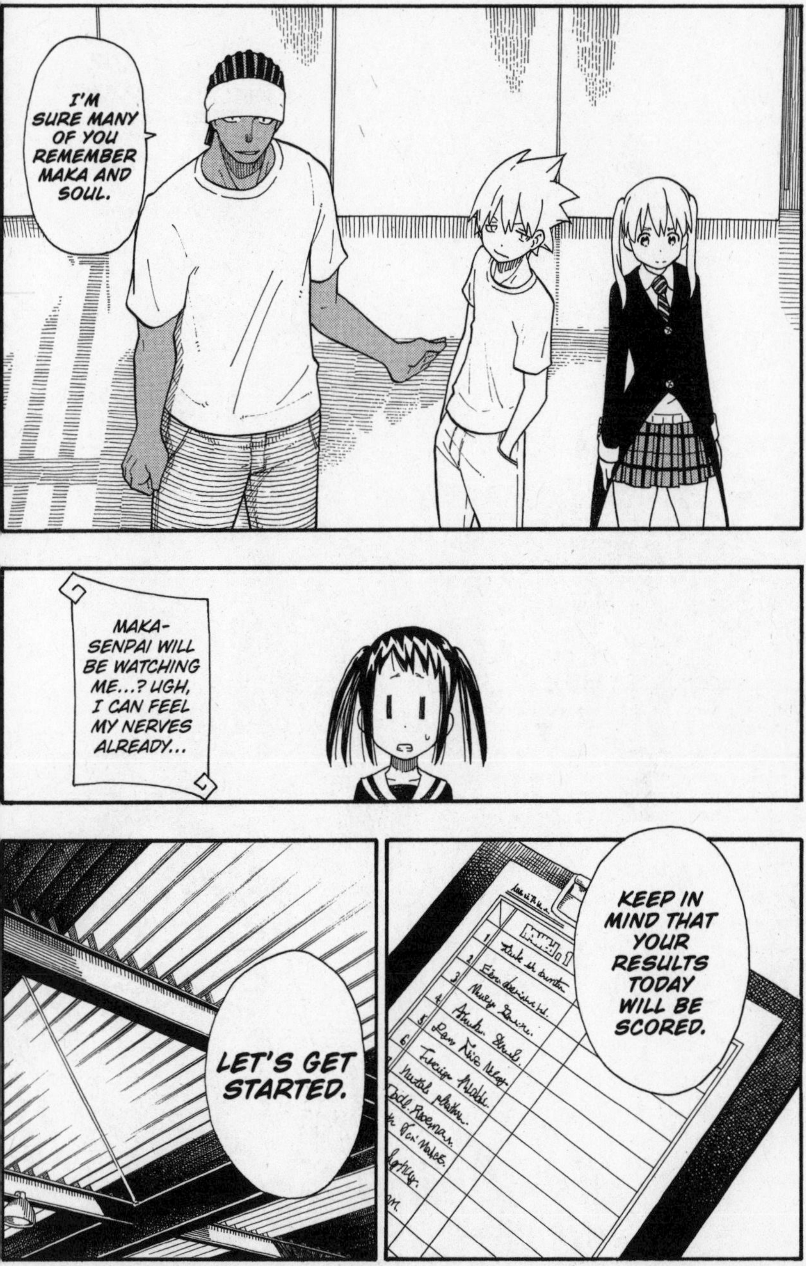
I'M SURE MANY OF YOU REMEMBER MAKA AND SOUL.
MAKA-SENPAI WILL BE WATCHING ME...? UGH, I CAN FEEL MY NERVES ALREADY...
KEEP IN MIND THAT YOUR RESULTS TODAY WILL BE SCORED.
LET'S GET STARTED.

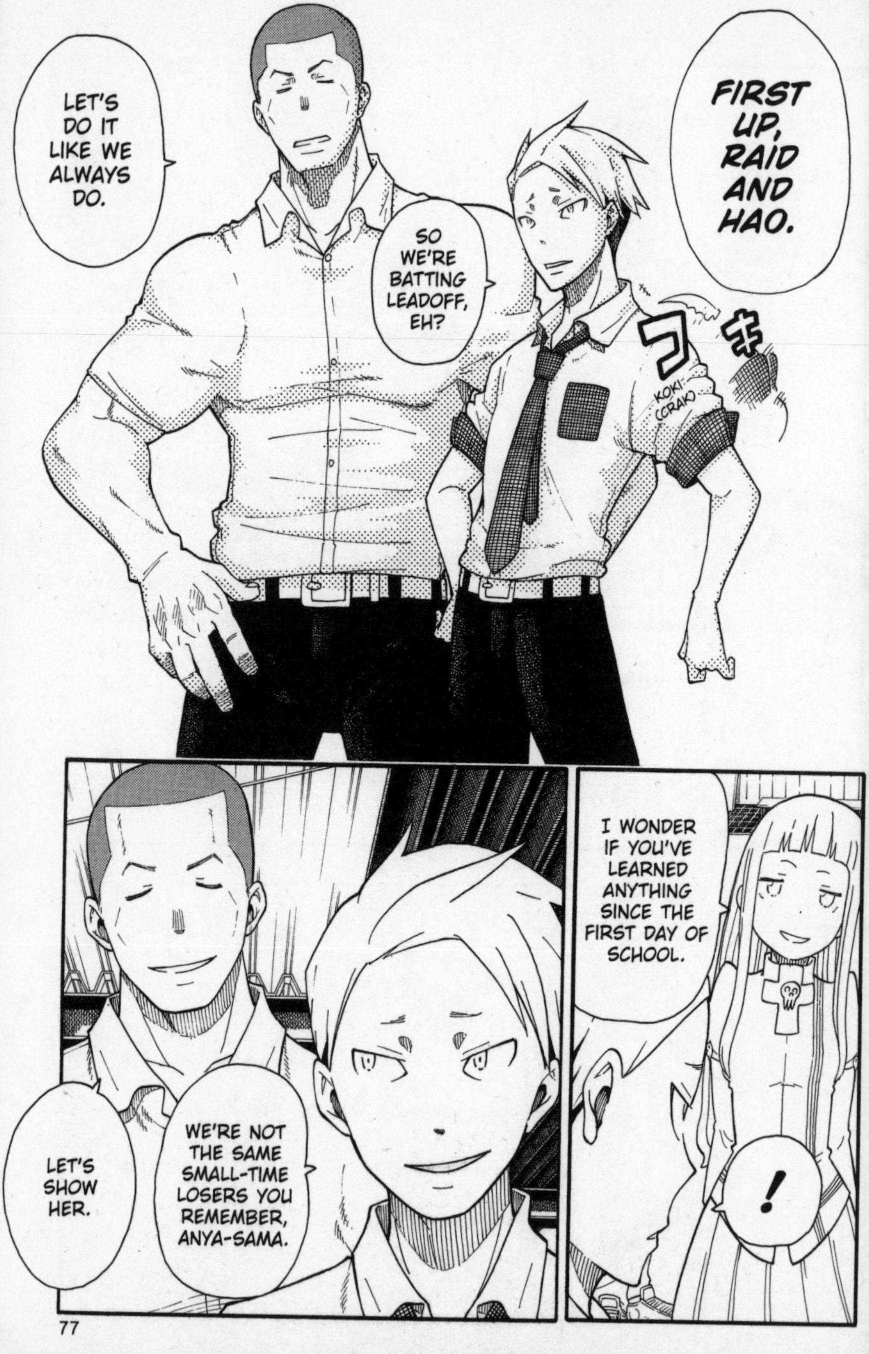
FIRST UP, RAID AND HAO.
LET'S DO IT LIKE WE ALWAYS DO.
SO WE'RE BATTING LEADOFF, EH?
KOKI (CRAK)
I WONDER IF YOU'VE LEARNED ANYTHING SINCE THE FIRST DAY OF SCHOOL.
!
WE'RE NOT THE SAME SMALL-TIME LOSERS YOU REMEMBER, ANYA-SAMA.
LET'S SHOW HER.

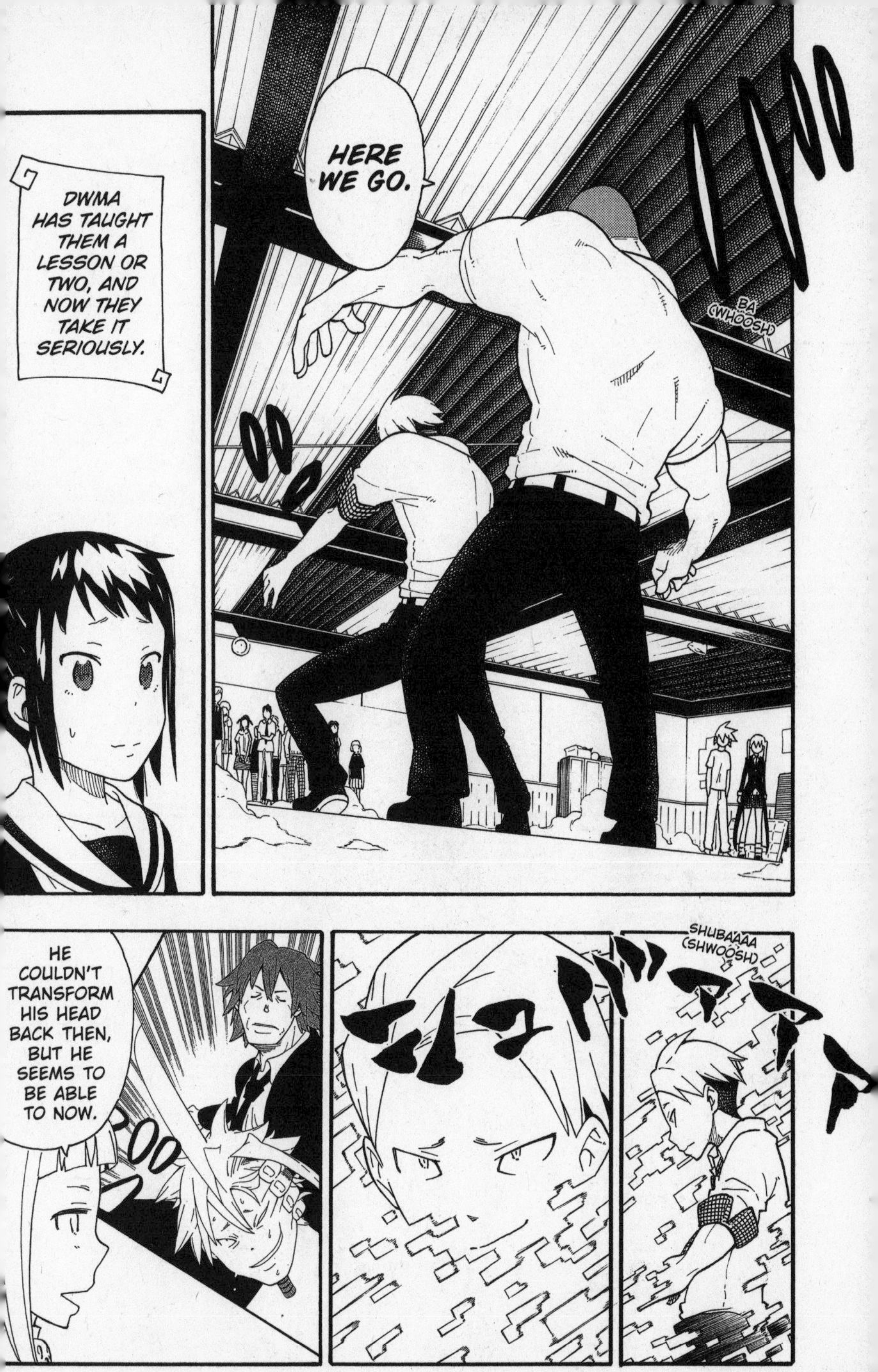
HERE WE GO.
BA (WHOOSH)
DWMA HAS TAUGHT THEM A LESSON OR TWO, AND NOW THEY TAKE IT SERIOUSLY.
SHUBAAAA (SHWOOSH)
HE COULDN'T TRANSFORM HIS HEAD BACK THEN, BUT HE SEEMS TO BE ABLE TO NOW.

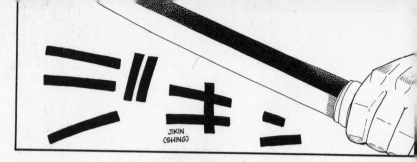

JIKIN
(SHING)

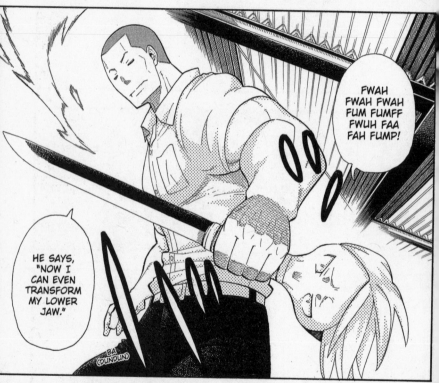

FWAH FWAH FWAH FUM FUMFF FWUH FAA FAH FUMP!

HE SAYS, "NOW I CAN EVEN TRANSFORM MY LOWER JAW."

BA (CLUNCLUN)

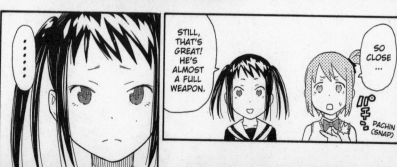

· · · · ·

STILL, THAT'S GREAT! HE'S ALMOST A FULL WEAPON.

SO CLOSE...

PACHIN (SNAP)

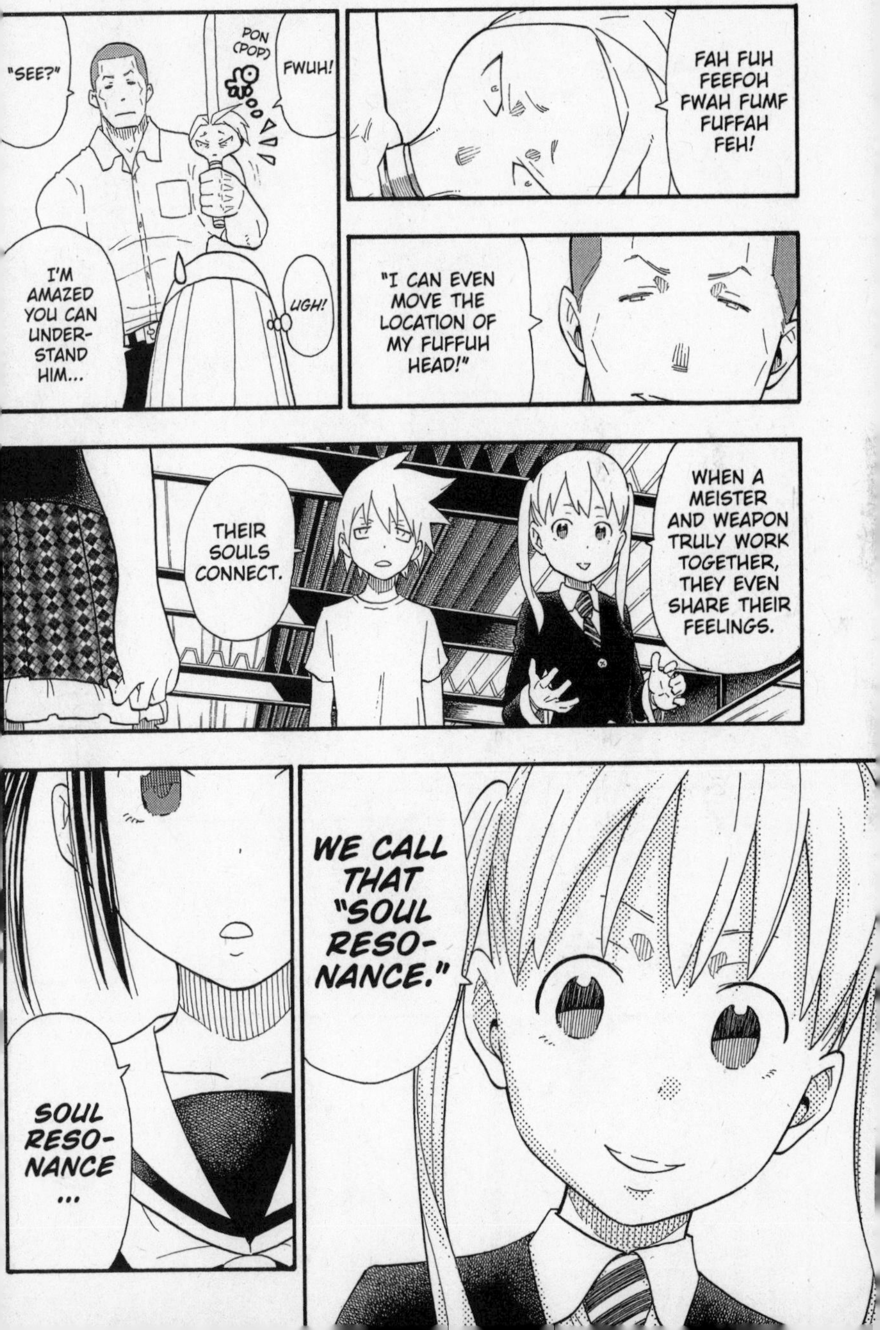
FAH FUH FEEFOH FWAH FUMF FUFFAH FEH!
"I CAN EVEN MOVE THE LOCATION OF MY FUFFUH HEAD!"
FWUH!
PON (POP)
"SEE?"
UGH!
I'M AMAZED YOU CAN UNDER-STAND HIM...
WHEN A MEISTER AND WEAPON TRULY WORK TOGETHER, THEY EVEN SHARE THEIR FEELINGS.
THEIR SOULS CONNECT.
WE CALL THAT "SOUL RESO-NANCE."
SOUL RESO-NANCE ...

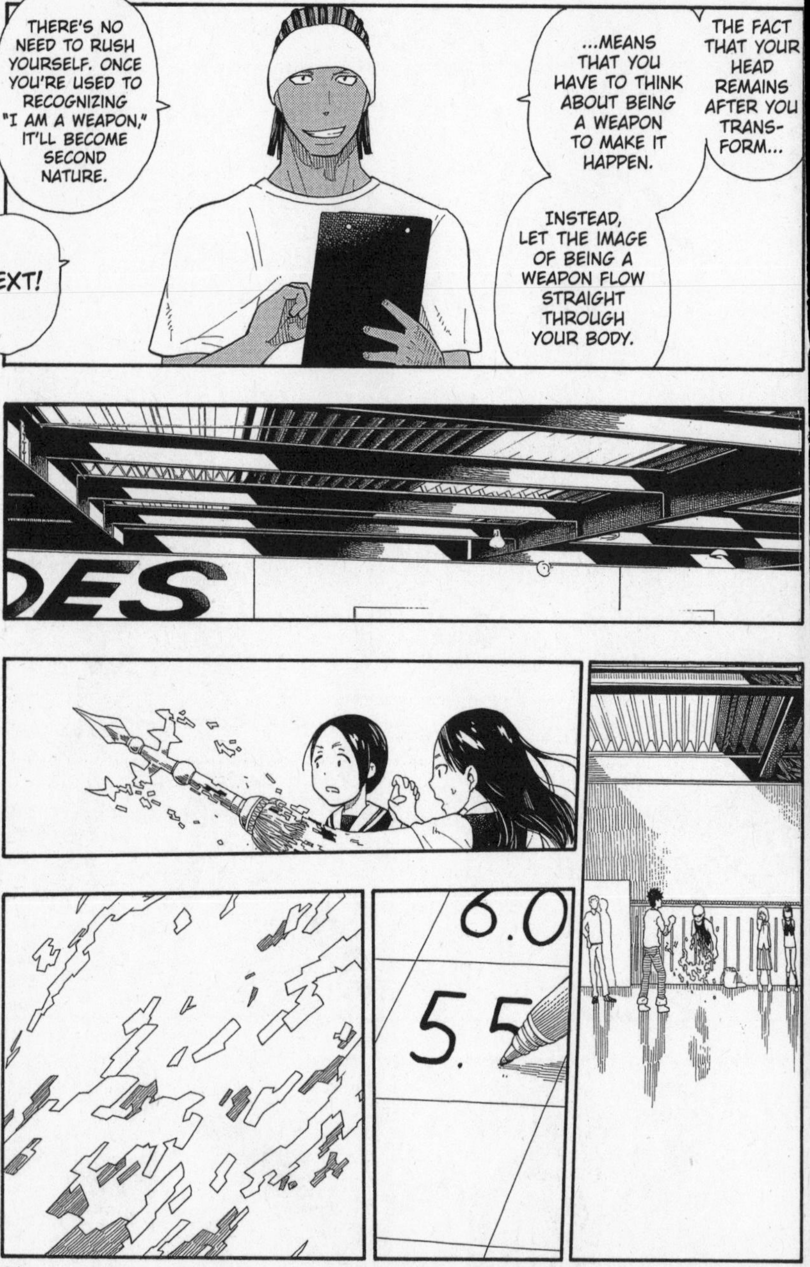
THE FACT THAT YOUR HEAD REMAINS AFTER YOU TRANS-FORM...
...MEANS THAT YOU HAVE TO THINK ABOUT BEING A WEAPON TO MAKE IT HAPPEN.
INSTEAD, LET THE IMAGE OF BEING A WEAPON FLOW STRAIGHT THROUGH YOUR BODY.
THERE'S NO NEED TO RUSH YOURSELF. ONCE YOU'RE USED TO RECOGNIZING "I AM A WEAPON," IT'LL BECOME SECOND NATURE.
NEXT!
DES
6.0
5.5

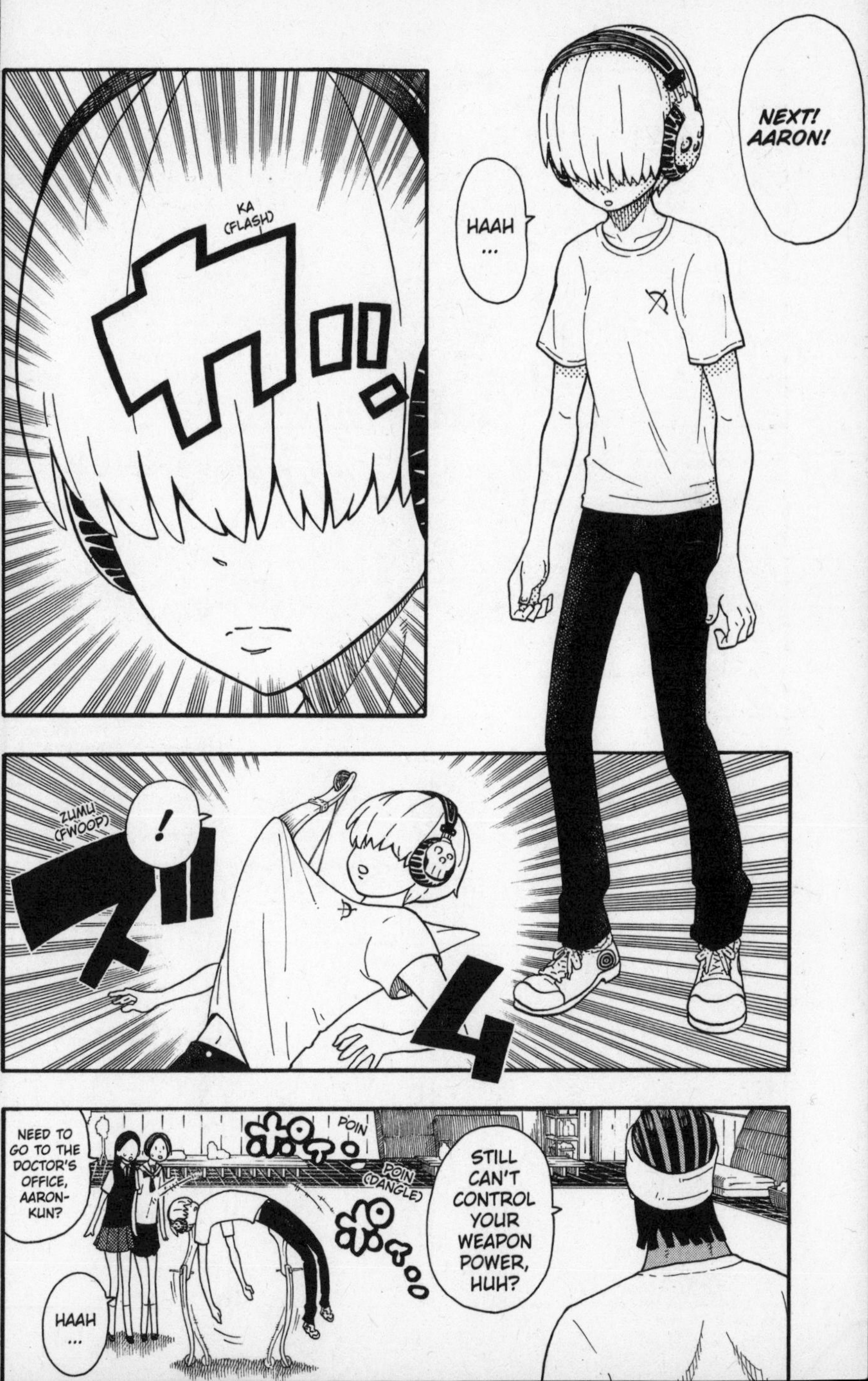
NEXT! AARON!
HAAH ...
KA (FLASH)
ZUMU (FWOOP)
!
STILL CAN'T CONTROL YOUR WEAPON POWER, HUH?
POIN
POIN (DANGLE)
NEED TO GO TO THE DOCTOR'S OFFICE, AARON-KUN?
HAAH ...

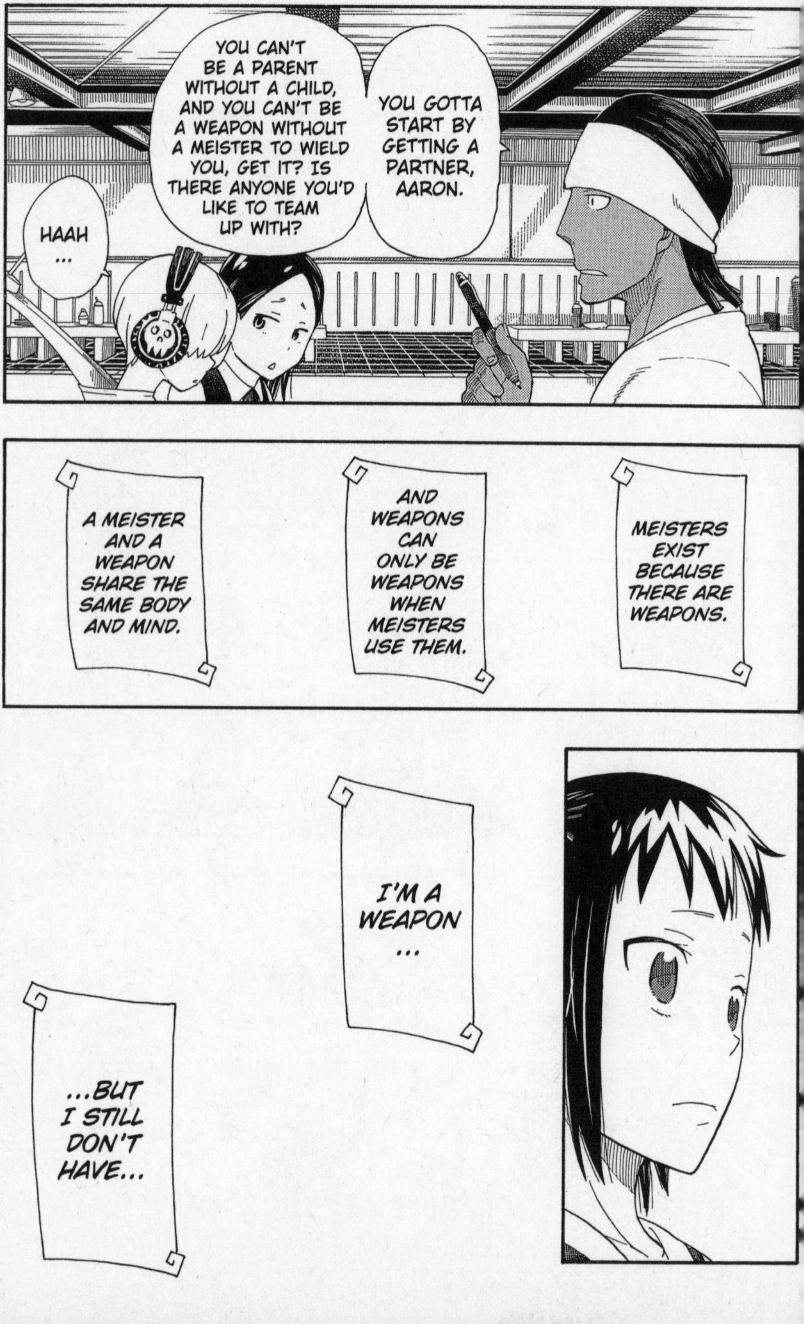
YOU GOTTA START BY GETTING A PARTNER, AARON.
YOU CAN'T BE A PARENT WITHOUT A CHILD, AND YOU CAN'T BE A WEAPON WITHOUT A MEISTER TO WIELD YOU, GET IT? IS THERE ANYONE YOU'D LIKE TO TEAM UP WITH?
HAAH ...
MEISTERS EXIST BECAUSE THERE ARE WEAPONS.
AND WEAPONS CAN ONLY BE WEAPONS WHEN MEISTERS USE THEM.
A MEISTER AND A WEAPON SHARE THE SAME BODY AND MIND.
I'M A WEAPON ...
...BUT I STILL DON'T HAVE...

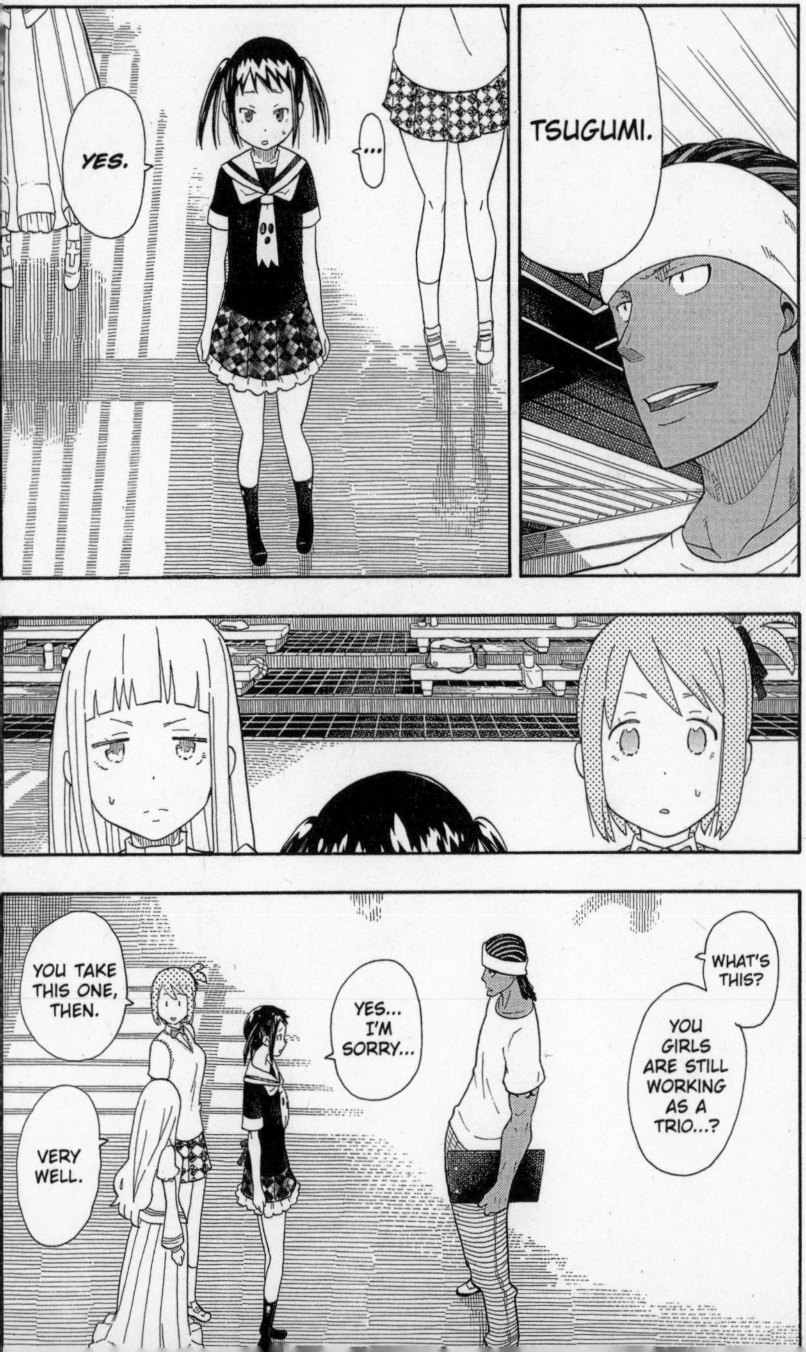
TSUGUMI.
...
YES.
WHAT'S THIS?
YOU GIRLS ARE STILL WORKING AS A TRIO...?
YES... I'M SORRY...
YOU TAKE THIS ONE, THEN.
VERY WELL.

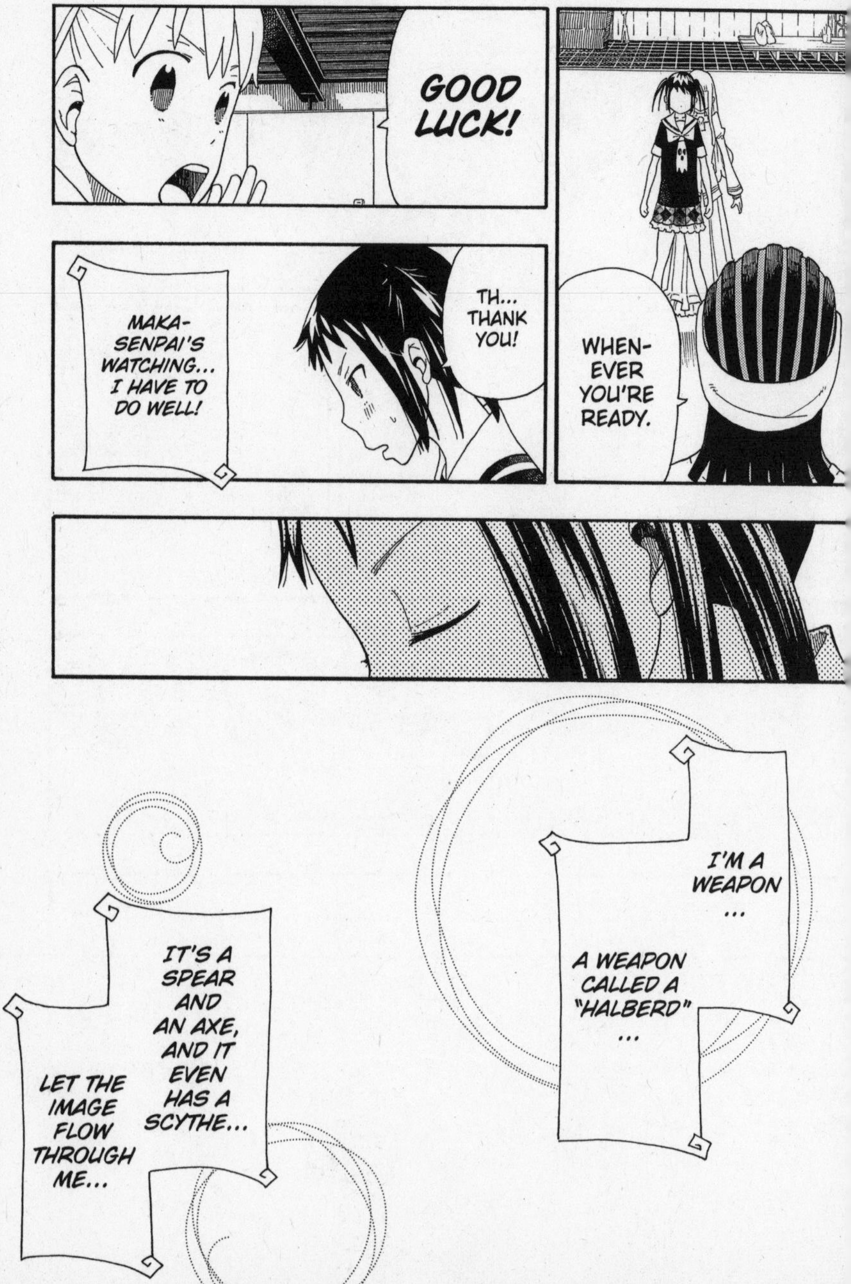
WHENEVER YOU'RE READY.
GOOD LUCK!
TH... THANK YOU!
MAKA-SENPAI'S WATCHING... I HAVE TO DO WELL!
I'M A WEAPON ...
A WEAPON CALLED A "HALBERD" ...
IT'S A SPEAR AND AN AXE, AND IT EVEN HAS A SCYTHE...
LET THE IMAGE FLOW THROUGH ME...

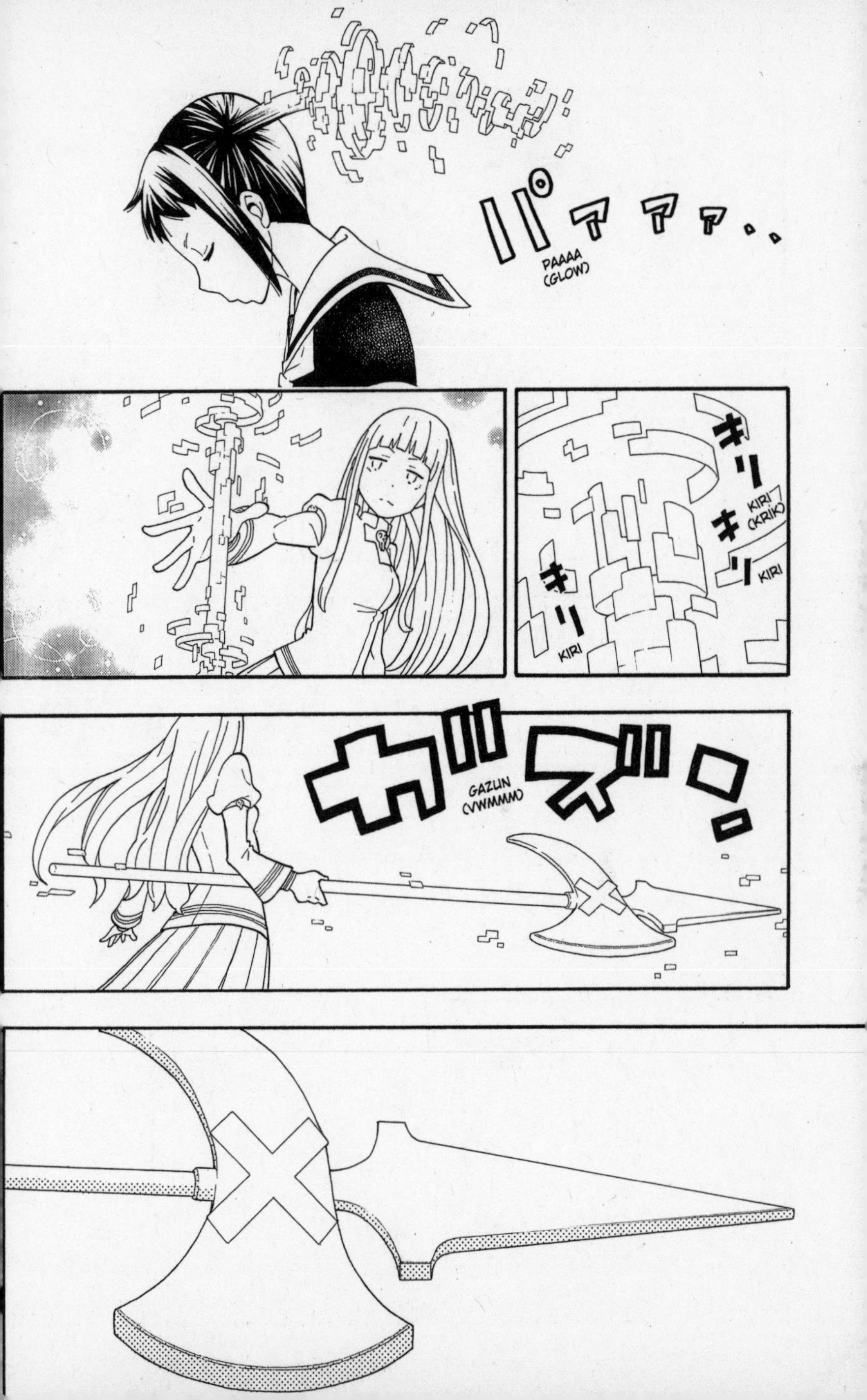
パァァァ。。
PAAAA (GLOW)
キリキリ
KIRI (KRIK)
KIRI
キリ
KIRI
ガズン。
GAZUN (VWMMM)

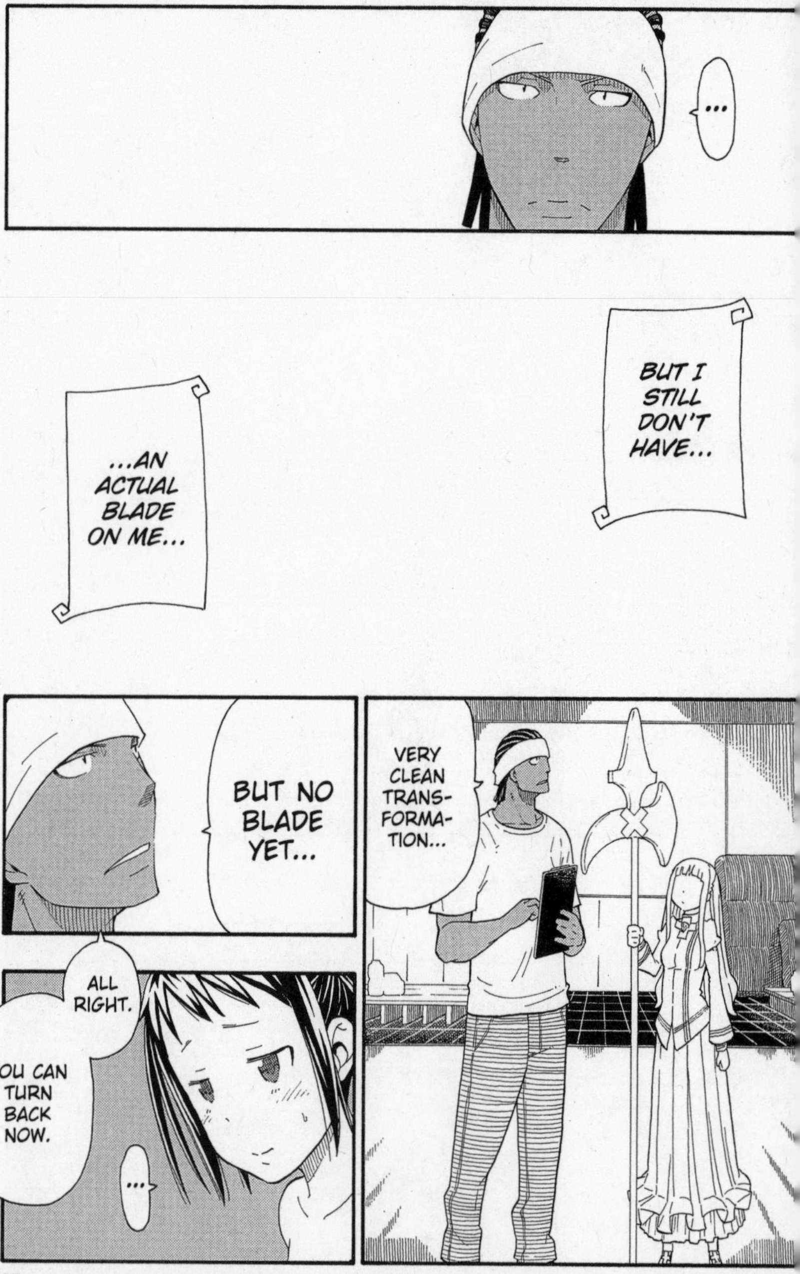
...
BUT I STILL DON'T HAVE...
...AN ACTUAL BLADE ON ME...
VERY CLEAN TRANS-FORMA-TION...
BUT NO BLADE YET...
ALL RIGHT.
YOU CAN TURN BACK NOW.
...

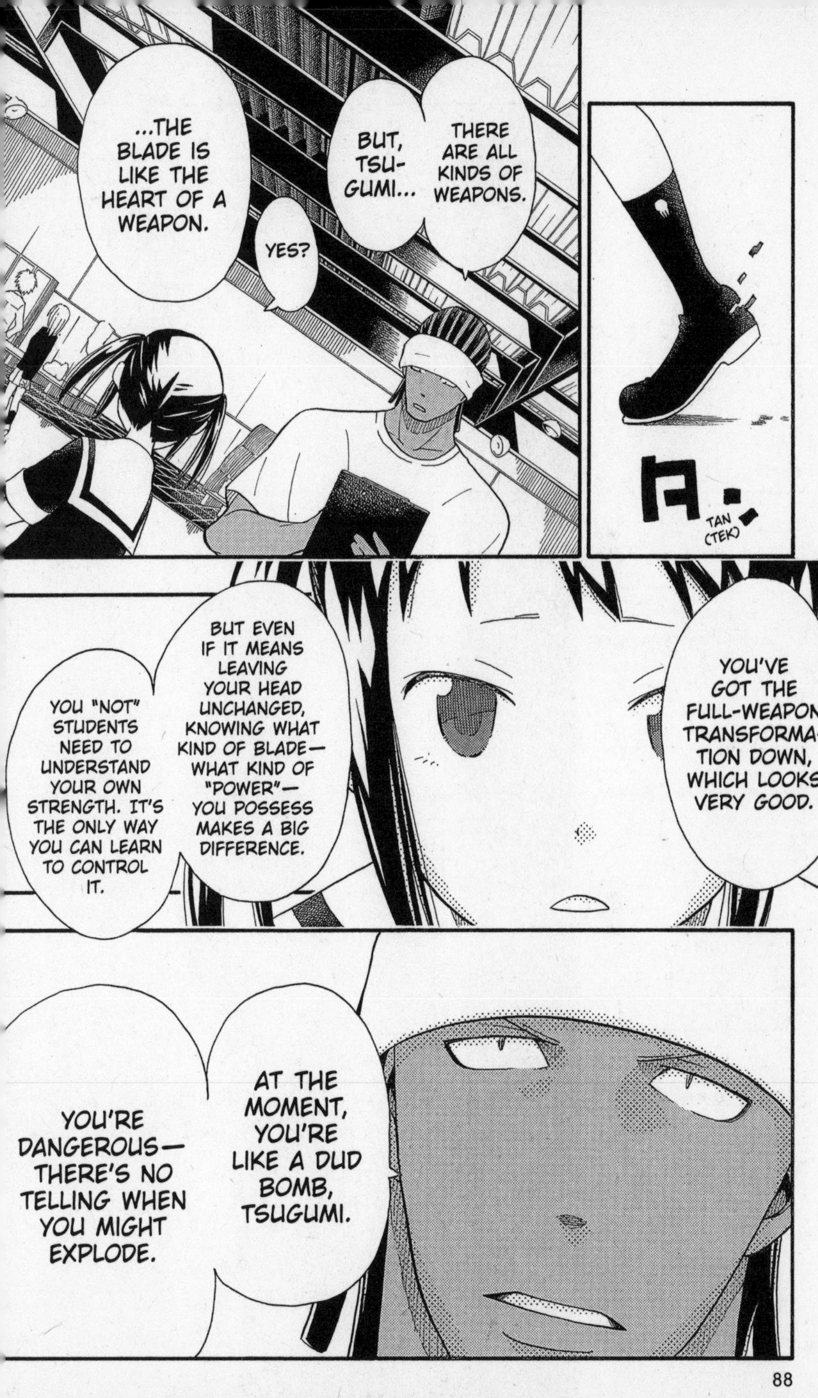
TAN (TEK)
THERE ARE ALL KINDS OF WEAPONS.
BUT, TSUGUMI...
...THE BLADE IS LIKE THE HEART OF A WEAPON.
YES?
YOU'VE GOT THE FULL-WEAPON TRANSFORMATION DOWN, WHICH LOOKS VERY GOOD.
BUT EVEN IF IT MEANS LEAVING YOUR HEAD UNCHANGED, KNOWING WHAT KIND OF BLADE—WHAT KIND OF "POWER"—YOU POSSESS MAKES A BIG DIFFERENCE.
YOU "NOT" STUDENTS NEED TO UNDERSTAND YOUR OWN STRENGTH. IT'S THE ONLY WAY YOU CAN LEARN TO CONTROL IT.
AT THE MOMENT, YOU'RE LIKE A DUD BOMB, TSUGUMI.
YOU'RE DANGEROUS—THERE'S NO TELLING WHEN YOU MIGHT EXPLODE.

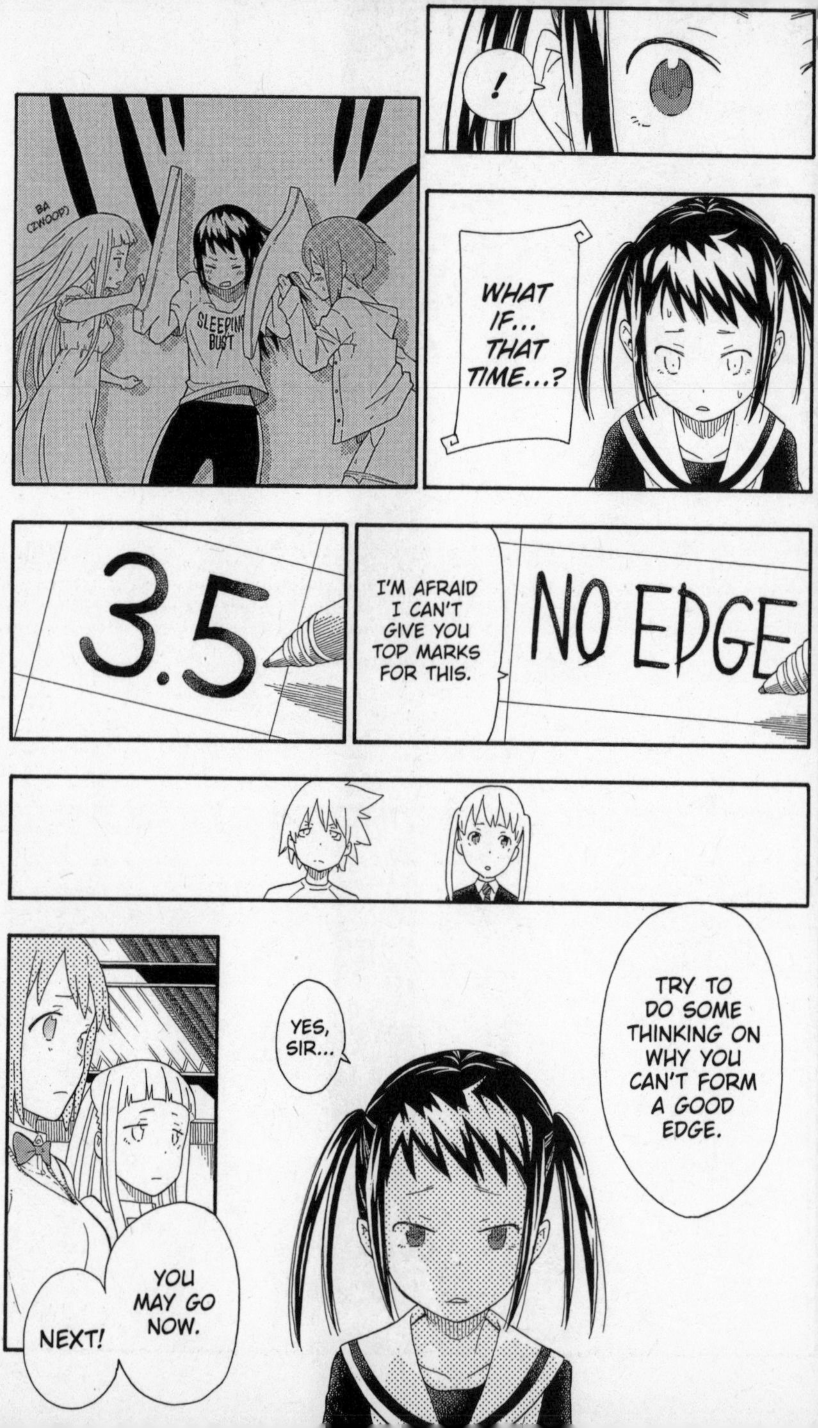
!
WHAT IF... THAT TIME...?
BA (ZWOOP)
NO EDGE
I'M AFRAID I CAN'T GIVE YOU TOP MARKS FOR THIS.
3.5
TRY TO DO SOME THINKING ON WHY YOU CAN'T FORM A GOOD EDGE.
YES, SIR...
YOU MAY GO NOW.
NEXT!

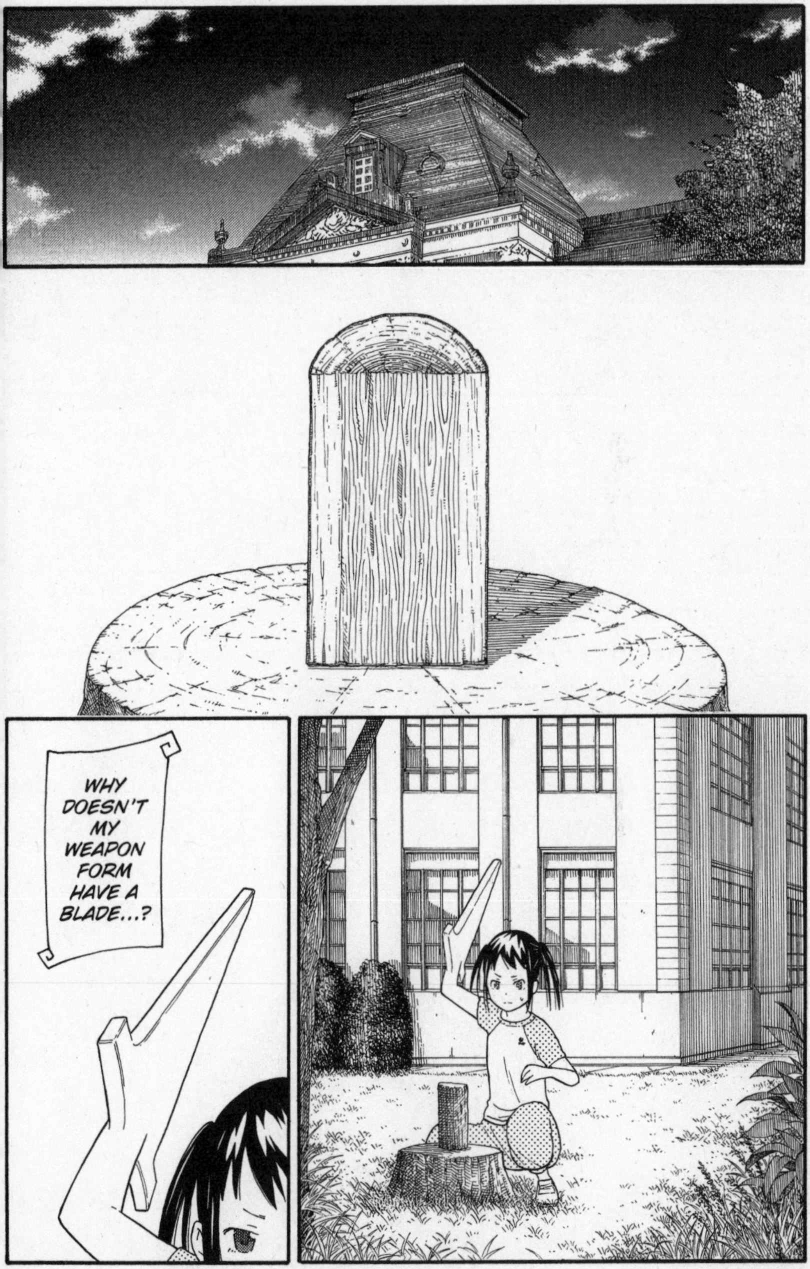
WHY DOESN'T MY WEAPON FORM HAVE A BLADE...?

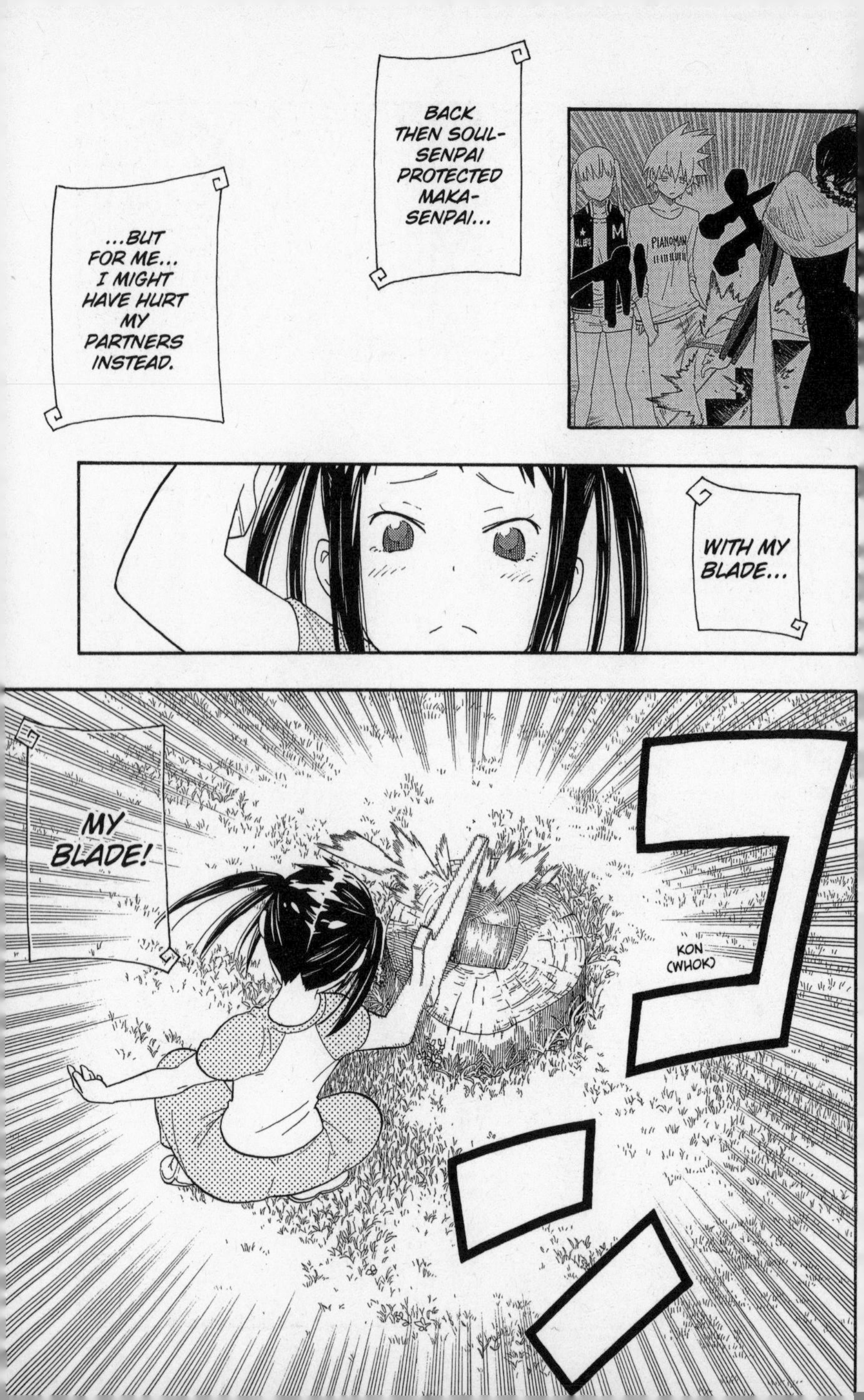
PIANOMAN
BACK THEN SOUL-SENPAI PROTECTED MAKA-SENPAI...
...BUT FOR ME... I MIGHT HAVE HURT MY PARTNERS INSTEAD.
WITH MY BLADE...
MY BLADE!
KON (WHOK)

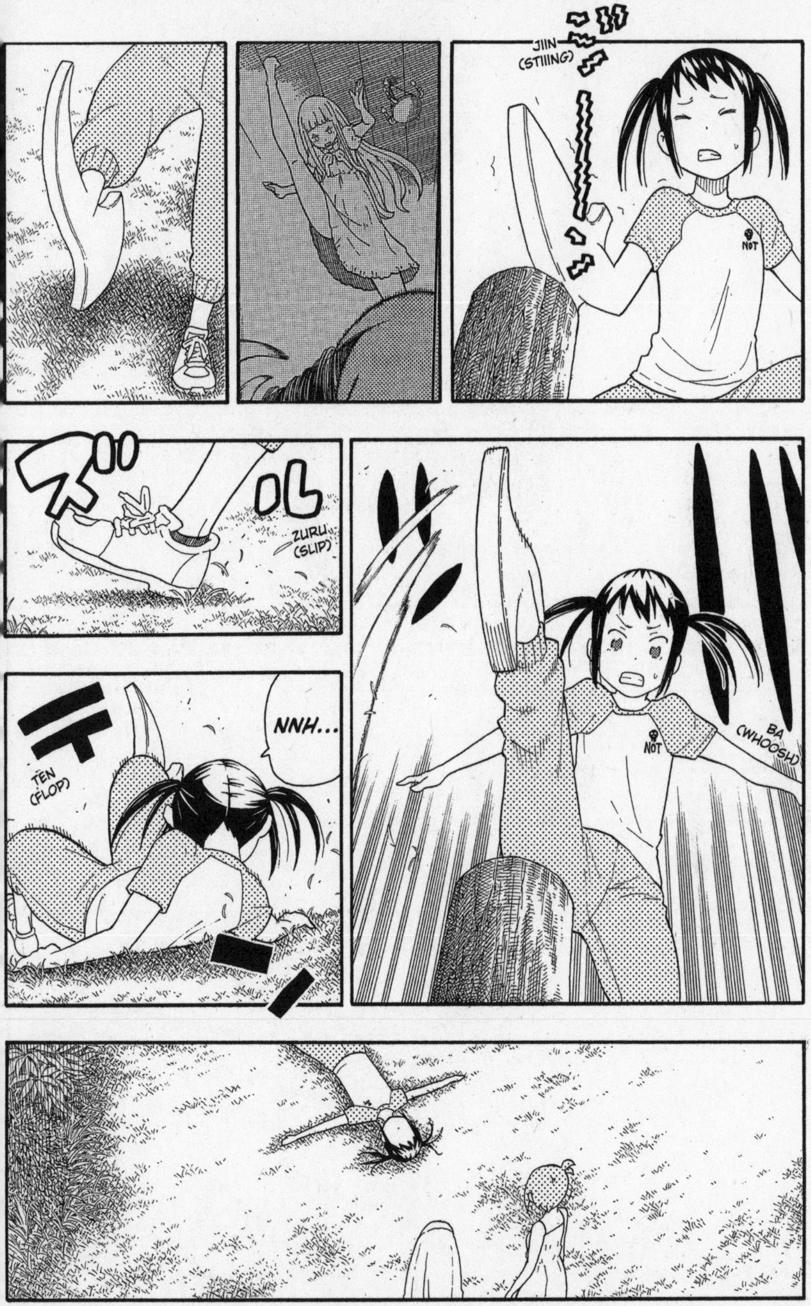
JIIN (STIIING)
BA (WHOOSH)
ZURU (SLIP)
NNH...
TEN (FLOP)

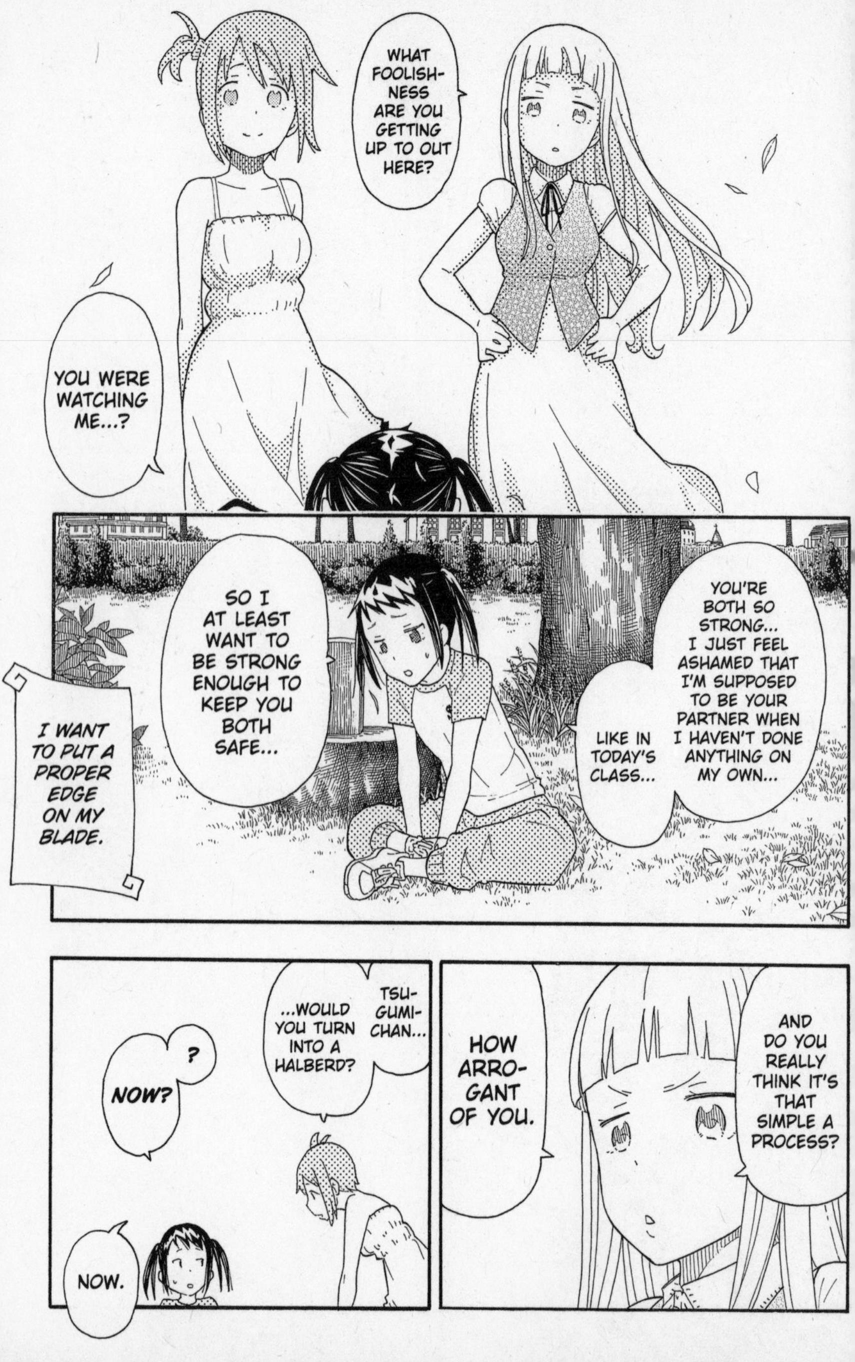
WHAT FOOLISHNESS ARE YOU GETTING UP TO OUT HERE?
YOU WERE WATCHING ME...?
YOU'RE BOTH SO STRONG... I JUST FEEL ASHAMED THAT I'M SUPPOSED TO BE YOUR PARTNER WHEN I HAVEN'T DONE ANYTHING ON MY OWN...
LIKE IN TODAY'S CLASS...
SO I AT LEAST WANT TO BE STRONG ENOUGH TO KEEP YOU BOTH SAFE...
I WANT TO PUT A PROPER EDGE ON MY BLADE.
AND DO YOU REALLY THINK IT'S THAT SIMPLE A PROCESS?
HOW ARROGANT OF YOU.
TSUGUMI-CHAN...
...WOULD YOU TURN INTO A HALBERD?
?
NOW?
NOW.

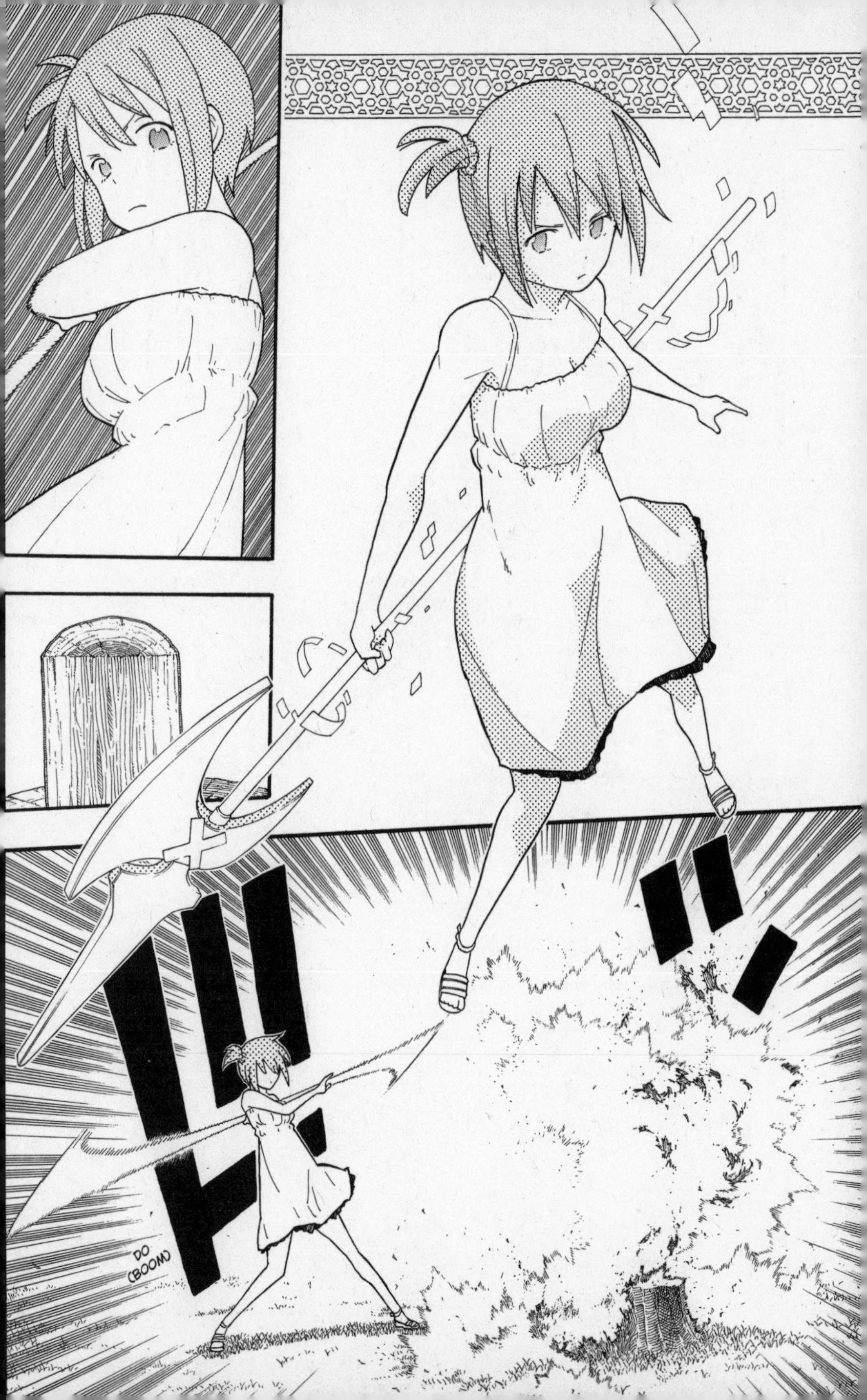
DO
(BOOM)

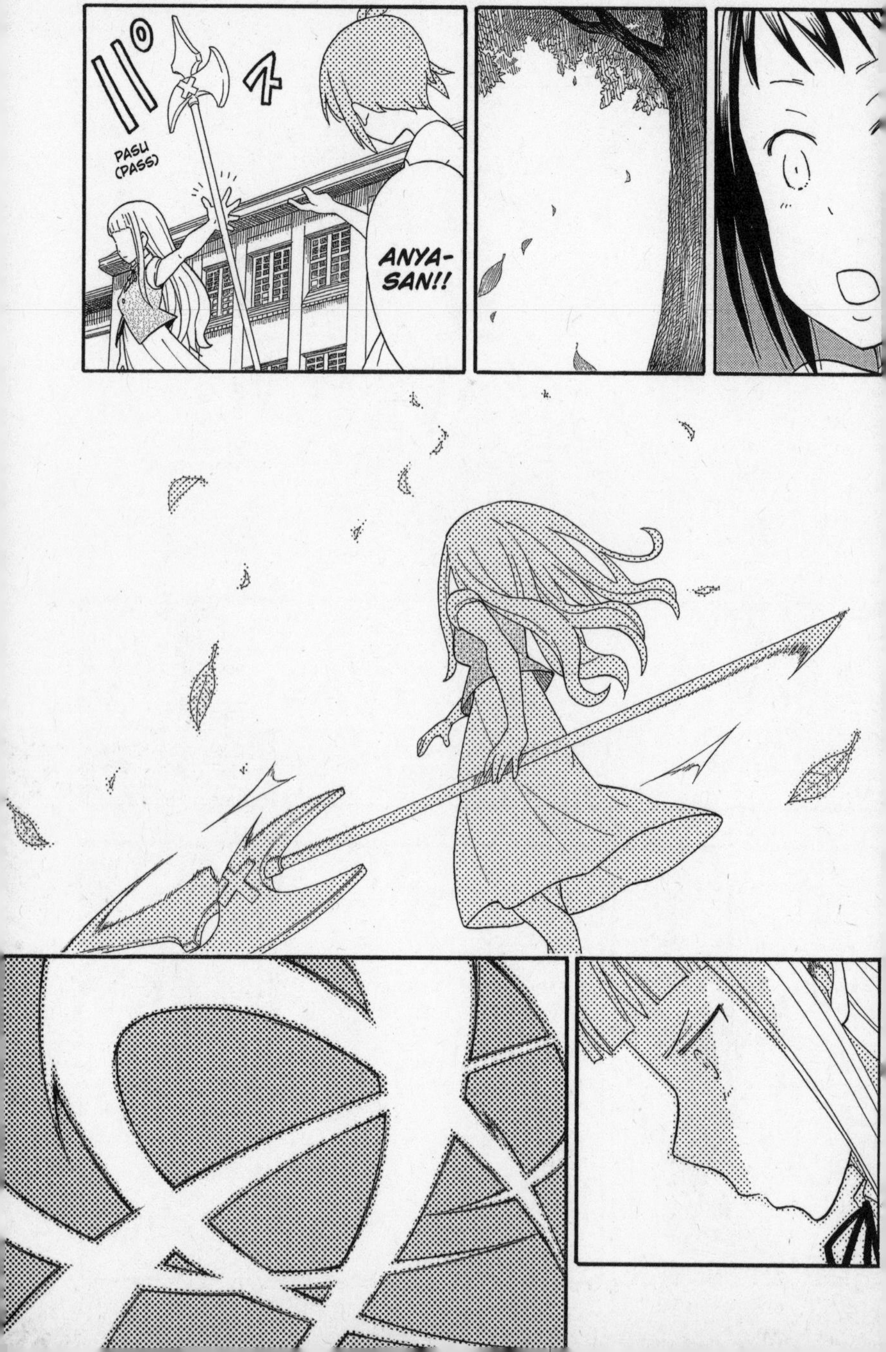
ANYA-SAN!!
パス
PASU (PASS)

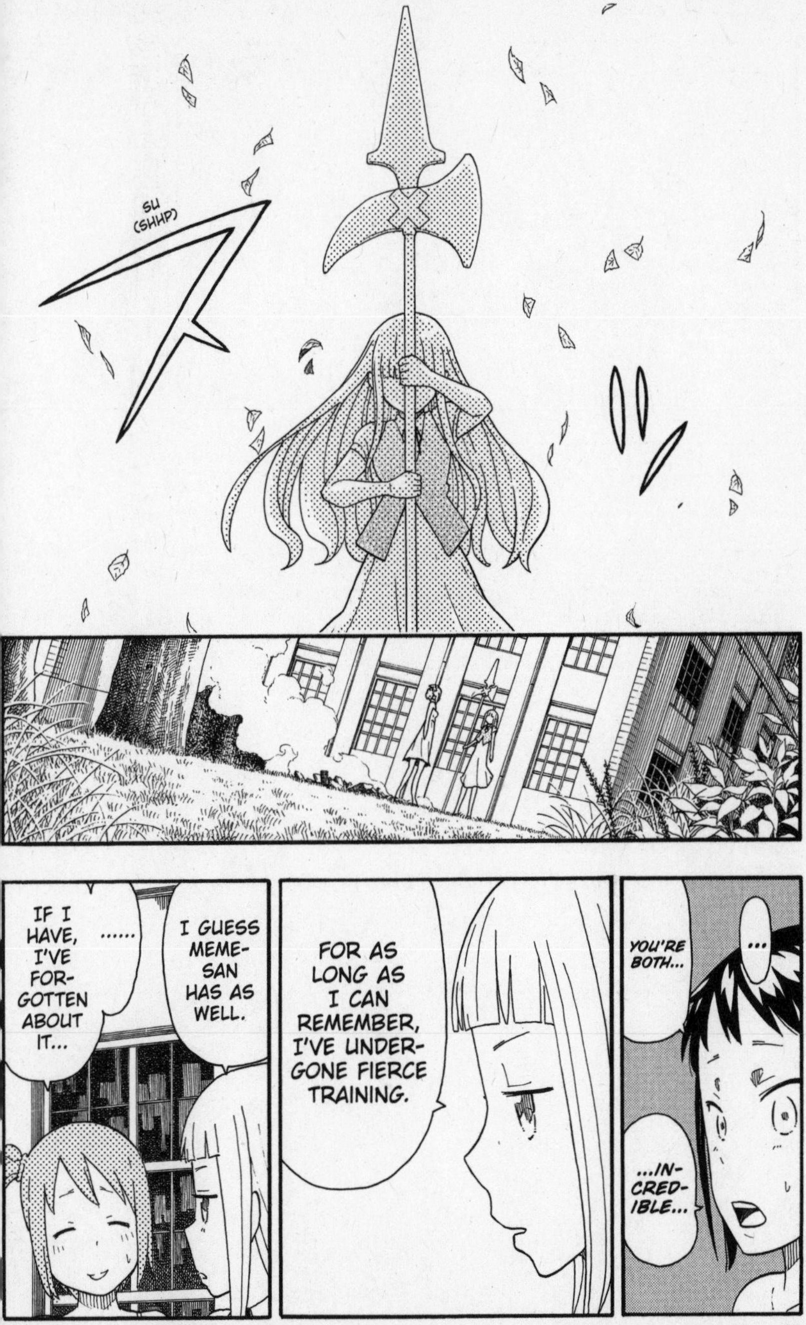
SU (SHHP)
...
YOU'RE BOTH...
...INCREDIBLE...
FOR AS LONG AS I CAN REMEMBER, I'VE UNDERGONE FIERCE TRAINING.
I GUESS MEME-SAN HAS AS WELL.
......
IF I HAVE, I'VE FORGOTTEN ABOUT IT...

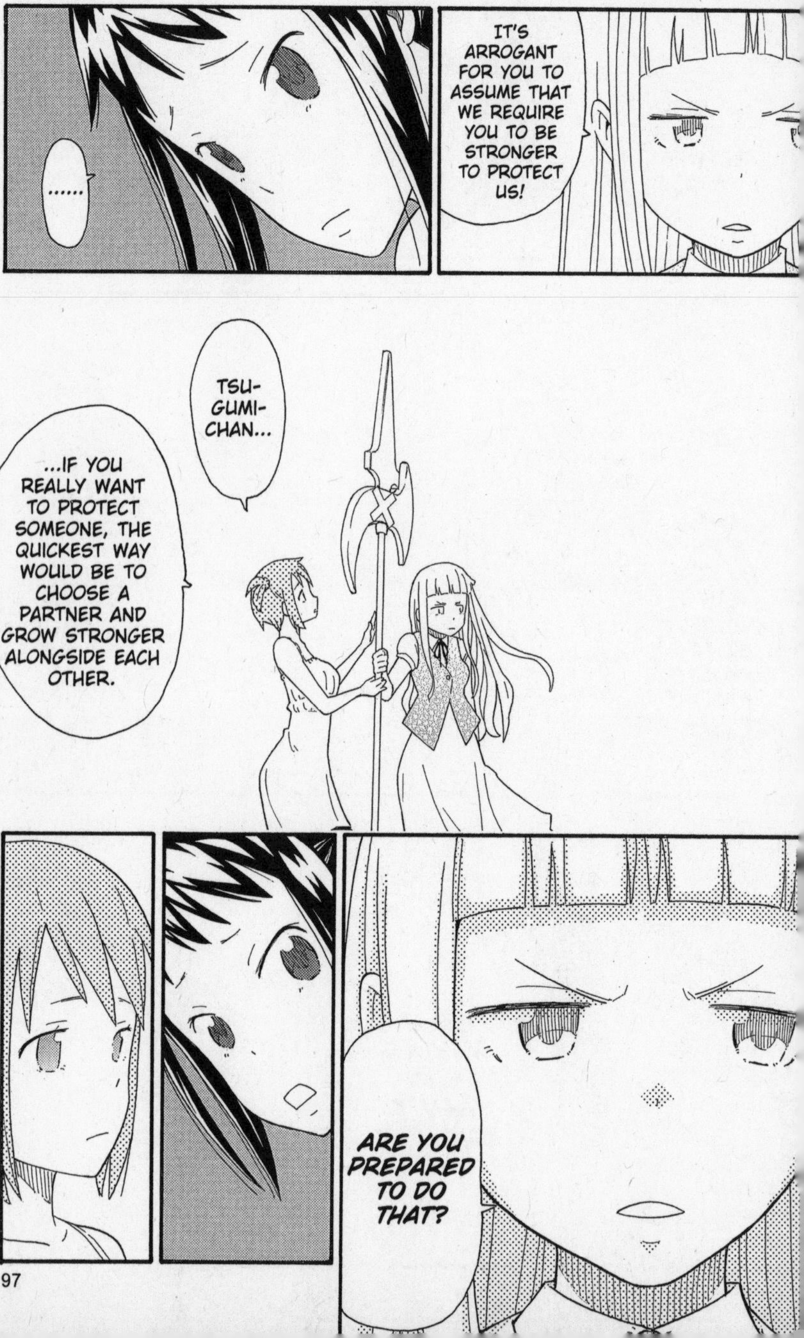
IT'S ARROGANT FOR YOU TO ASSUME THAT WE REQUIRE YOU TO BE STRONGER TO PROTECT US!
......
TSU-GUMI-CHAN...
...IF YOU REALLY WANT TO PROTECT SOMEONE, THE QUICKEST WAY WOULD BE TO CHOOSE A PARTNER AND GROW STRONGER ALONGSIDE EACH OTHER.
ARE YOU PREPARED TO DO THAT?

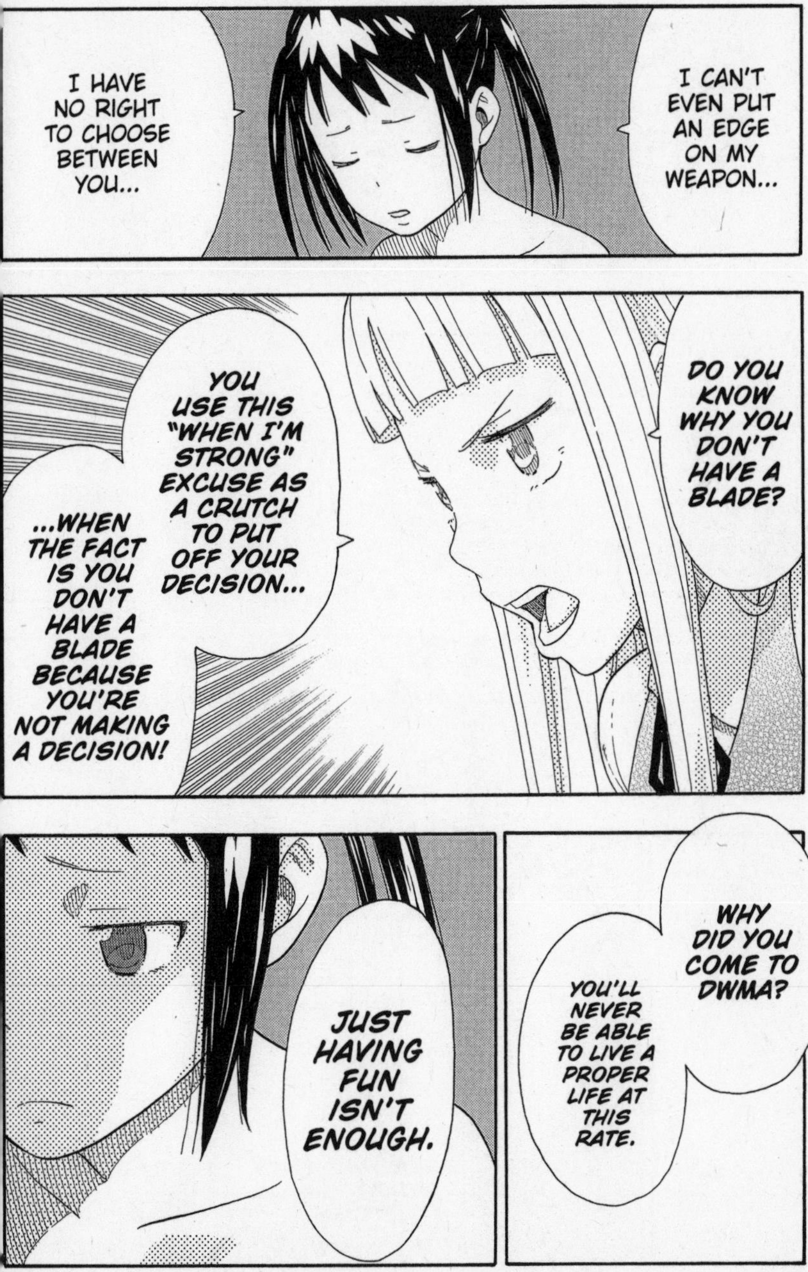

I CAN'T EVEN PUT AN EDGE ON MY WEAPON...
I HAVE NO RIGHT TO CHOOSE BETWEEN YOU...
DO YOU KNOW WHY YOU DON'T HAVE A BLADE?
YOU USE THIS "WHEN I'M STRONG" EXCUSE AS A CRUTCH TO PUT OFF YOUR DECISION...
...WHEN THE FACT IS YOU DON'T HAVE A BLADE BECAUSE YOU'RE NOT MAKING A DECISION!
WHY DID YOU COME TO DWMA?
YOU'LL NEVER BE ABLE TO LIVE A PROPER LIFE AT THIS RATE.
JUST HAVING FUN ISN'T ENOUGH.

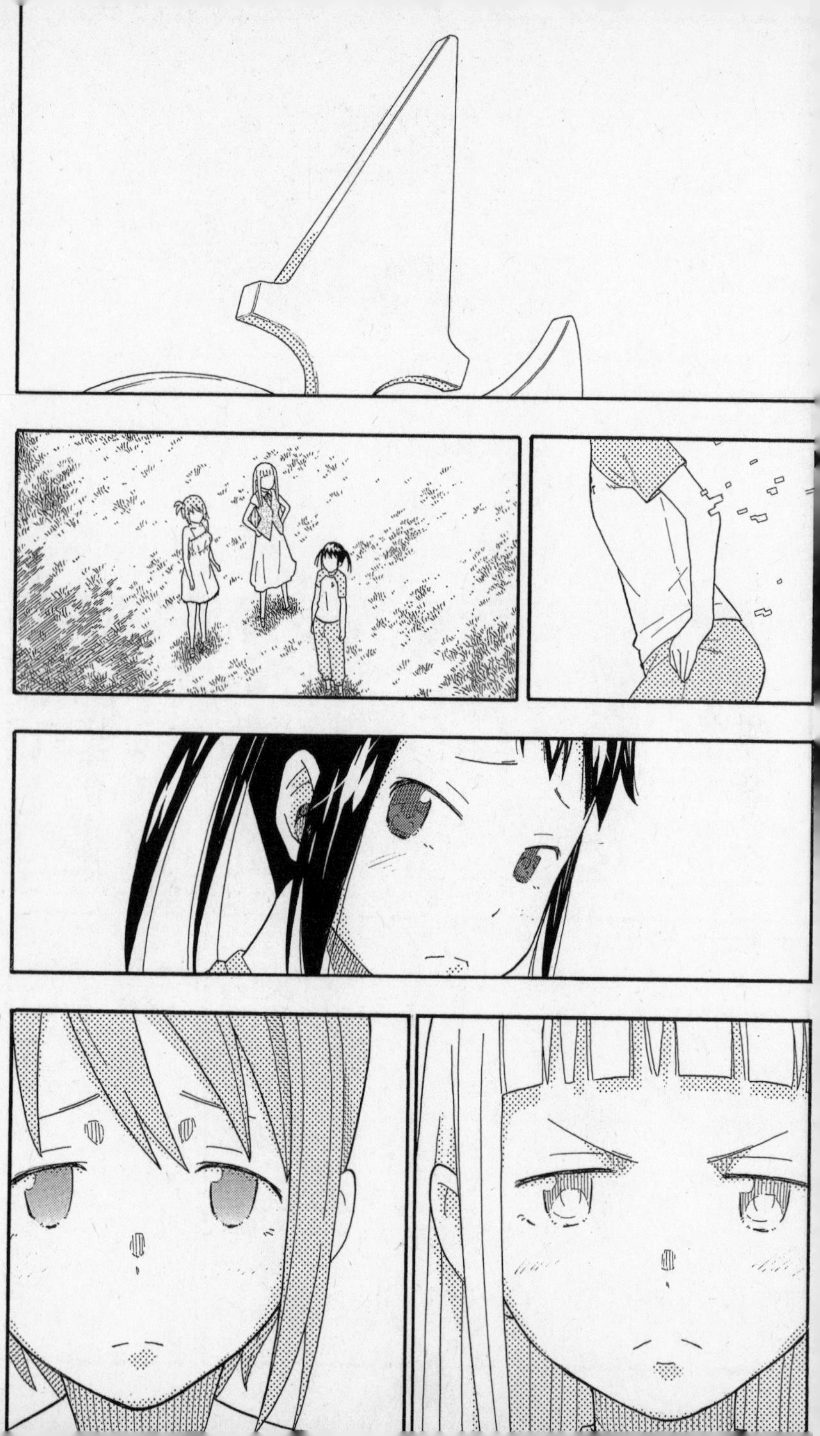

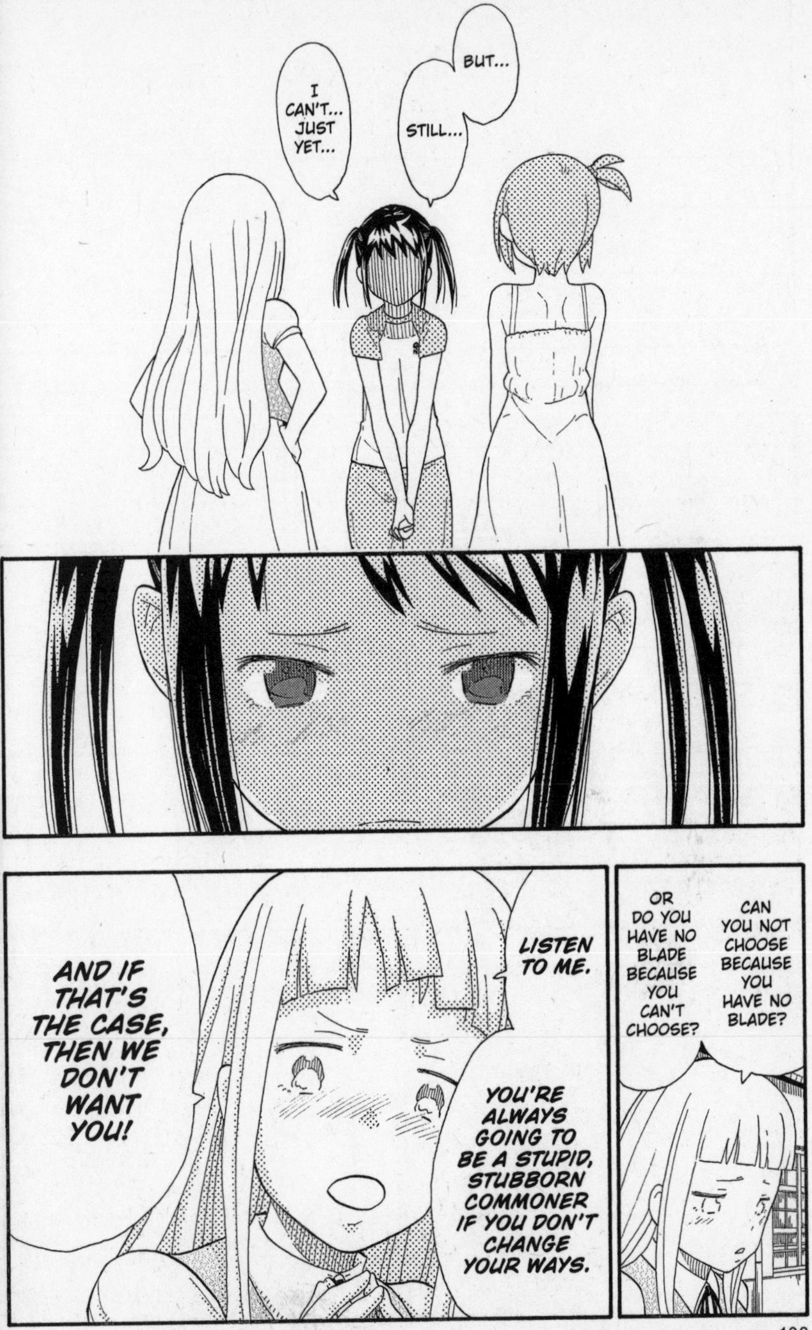
BUT... STILL...
I CAN'T... JUST YET...
CAN YOU NOT CHOOSE BECAUSE YOU HAVE NO BLADE?
OR DO YOU HAVE NO BLADE BECAUSE YOU CAN'T CHOOSE?
LISTEN TO ME.
YOU'RE ALWAYS GOING TO BE A STUPID, STUBBORN COMMONER IF YOU DON'T CHANGE YOUR WAYS.
AND IF THAT'S THE CASE, THEN WE DON'T WANT YOU!

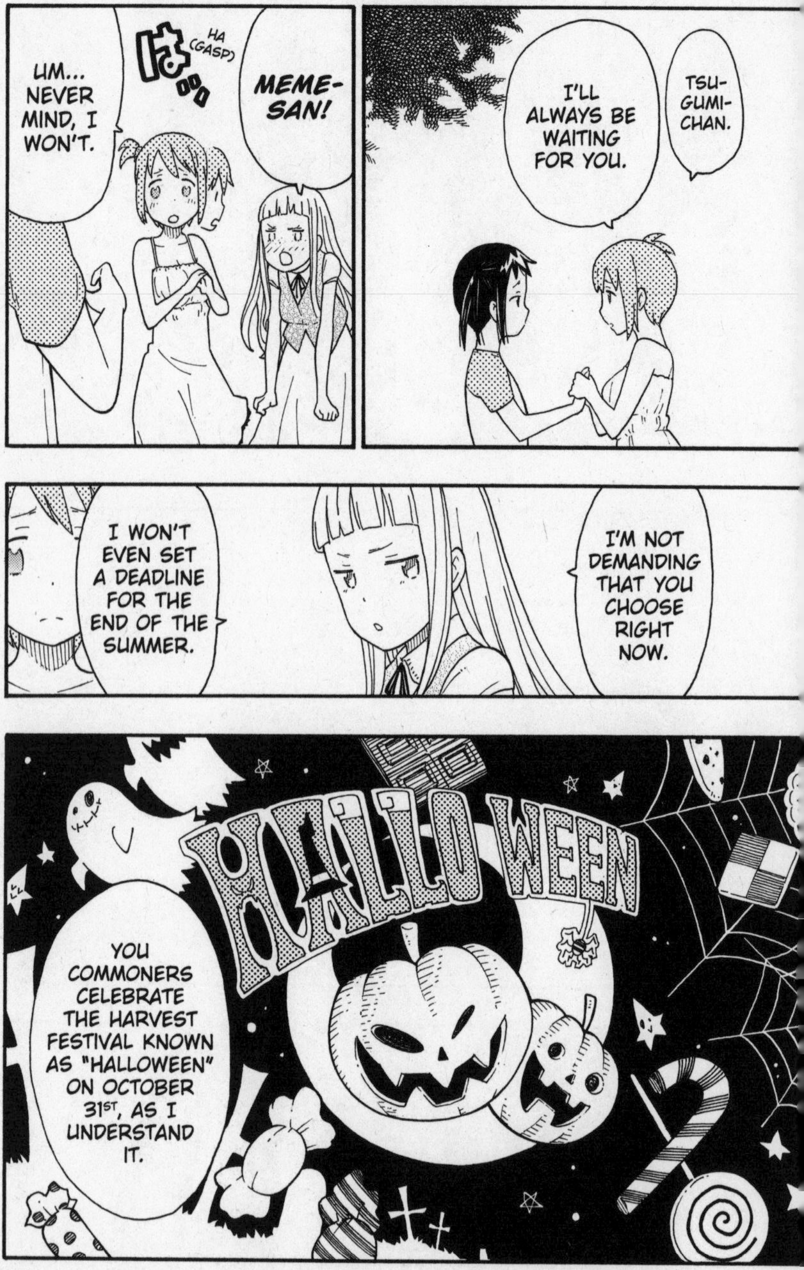
TSU-GUMI-CHAN.
I'LL ALWAYS BE WAITING FOR YOU.
MEME-SAN!
は
HA (GASP)
UM... NEVER MIND, I WON'T.
I'M NOT DEMANDING THAT YOU CHOOSE RIGHT NOW.
I WON'T EVEN SET A DEADLINE FOR THE END OF THE SUMMER.
HALLOWEEN
YOU COMMONERS CELEBRATE THE HARVEST FESTIVAL KNOWN AS "HALLOWEEN" ON OCTOBER 31st, AS I UNDERSTAND IT.

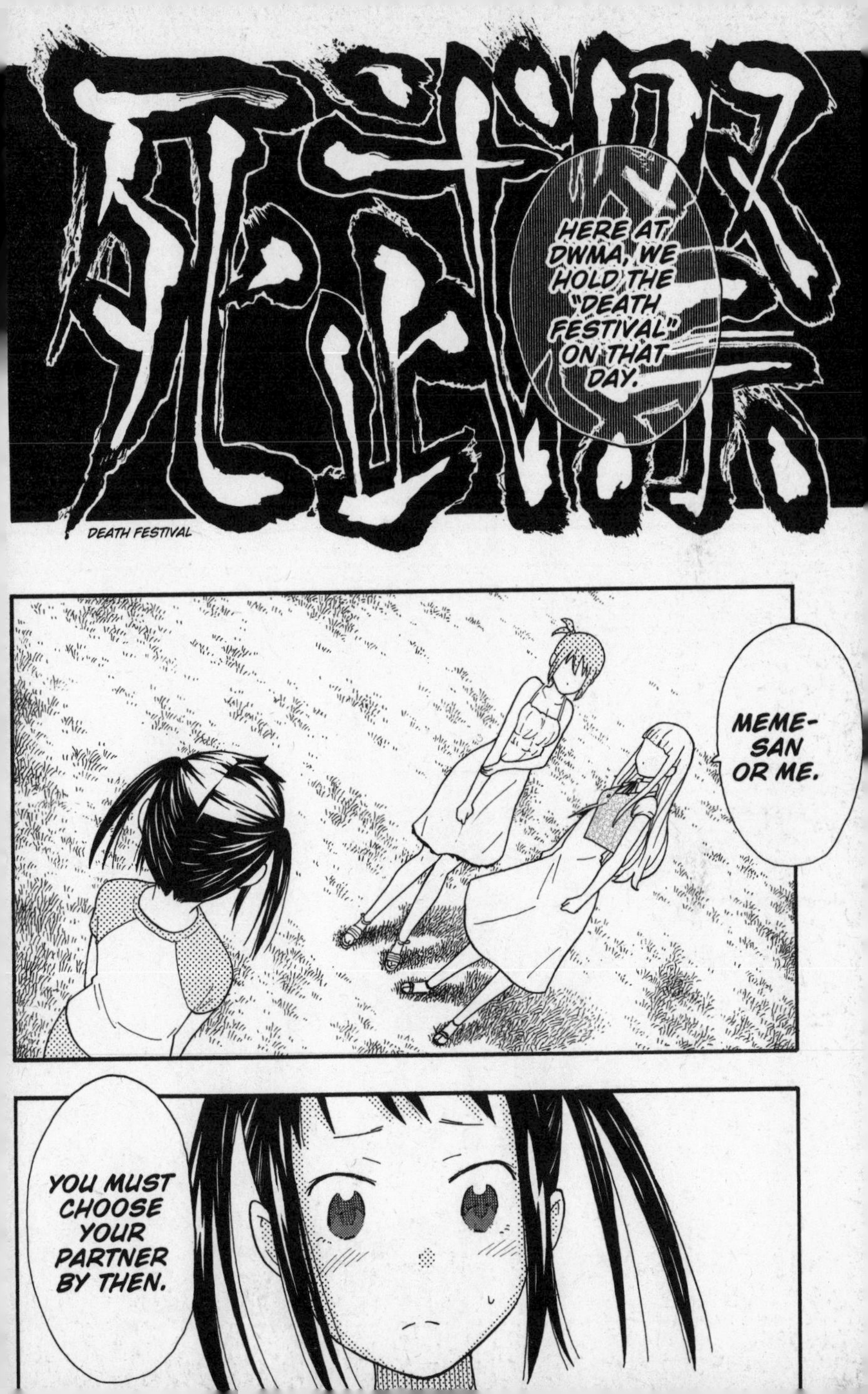
HERE AT DWMA, WE HOLD THE "DEATH FESTIVAL" ON THAT DAY.
DEATH FESTIVAL
MEME-SAN OR ME.
YOU MUST CHOOSE YOUR PARTNER BY THEN.

SOUL EATER NOT!

SOUL EATER

JOT!

ATSUSHI OHKUBO

PART 9

HANG ON A JOT

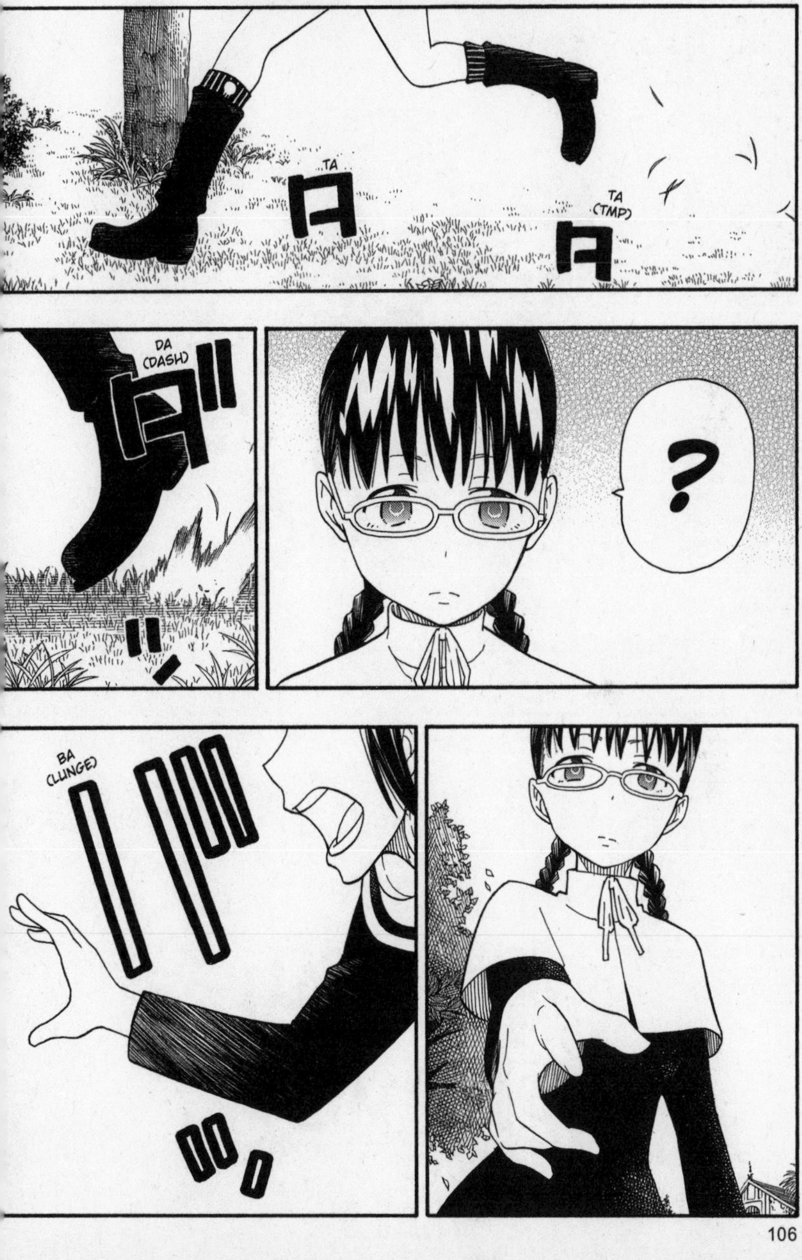
TA (TMP)
TA
?
DA (DASH)
BA (LUNGE)

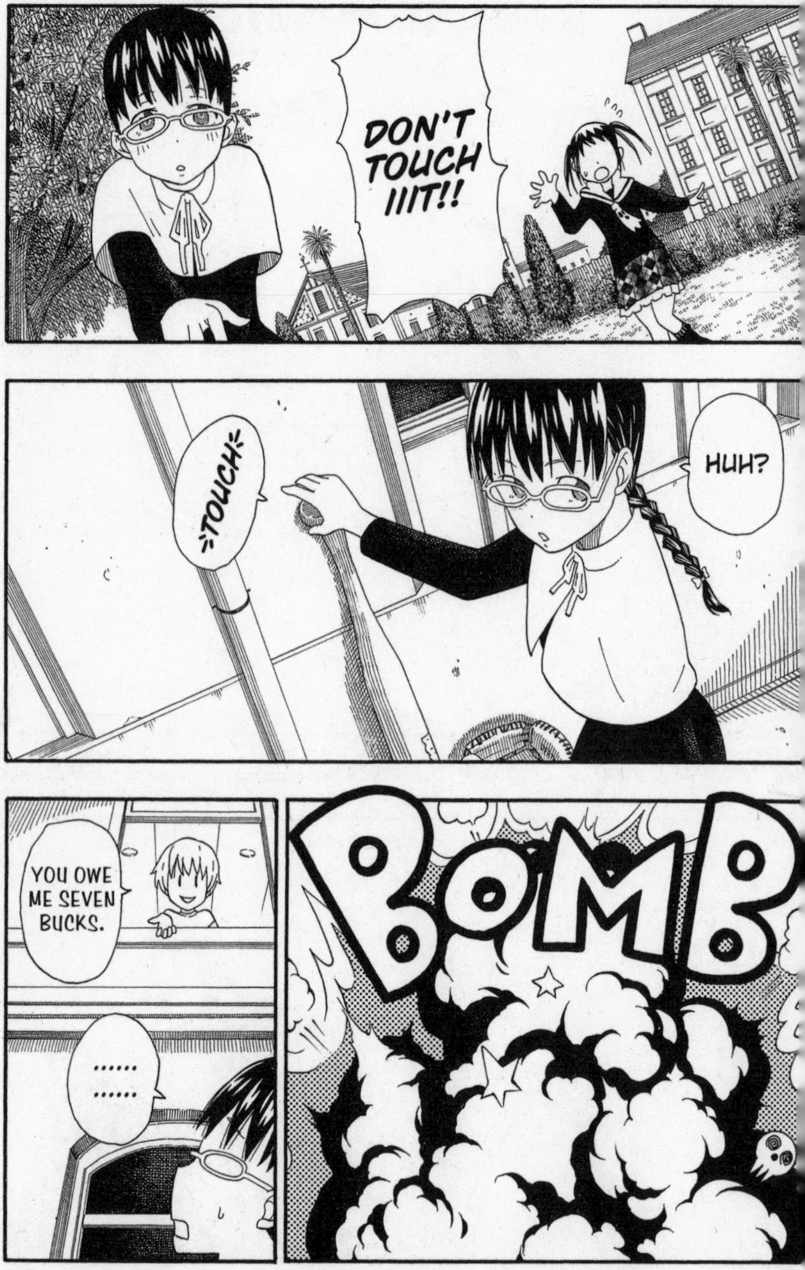
DON'T TOUCH IIIT!!
HUH?
TOUCH
BOMB
YOU OWE ME SEVEN BUCKS.
......
......

A JOT AT A TIME

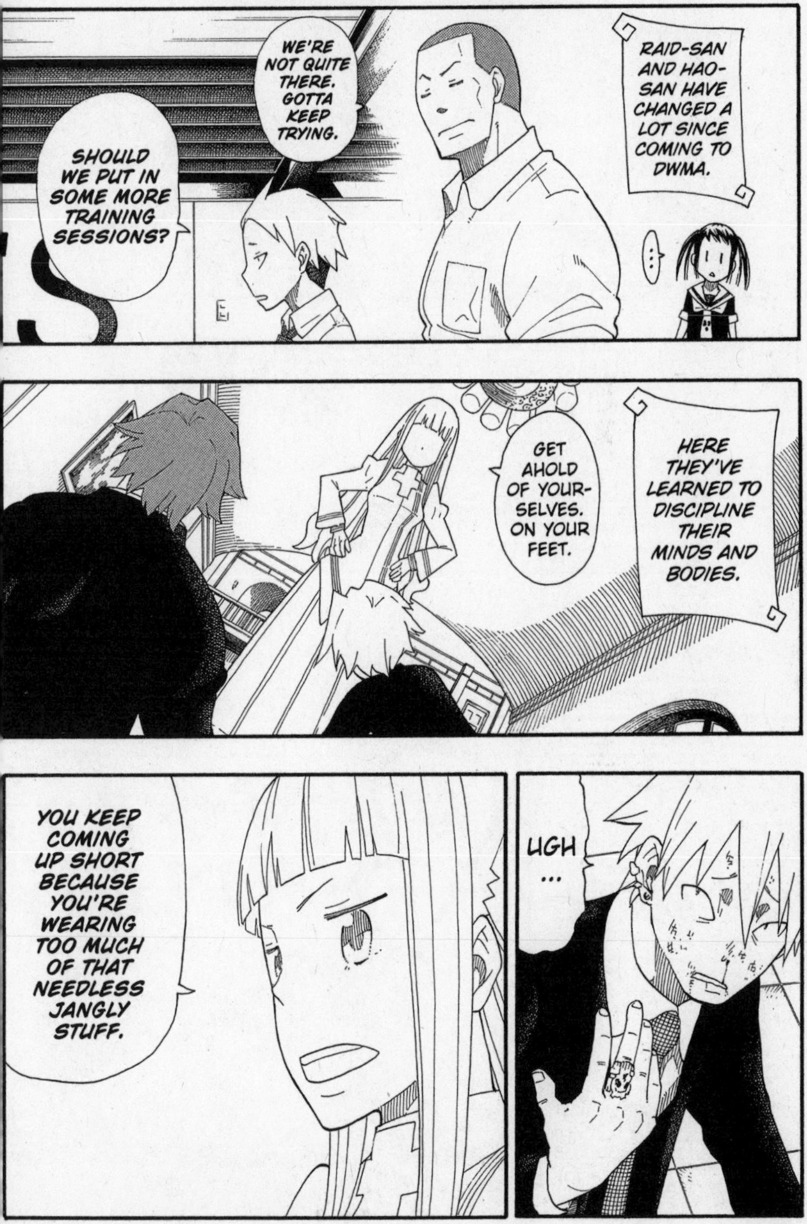
RAID-SAN AND HAO-SAN HAVE CHANGED A LOT SINCE COMING TO DWMA.
...
WE'RE NOT QUITE THERE. GOTTA KEEP TRYING.
SHOULD WE PUT IN SOME MORE TRAINING SESSIONS?
HERE THEY'VE LEARNED TO DISCIPLINE THEIR MINDS AND BODIES.
GET AHOLD OF YOUR-SELVES. ON YOUR FEET.
UGH ...
YOU KEEP COMING UP SHORT BECAUSE YOU'RE WEARING TOO MUCH OF THAT NEEDLESS JANGLY STUFF.

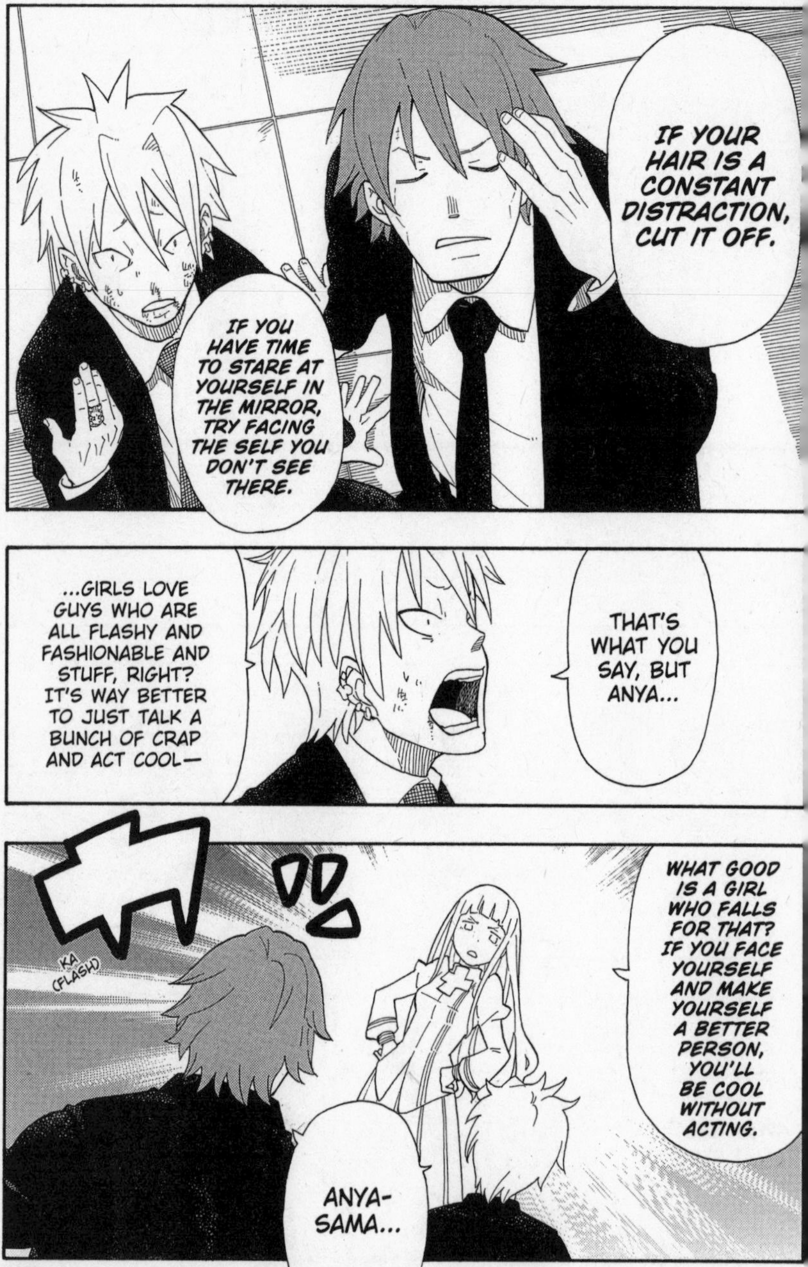
IF YOUR HAIR IS A CONSTANT DISTRACTION, CUT IT OFF.
IF YOU HAVE TIME TO STARE AT YOURSELF IN THE MIRROR, TRY FACING THE SELF YOU DON'T SEE THERE.
THAT'S WHAT YOU SAY, BUT ANYA...
...GIRLS LOVE GUYS WHO ARE ALL FLASHY AND FASHIONABLE AND STUFF, RIGHT? IT'S WAY BETTER TO JUST TALK A BUNCH OF CRAP AND ACT COOL—
WHAT GOOD IS A GIRL WHO FALLS FOR THAT? IF YOU FACE YOURSELF AND MAKE YOURSELF A BETTER PERSON, YOU'LL BE COOL WITHOUT ACTING.
KA (FLASH)
ANYA-SAMA...

A JOT IMPOSSIBLE

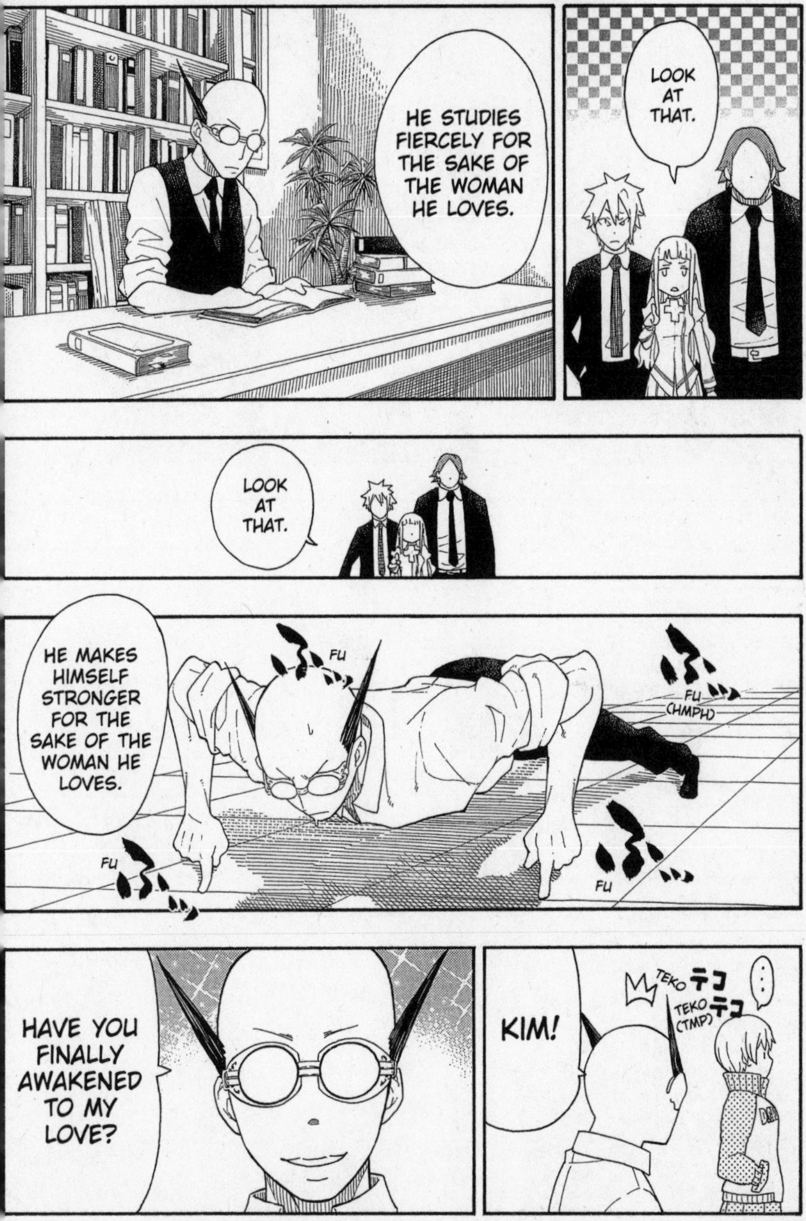
LOOK AT THAT.
HE STUDIES FIERCELY FOR THE SAKE OF THE WOMAN HE LOVES.
LOOK AT THAT.
FU
FU (HMPH)
HE MAKES HIMSELF STRONGER FOR THE SAKE OF THE WOMAN HE LOVES.
FU
FU
…
TEKO テコ TEKO テコ (TMP)
KIM!
HAVE YOU FINALLY AWAKENED TO MY LOVE?

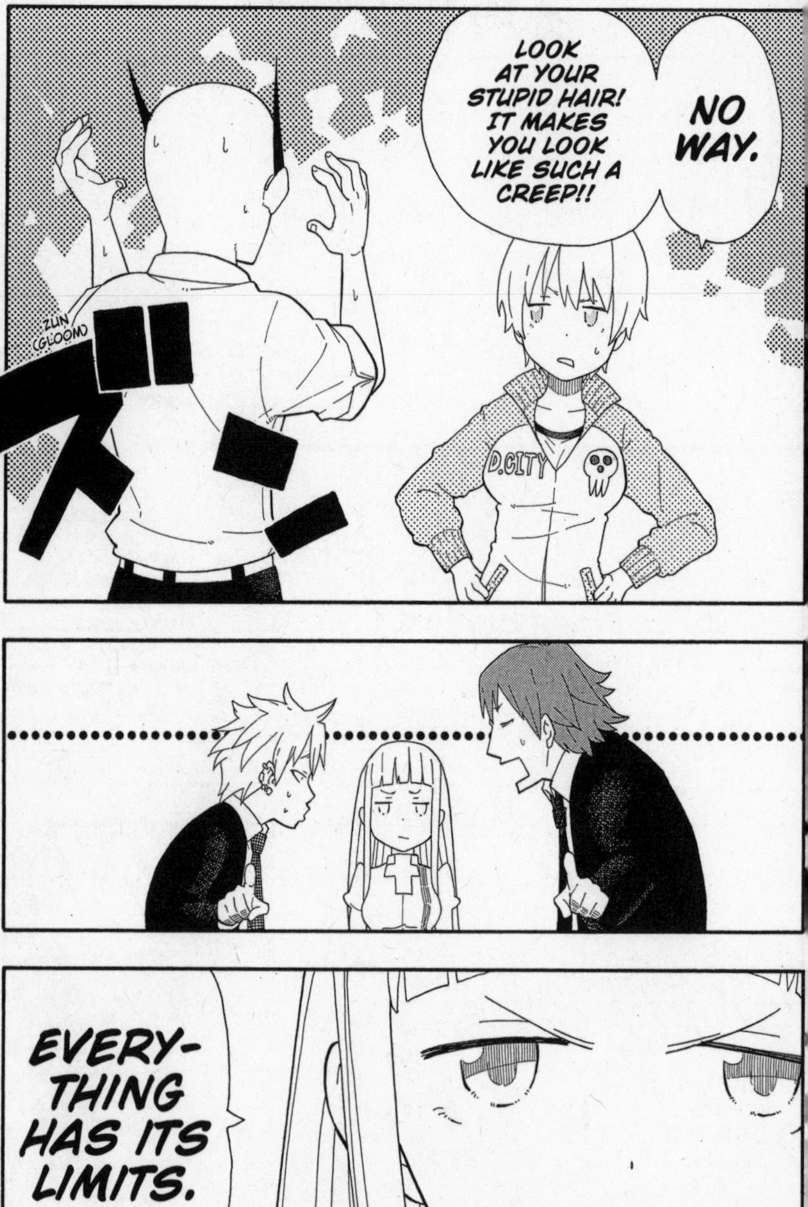
NO WAY.
LOOK AT YOUR STUPID HAIR! IT MAKES YOU LOOK LIKE SUCH A CREEP!!
ZUN (GLOOM)
....
EVERY-THING HAS ITS LIMITS.

A JOT WRONG

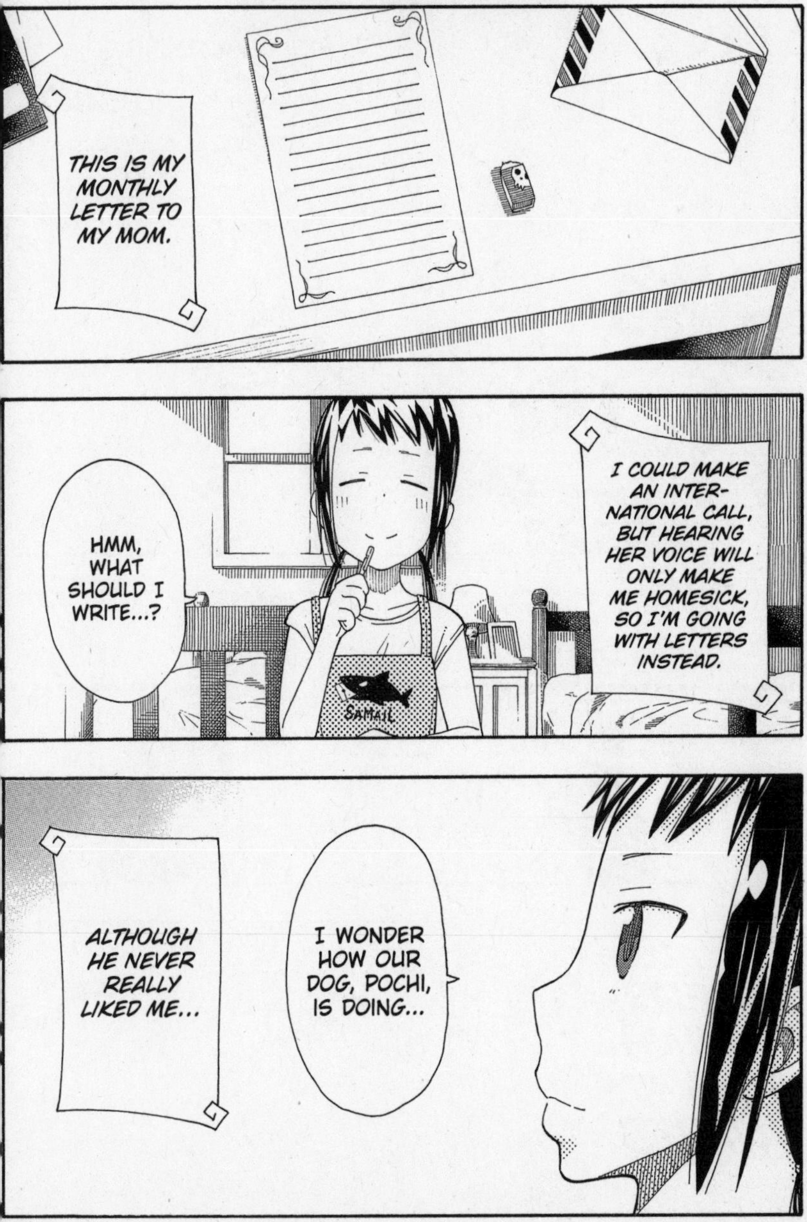
THIS IS MY MONTHLY LETTER TO MY MOM.
I COULD MAKE AN INTER- NATIONAL CALL, BUT HEARING HER VOICE WILL ONLY MAKE ME HOMESICK, SO I'M GOING WITH LETTERS INSTEAD.
HMM, WHAT SHOULD I WRITE...?
SAMAIL
I WONDER HOW OUR DOG, POCHI, IS DOING...
ALTHOUGH HE NEVER REALLY LIKED ME...

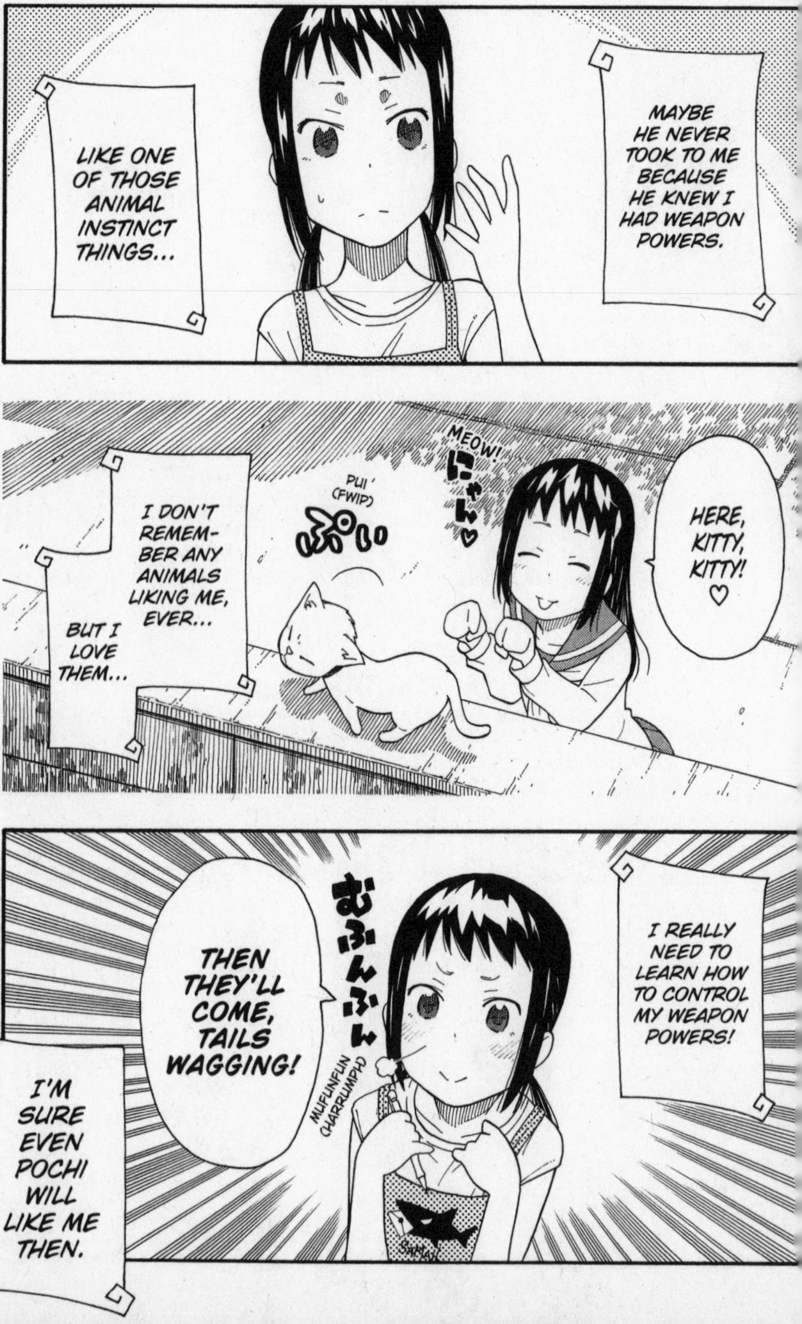
MAYBE HE NEVER TOOK TO ME BECAUSE HE KNEW I HAD WEAPON POWERS.
LIKE ONE OF THOSE ANIMAL INSTINCT THINGS...
HERE, KITTY, KITTY! ♡
MEOW!
にゃん♡
PUI (FWIP)
ぷい
I DON'T REMEMBER ANY ANIMALS LIKING ME, EVER...
BUT I LOVE THEM...
I REALLY NEED TO LEARN HOW TO CONTROL MY WEAPON POWERS!
むふんふん
MUFUNFUN CHARRUMPH
THEN THEY'LL COME, TAILS WAGGING!
I'M SURE EVEN POCHI WILL LIKE ME THEN.

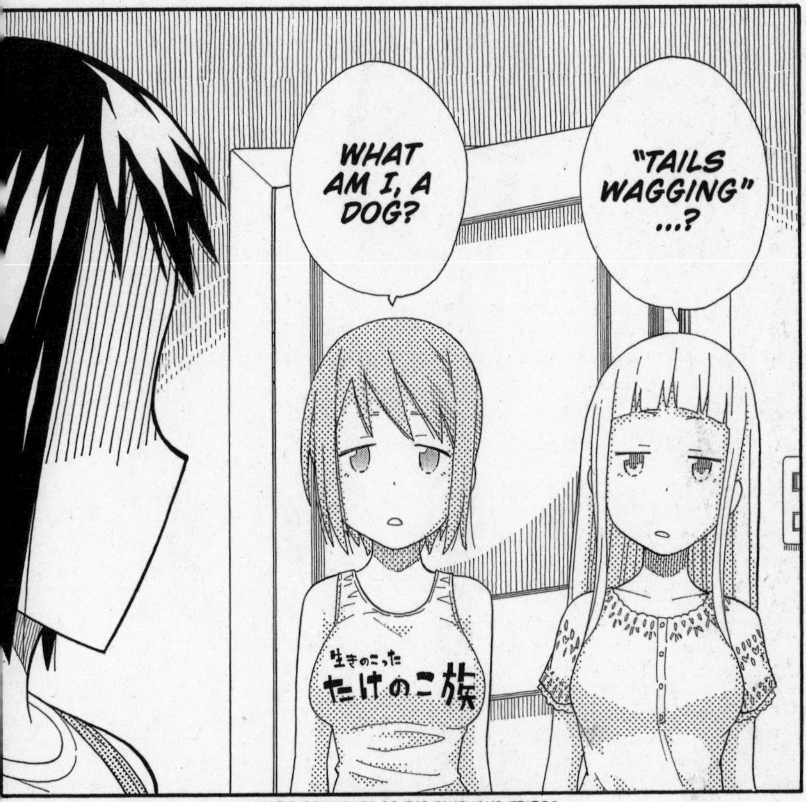
"TAILS WAGGING" ...?
WHAT AM I, A DOG?
生きのこった たけのこ族
SHIRT: REMNANTS OF THE TAKENOKO TRIBES

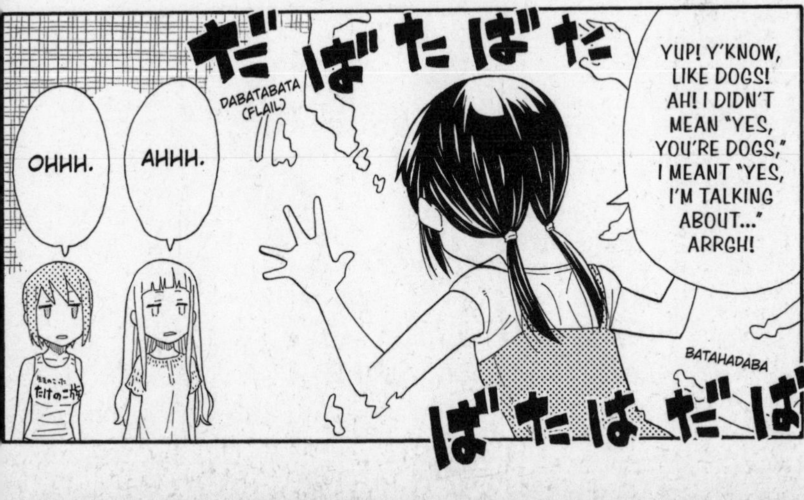
YUP! Y'KNOW, LIKE DOGS! AH! I DIDN'T MEAN "YES, YOU'RE DOGS," I MEANT "YES, I'M TALKING ABOUT..." ARRGH!
だばたばた
DABATABATA (FLAIL)
AHHH.
OHHH.
BATAHADABA
ばたはだば

SOUL EATER NOT!

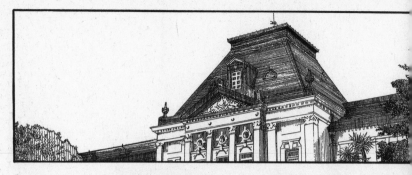

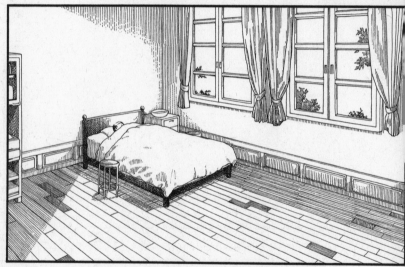

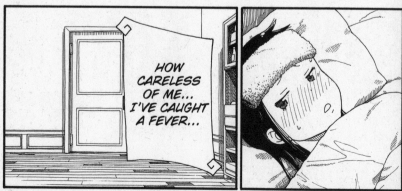

HOW CARELESS OF ME... I'VE CAUGHT A FEVER...

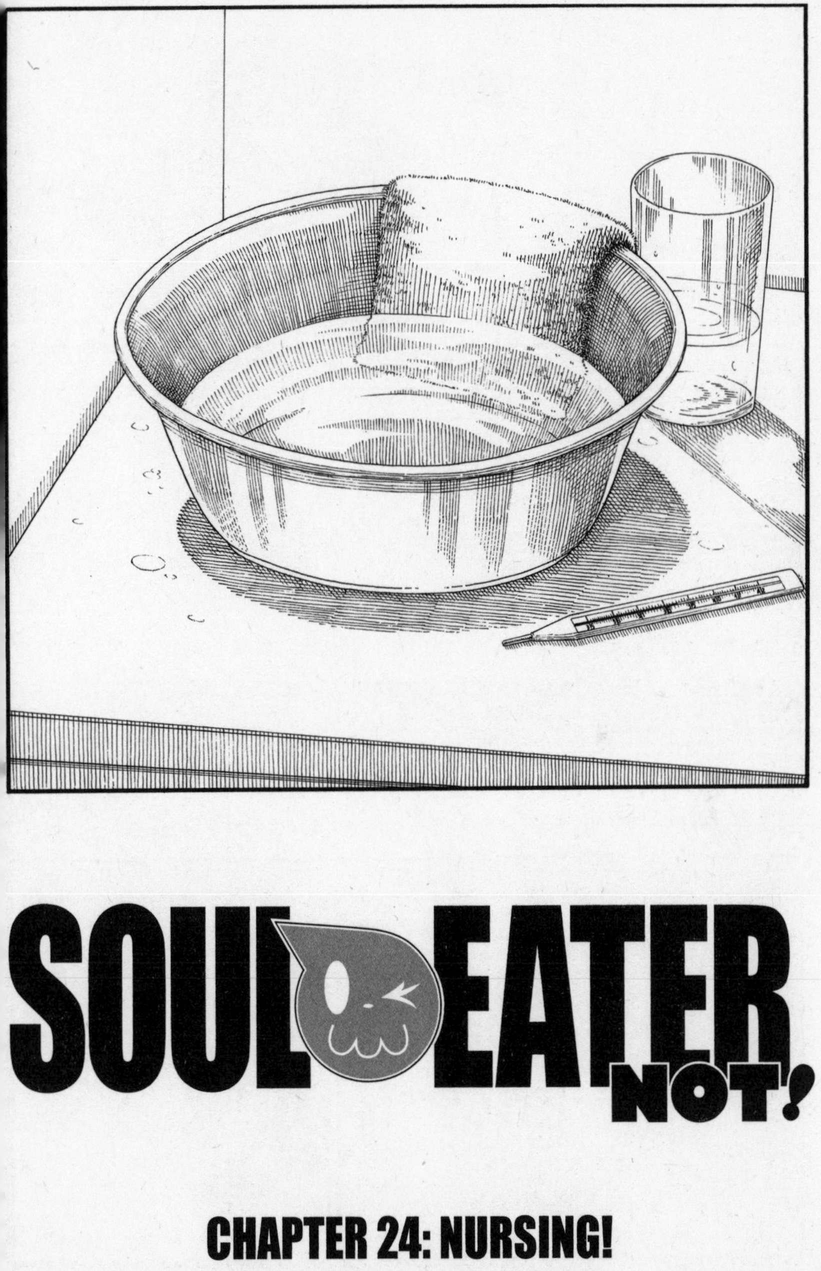

SOUL EATER NOT!

CHAPTER 24: NURSING!

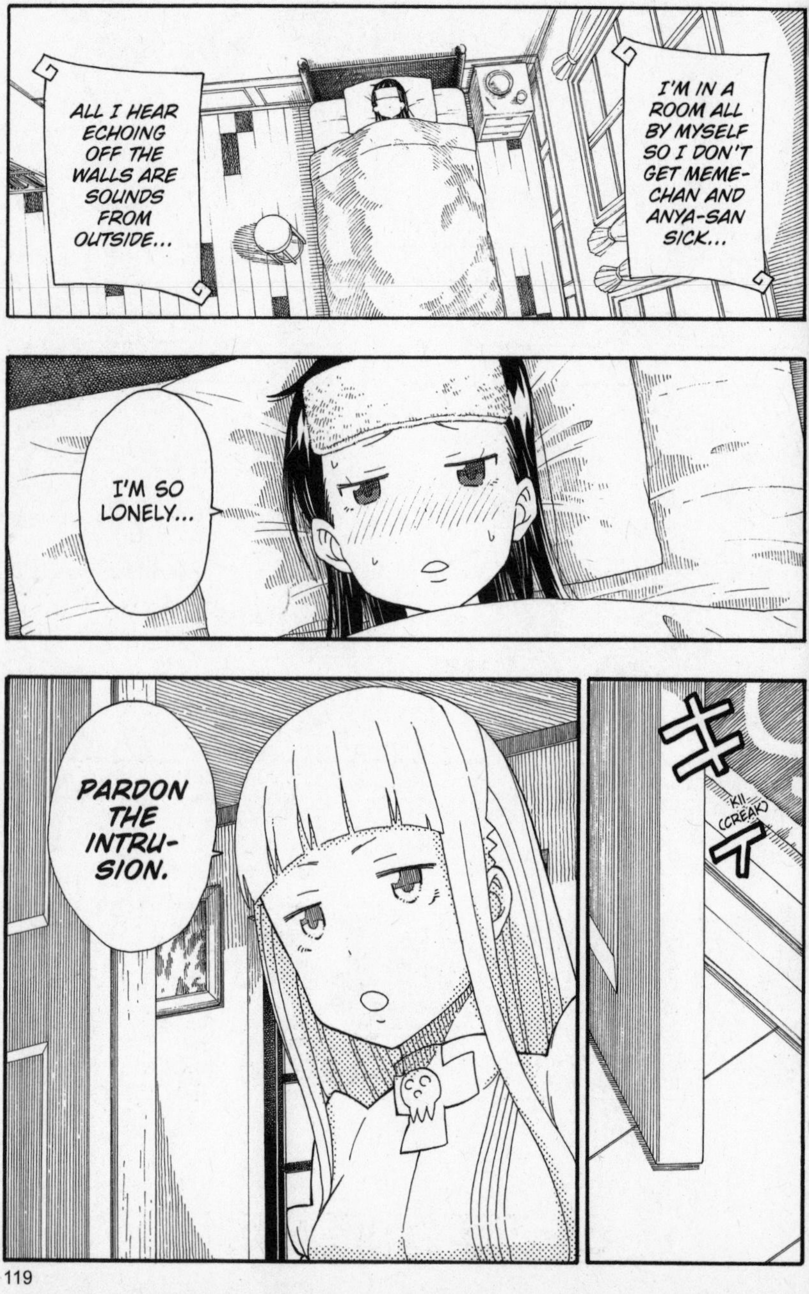
I'M IN A ROOM ALL BY MYSELF SO I DON'T GET MEME-CHAN AND ANYA-SAN SICK...
ALL I HEAR ECHOING OFF THE WALLS ARE SOUNDS FROM OUTSIDE...
I'M SO LONELY...
KII (CREAK)
PARDON THE INTRU-SION.

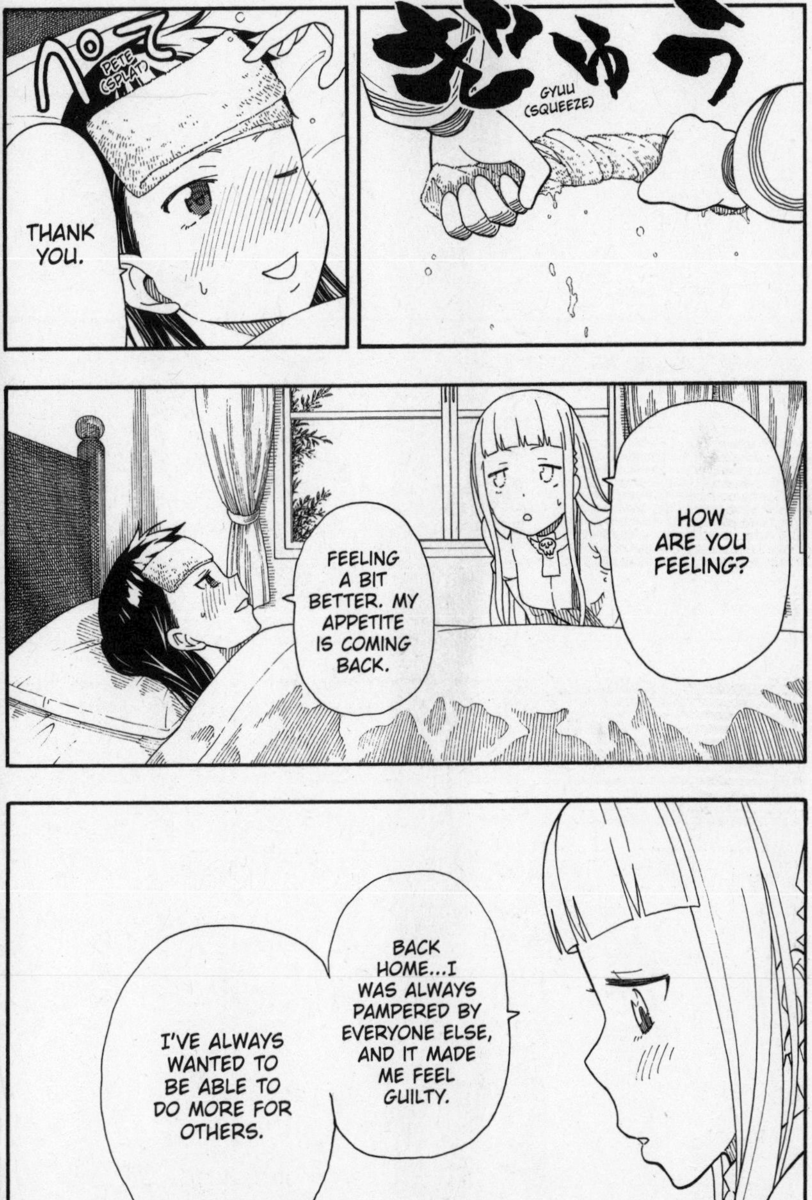
ぎゅう
GYUU (SQUEEZE)
ぺて
PETE (SPLAT)
THANK YOU.
HOW ARE YOU FEELING?
FEELING A BIT BETTER. MY APPETITE IS COMING BACK.
BACK HOME...I WAS ALWAYS PAMPERED BY EVERYONE ELSE, AND IT MADE ME FEEL GUILTY.
I'VE ALWAYS WANTED TO BE ABLE TO DO MORE FOR OTHERS.

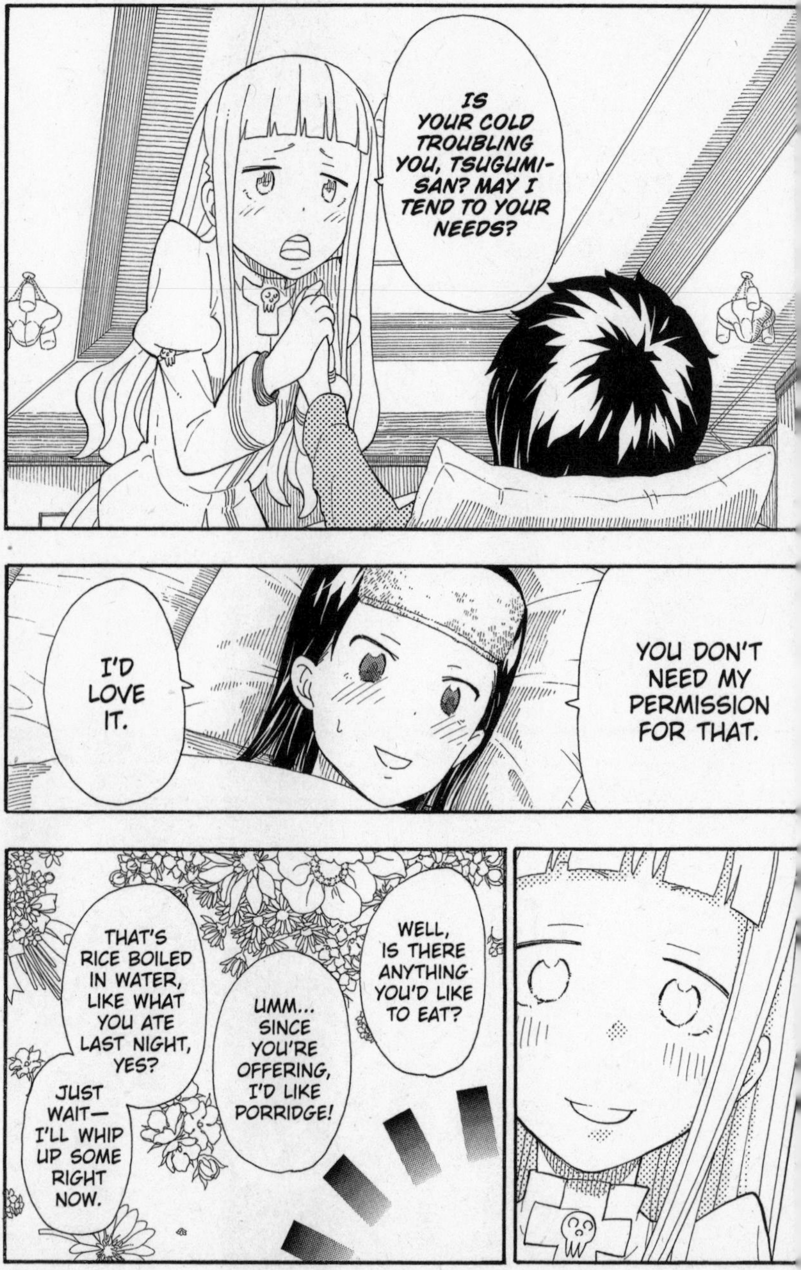
IS YOUR COLD TROUBLING YOU, TSUGUMI-SAN? MAY I TEND TO YOUR NEEDS?
YOU DON'T NEED MY PERMISSION FOR THAT.
I'D LOVE IT.
WELL, IS THERE ANYTHING YOU'D LIKE TO EAT?
UMM... SINCE YOU'RE OFFERING, I'D LIKE PORRIDGE!
THAT'S RICE BOILED IN WATER, LIKE WHAT YOU ATE LAST NIGHT, YES?
JUST WAIT— I'LL WHIP UP SOME RIGHT NOW.

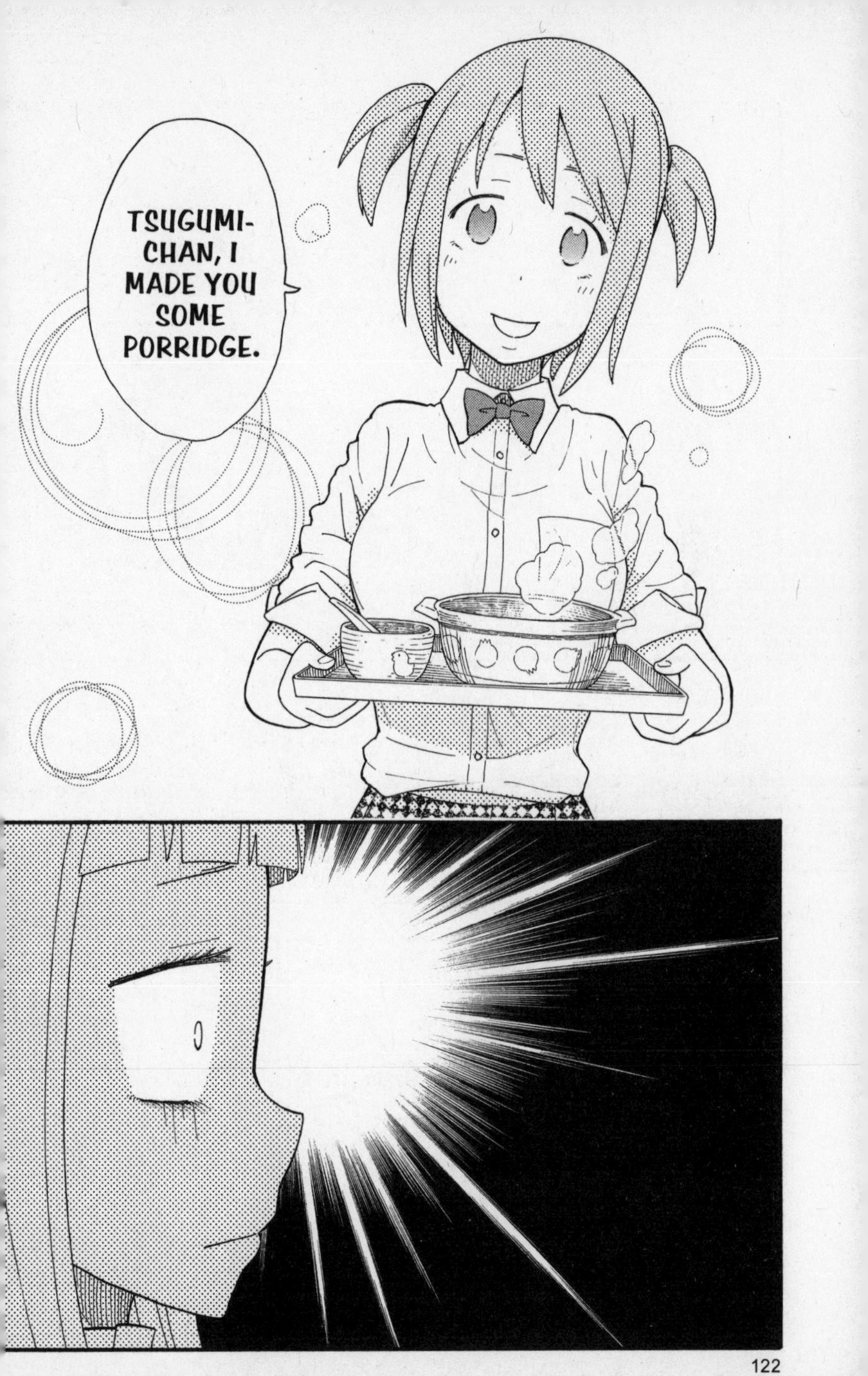
TSUGUMI-CHAN, I MADE YOU SOME PORRIDGE.

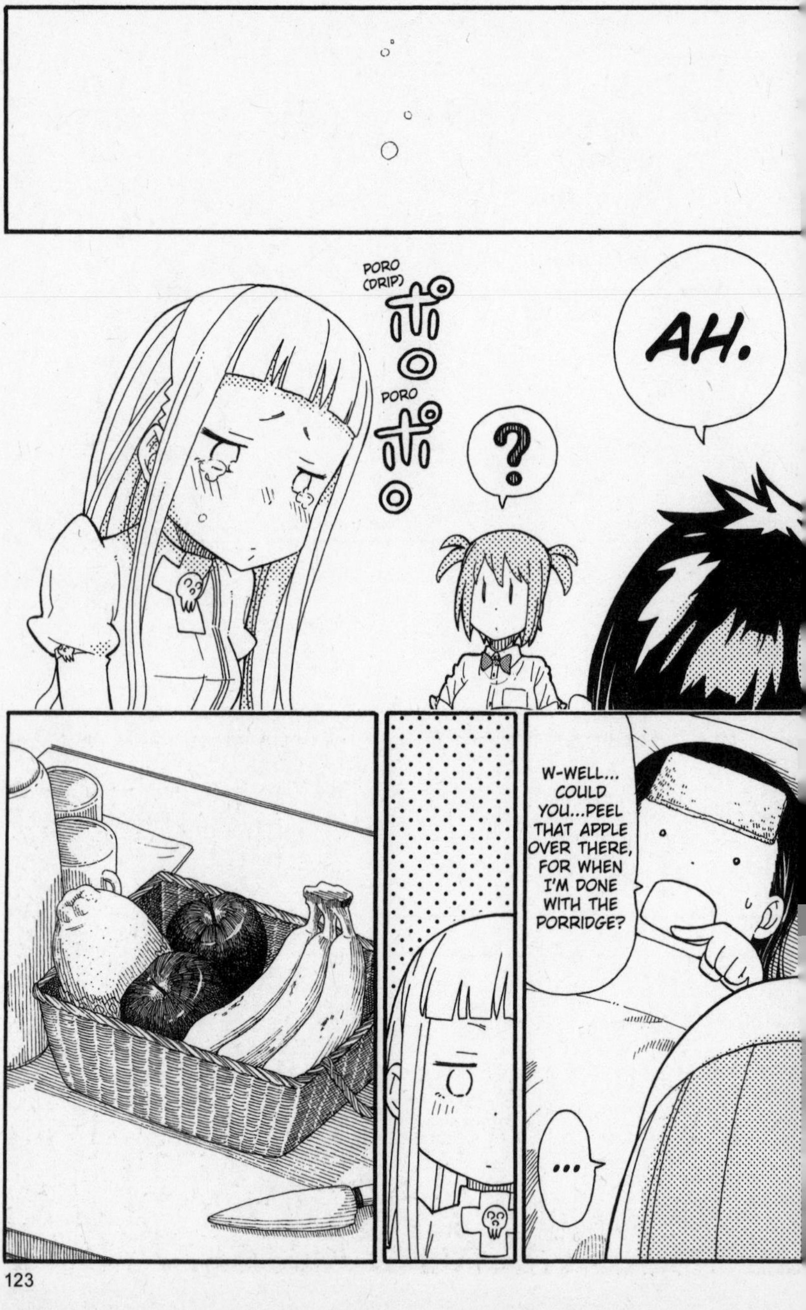
AH.
?
PORO (DRIP)
PORO
W-WELL... COULD YOU...PEEL THAT APPLE OVER THERE, FOR WHEN I'M DONE WITH THE PORRIDGE?
...

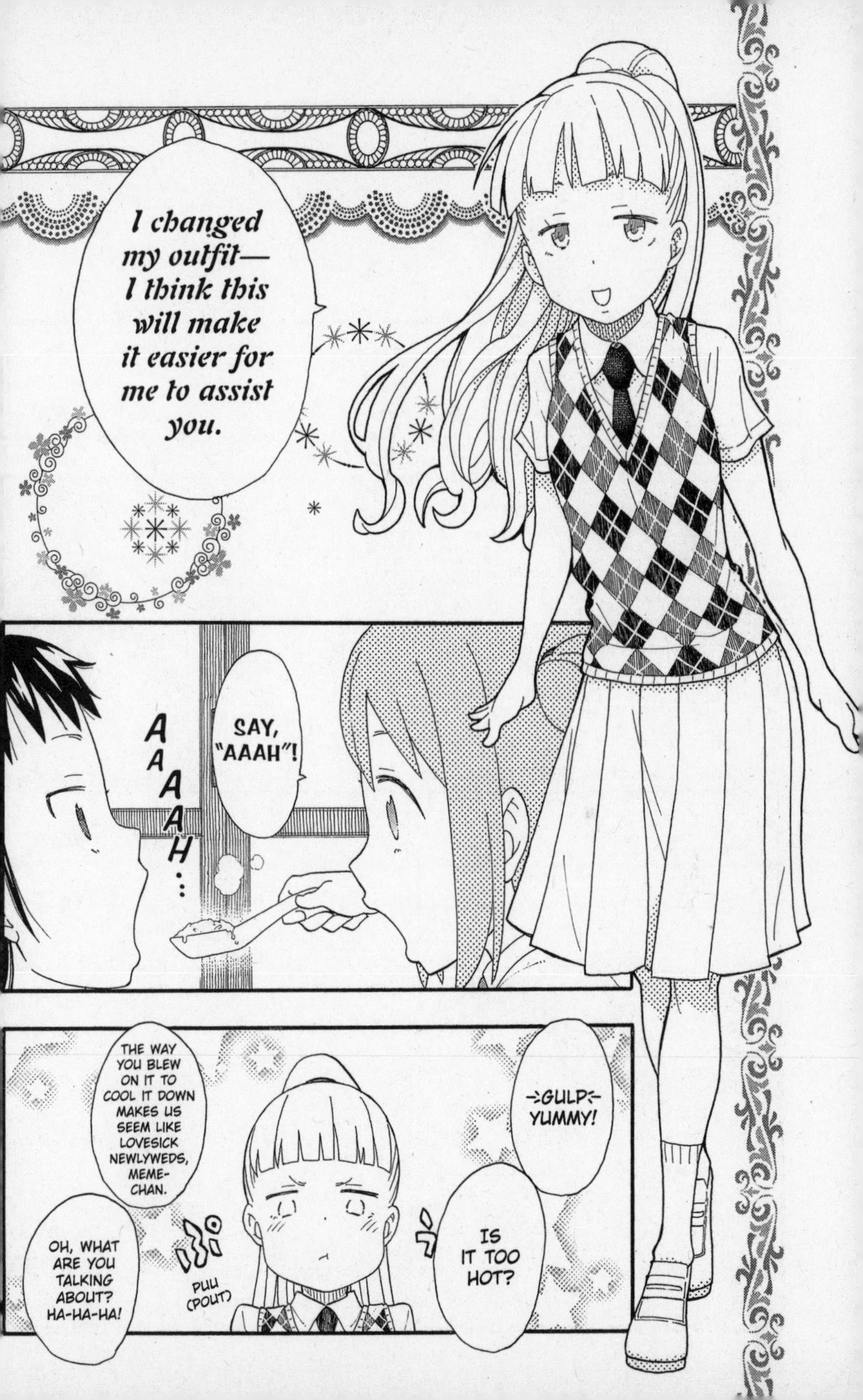

I changed my outfit—I think this will make it easier for me to assist you.
SAY, "AAAH"!
AAAAH...
-GULP- YUMMY!
IS IT TOO HOT?
THE WAY YOU BLEW ON IT TO COOL IT DOWN MAKES US SEEM LIKE LOVESICK NEWLYWEDS, MEME-CHAN.
PUU (POUT)
OH, WHAT ARE YOU TALKING ABOUT? HA-HA-HA!

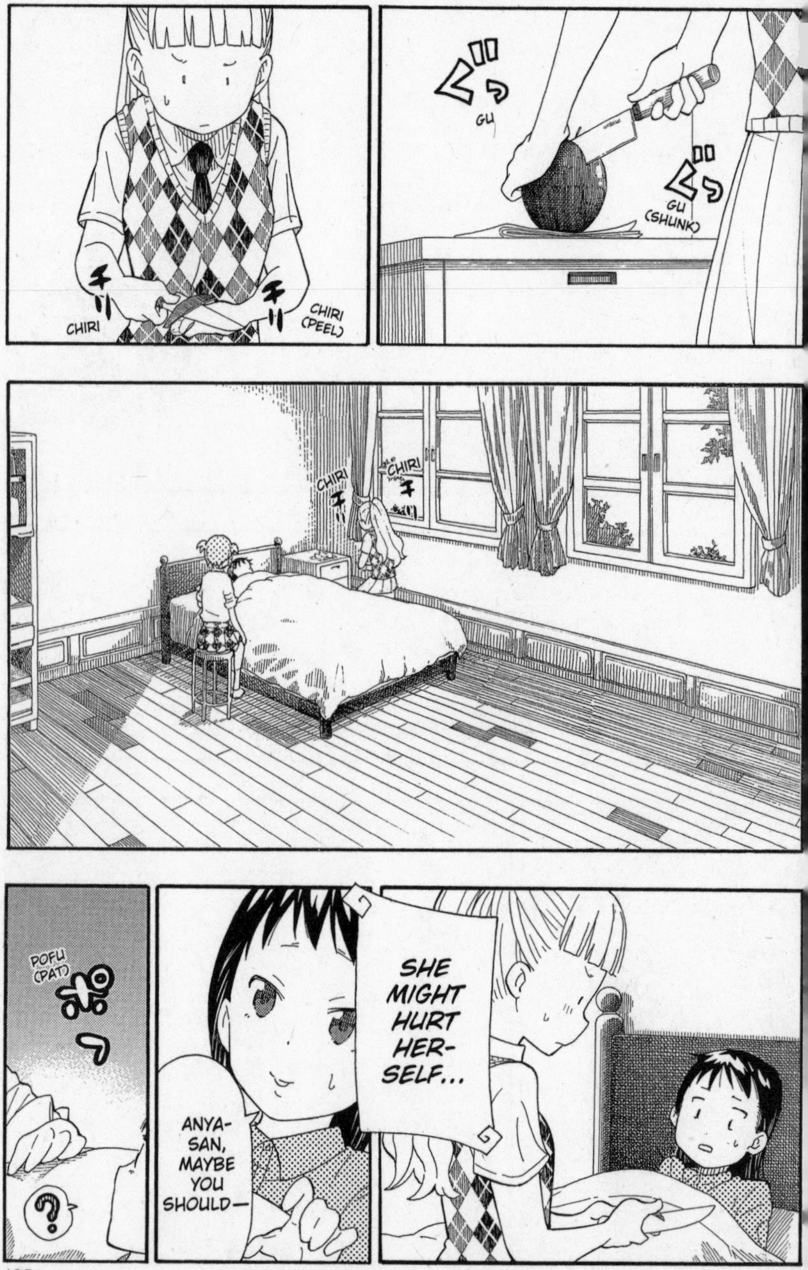
GU
GU (SHUNK)
CHIRI
CHIRI (PEEL)
CHIRI
CHIRI
SHE MIGHT HURT HER-SELF...
ANYA-SAN, MAYBE YOU SHOULD—
POFU (PAT)
?

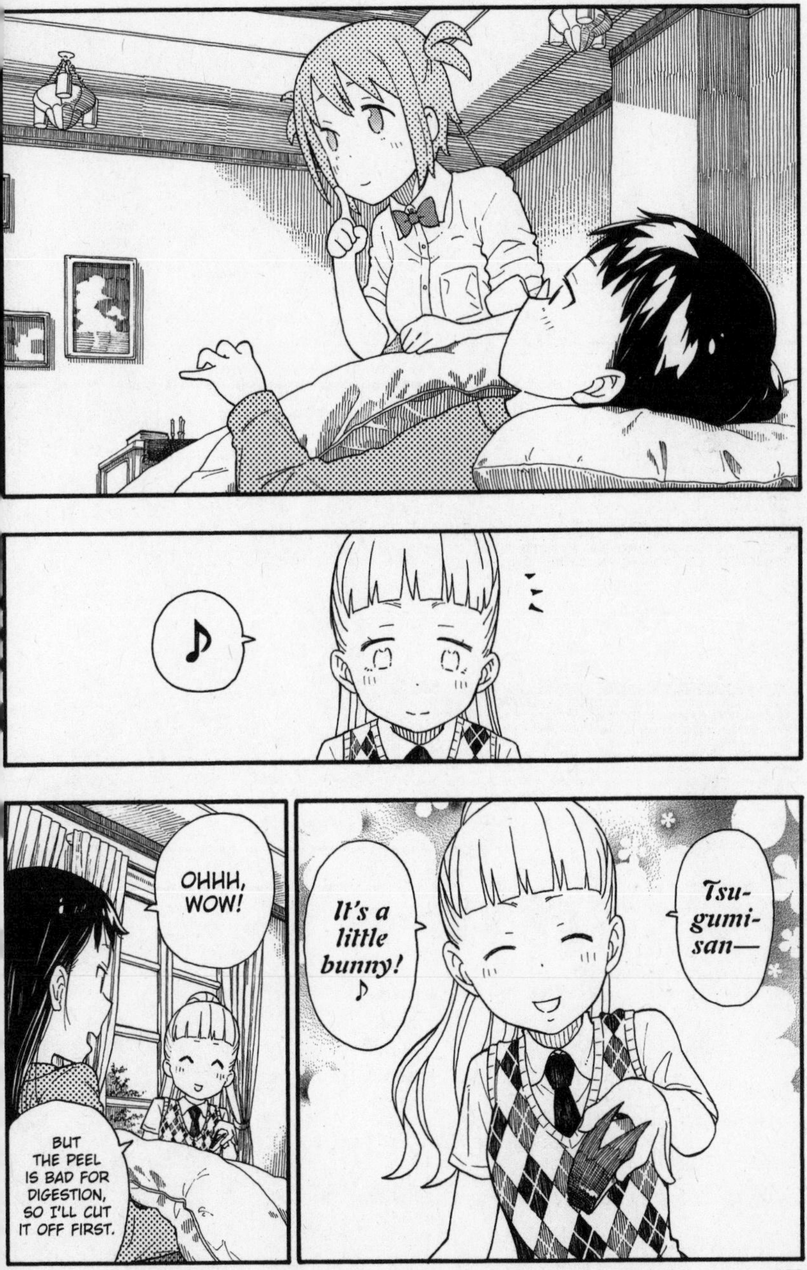
♪
Tsu-gumi-san—
It's a little bunny! ♪
OHHH, WOW!
BUT THE PEEL IS BAD FOR DIGESTION, SO I'LL CUT IT OFF FIRST.

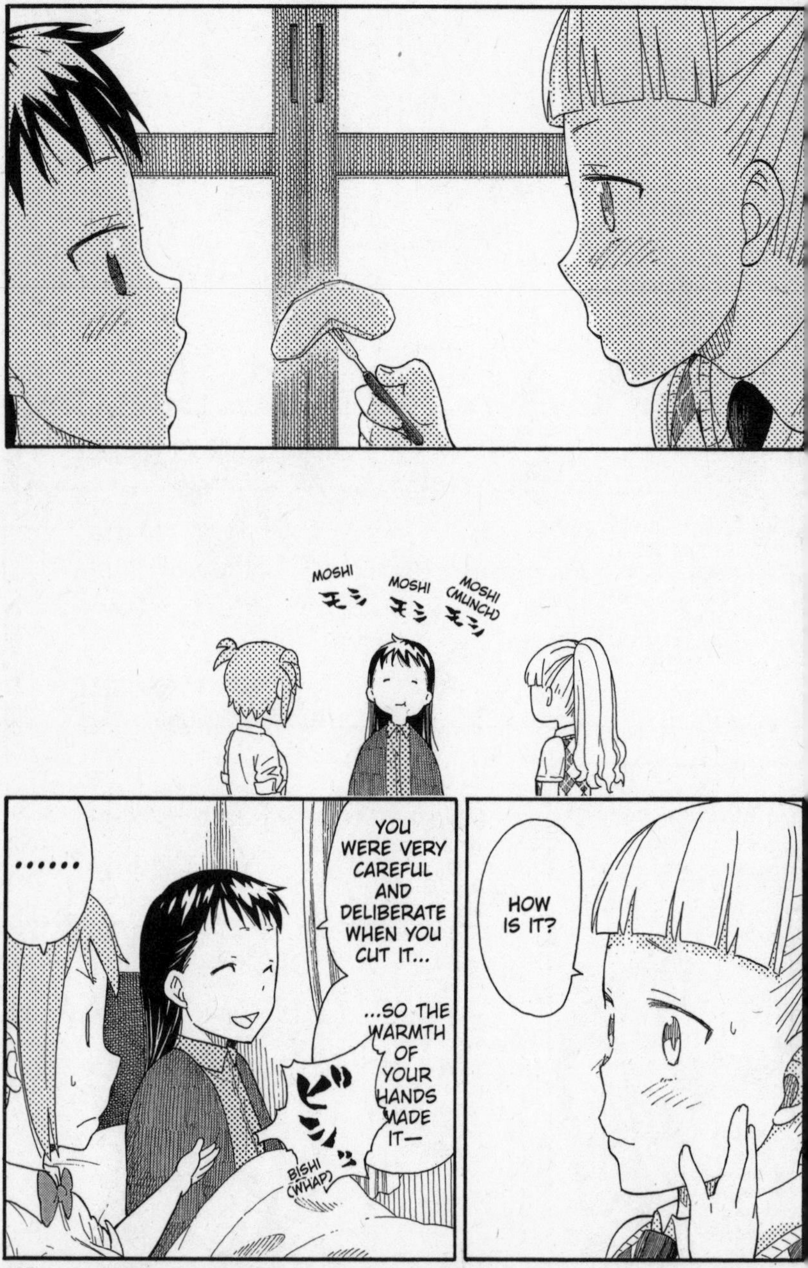
MOSHI (MUNCH) モシ
MOSHI モシ
MOSHI モシ
HOW IS IT?
YOU WERE VERY CAREFUL AND DELIBERATE WHEN YOU CUT IT...
...SO THE WARMTH OF YOUR HANDS MADE IT—
BISHI (WHAP)
......

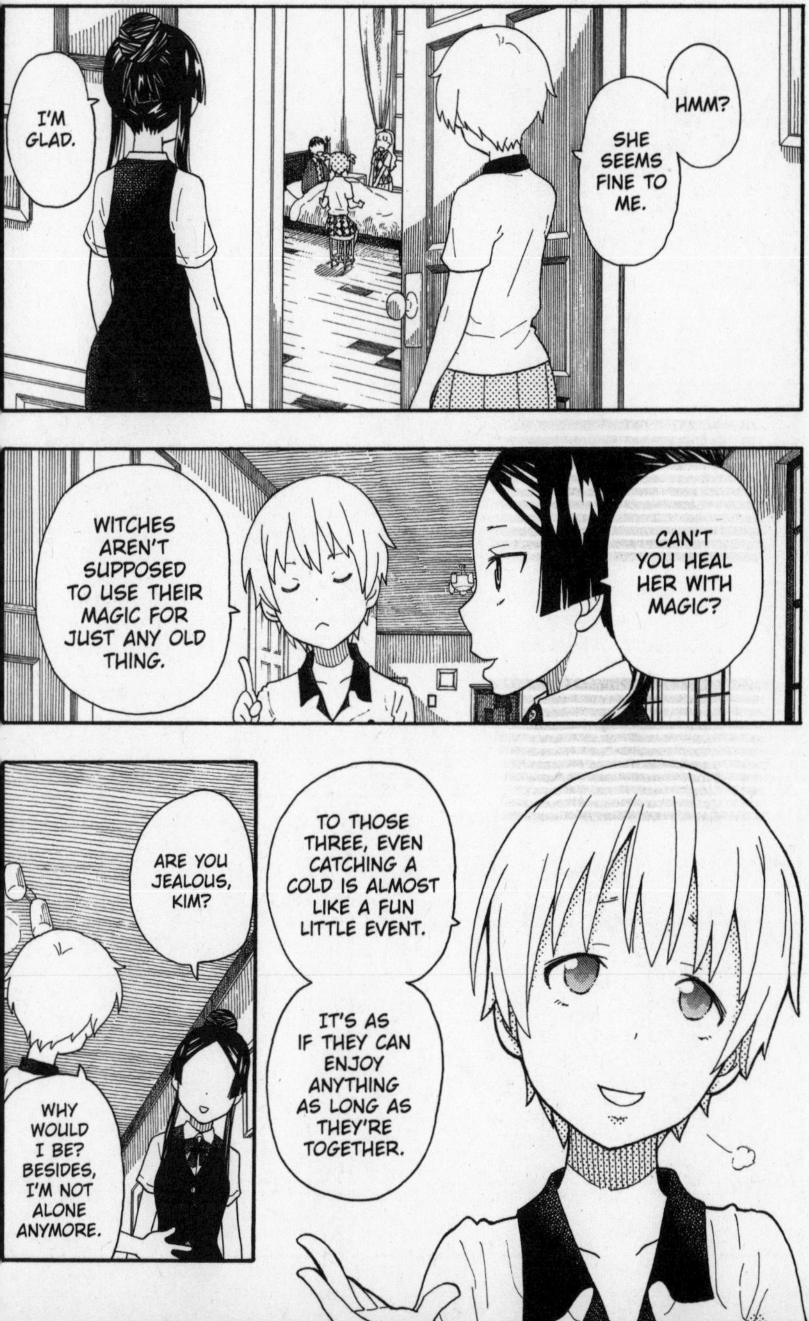
HMM?
SHE SEEMS FINE TO ME.
I'M GLAD.
CAN'T YOU HEAL HER WITH MAGIC?
WITCHES AREN'T SUPPOSED TO USE THEIR MAGIC FOR JUST ANY OLD THING.
TO THOSE THREE, EVEN CATCHING A COLD IS ALMOST LIKE A FUN LITTLE EVENT.
IT'S AS IF THEY CAN ENJOY ANYTHING AS LONG AS THEY'RE TOGETHER.
ARE YOU JEALOUS, KIM?
WHY WOULD I BE? BESIDES, I'M NOT ALONE ANYMORE.

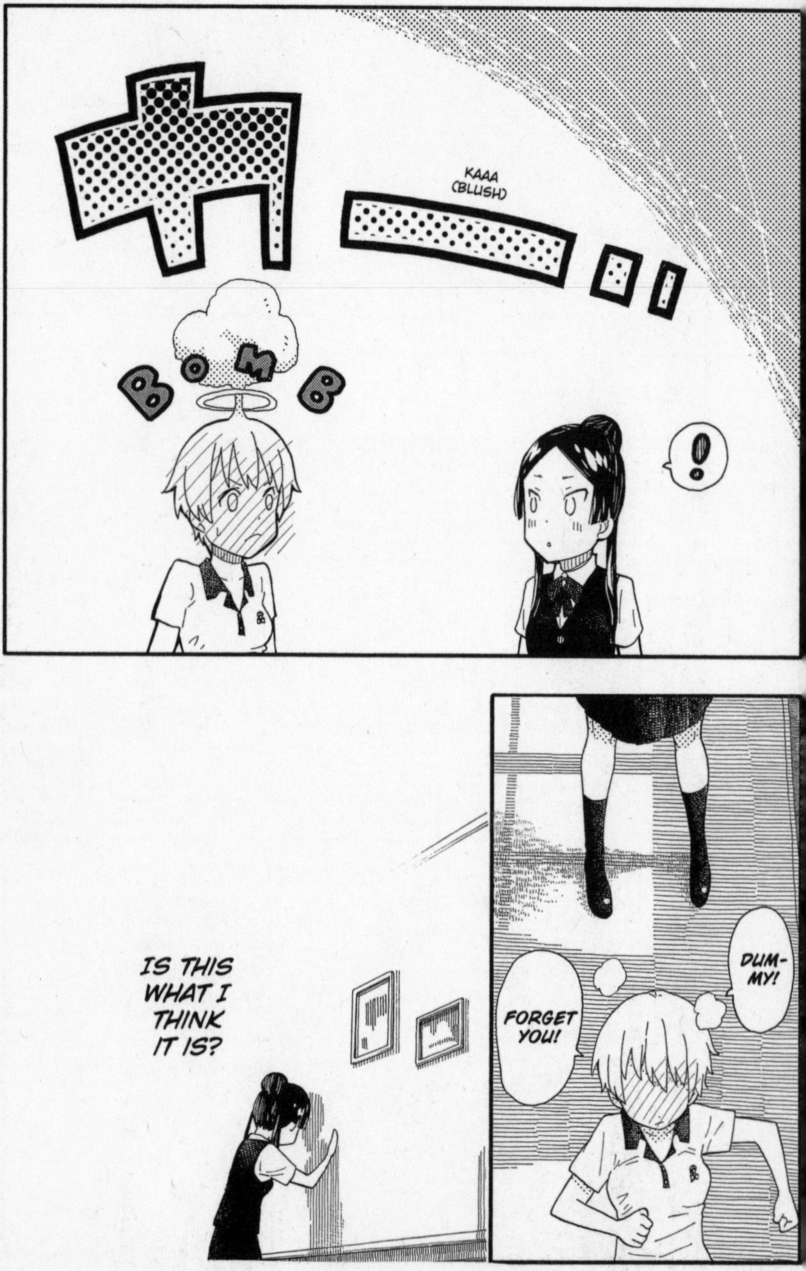
KAAA (BLUSH)
BOMB
!
DUM-MY!
FORGET YOU!
IS THIS WHAT I THINK IT IS?

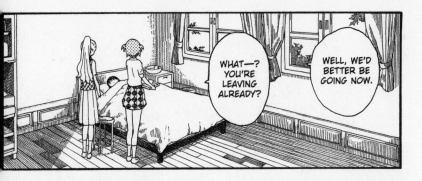

WELL, WE'D BETTER BE GOING NOW.

WHAT—? YOU'RE LEAVING ALREADY?

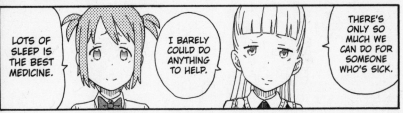

THERE'S ONLY SO MUCH WE CAN DO FOR SOMEONE WHO'S SICK.

I BARELY COULD DO ANYTHING TO HELP.

LOTS OF SLEEP IS THE BEST MEDICINE.

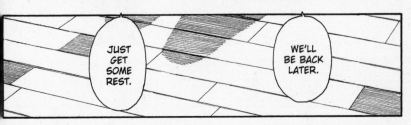

WE'LL BE BACK LATER.

JUST GET SOME REST.

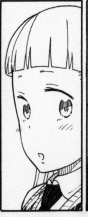

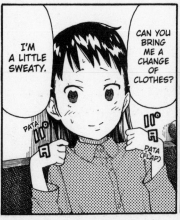

CAN YOU BRING ME A CHANGE OF CLOTHES?

I'M A LITTLE SWEATY.

PATA
PATA (FLAP)

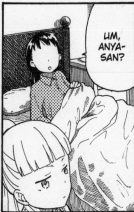

UM, ANYA-SAN?

130

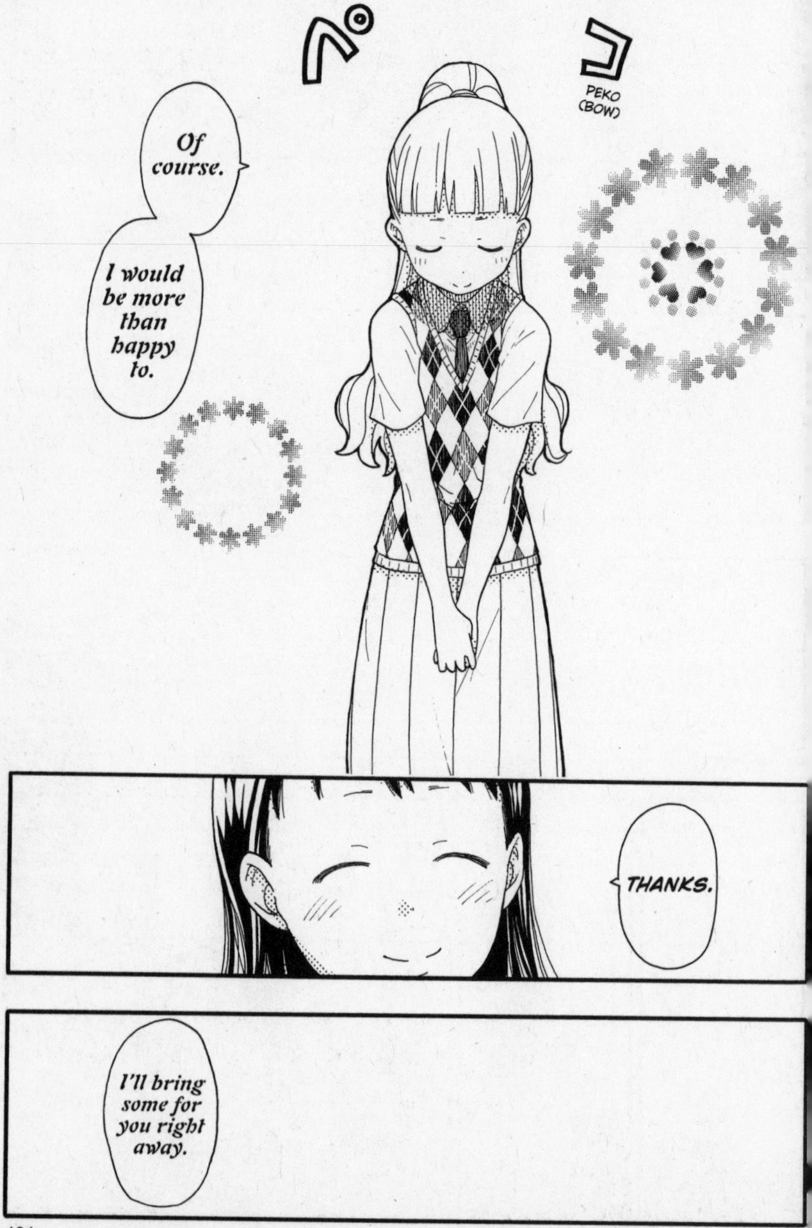
ペコ
PEKO (BOW)
Of course.
I would be more than happy to.
THANKS.
I'll bring some for you right away.

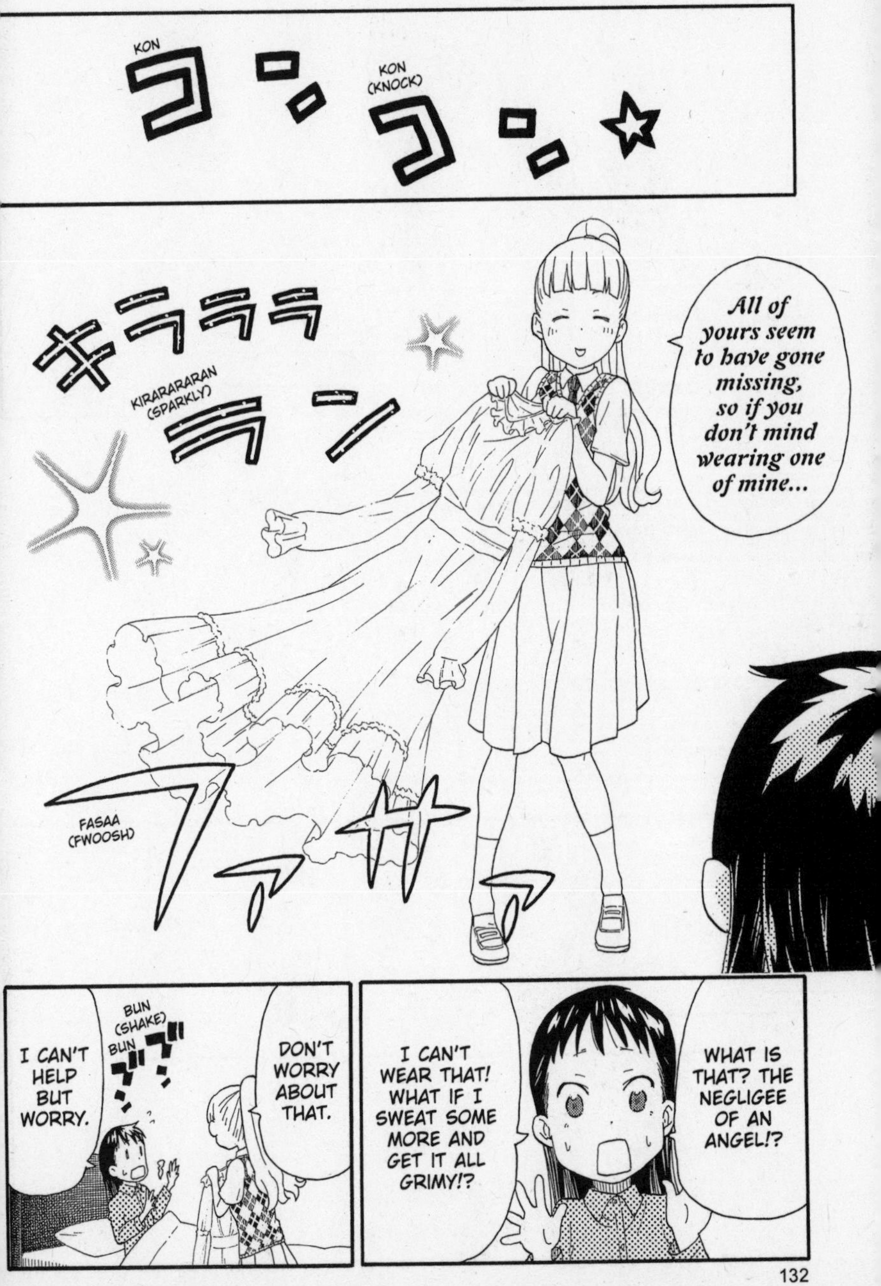

KON
KON (KNOCK)
KIRARARARAN (SPARKLY)
All of yours seem to have gone missing, so if you don't mind wearing one of mine...
FASAA (FWOOSH)
WHAT IS THAT? THE NEGLIGEE OF AN ANGEL!?
I CAN'T WEAR THAT! WHAT IF I SWEAT SOME MORE AND GET IT ALL GRIMY!?
DON'T WORRY ABOUT THAT.
BUN BUN (SHAKE)
I CAN'T HELP BUT WORRY.

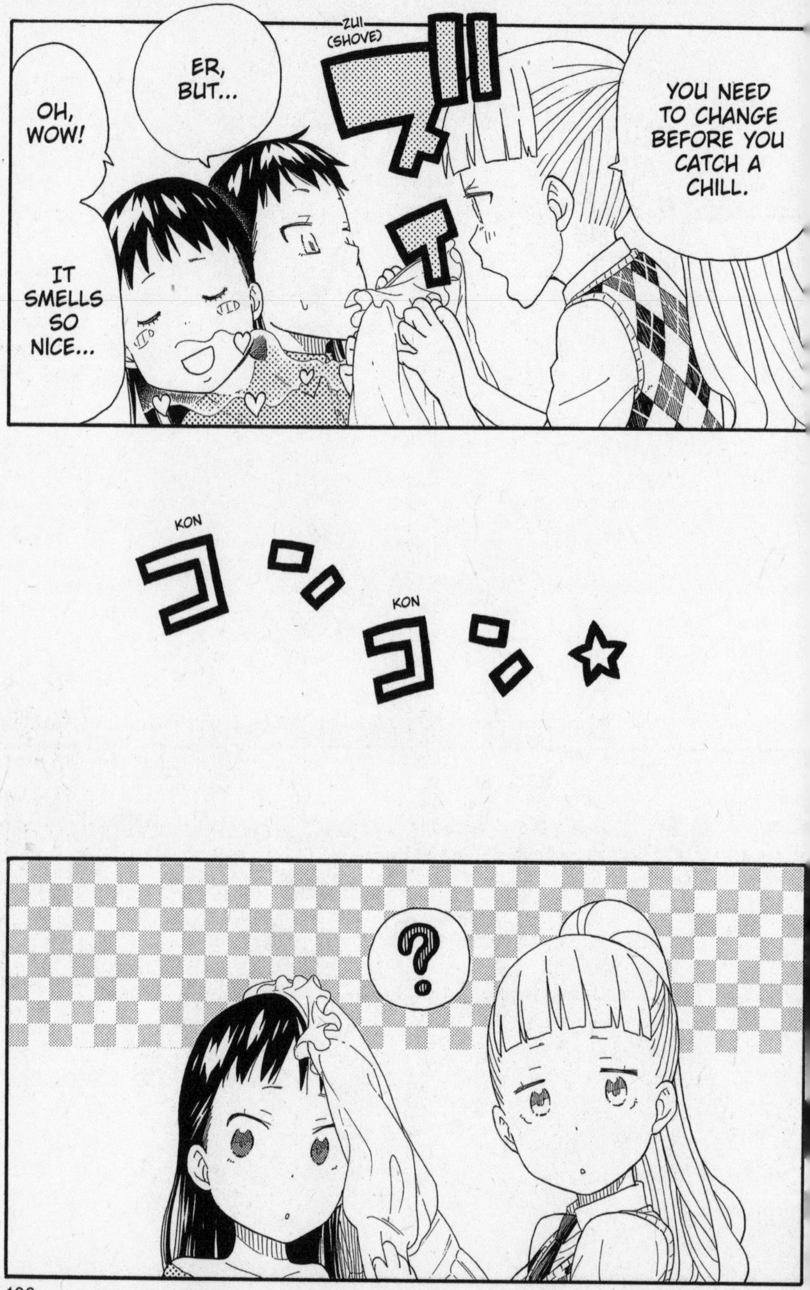
YOU NEED TO CHANGE BEFORE YOU CATCH A CHILL.
ZUI (SHOVE)
ER, BUT...
OH, WOW!
IT SMELLS SO NICE...
KON
KON
?

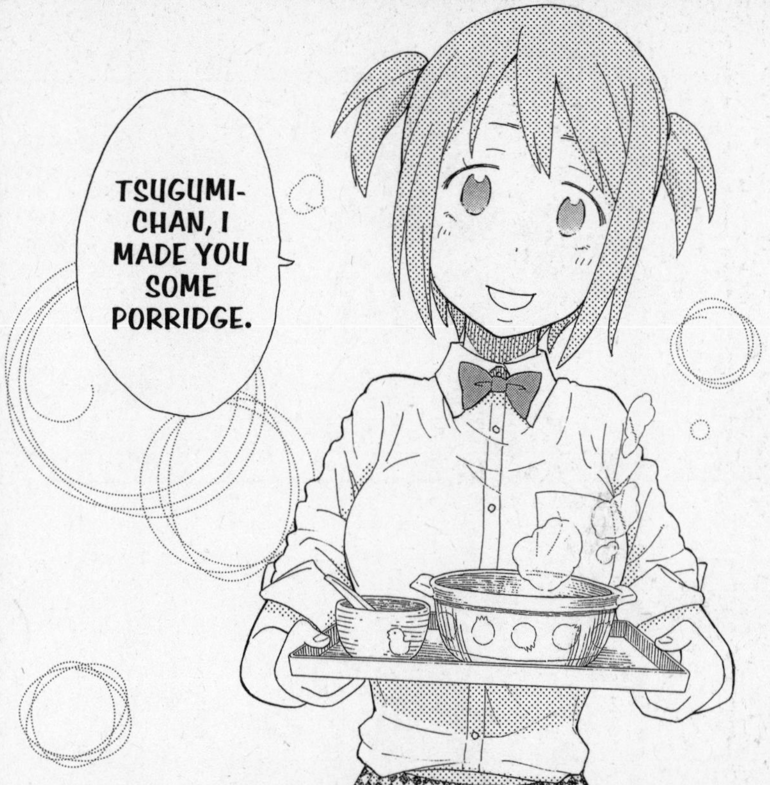
TSUGUMI-CHAN, I MADE YOU SOME PORRIDGE.
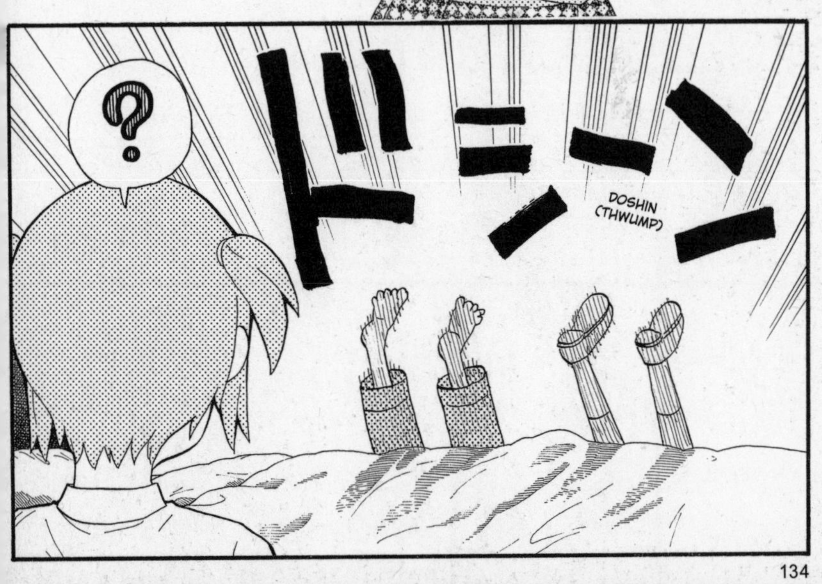
?
ドーン
DOSHIN (THWUMP)

SOUL EATER NOT!

SOUL EATER JOT! PART 10

A JOT TIRESOME

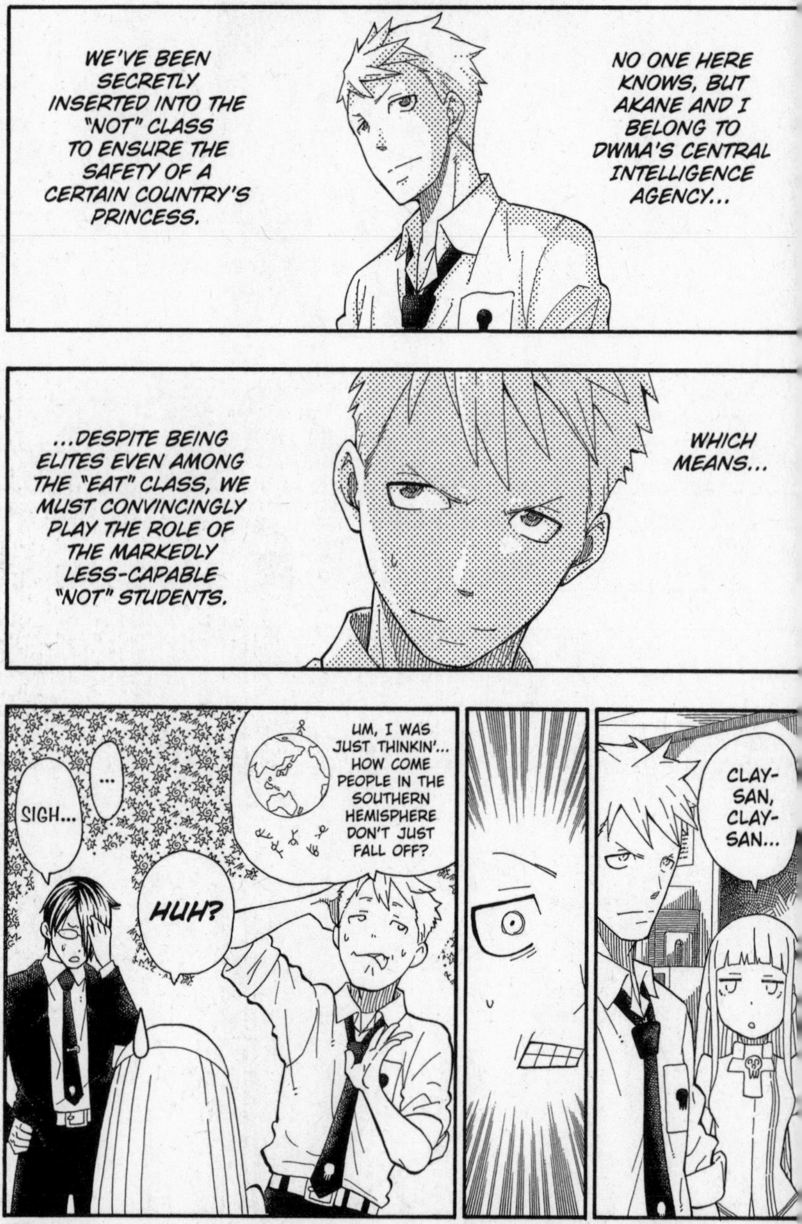
NO ONE HERE KNOWS, BUT AKANE AND I BELONG TO DWMA'S CENTRAL INTELLIGENCE AGENCY...
WE'VE BEEN SECRETLY INSERTED INTO THE "NOT" CLASS TO ENSURE THE SAFETY OF A CERTAIN COUNTRY'S PRINCESS.
...DESPITE BEING ELITES EVEN AMONG THE "EAT" CLASS, WE MUST CONVINCINGLY PLAY THE ROLE OF THE MARKEDLY LESS-CAPABLE "NOT" STUDENTS.
WHICH MEANS...
CLAY-SAN, CLAY-SAN...
UM, I WAS JUST THINKIN'... HOW COME PEOPLE IN THE SOUTHERN HEMISPHERE DON'T JUST FALL OFF?
HUH?
...
SIGH...

A JOT OF A PRANK

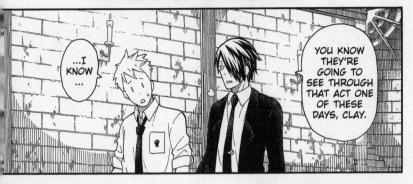

...I KNOW...

YOU KNOW THEY'RE GOING TO SEE THROUGH THAT ACT ONE OF THESE DAYS, CLAY.

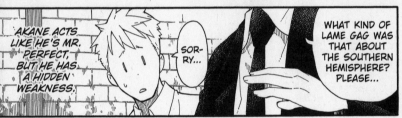

AKANE ACTS LIKE HE'S MR. PERFECT, BUT HE HAS A HIDDEN WEAKNESS.

SORRY...

WHAT KIND OF LAME GAG WAS THAT ABOUT THE SOUTHERN HEMISPHERE? PLEASE...

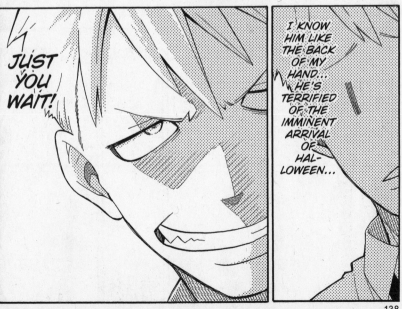

JUST YOU WAIT!

I KNOW HIM LIKE THE BACK OF MY HAND... HE'S TERRIFIED OF THE IMMINENT ARRIVAL OF HALLOWEEN...

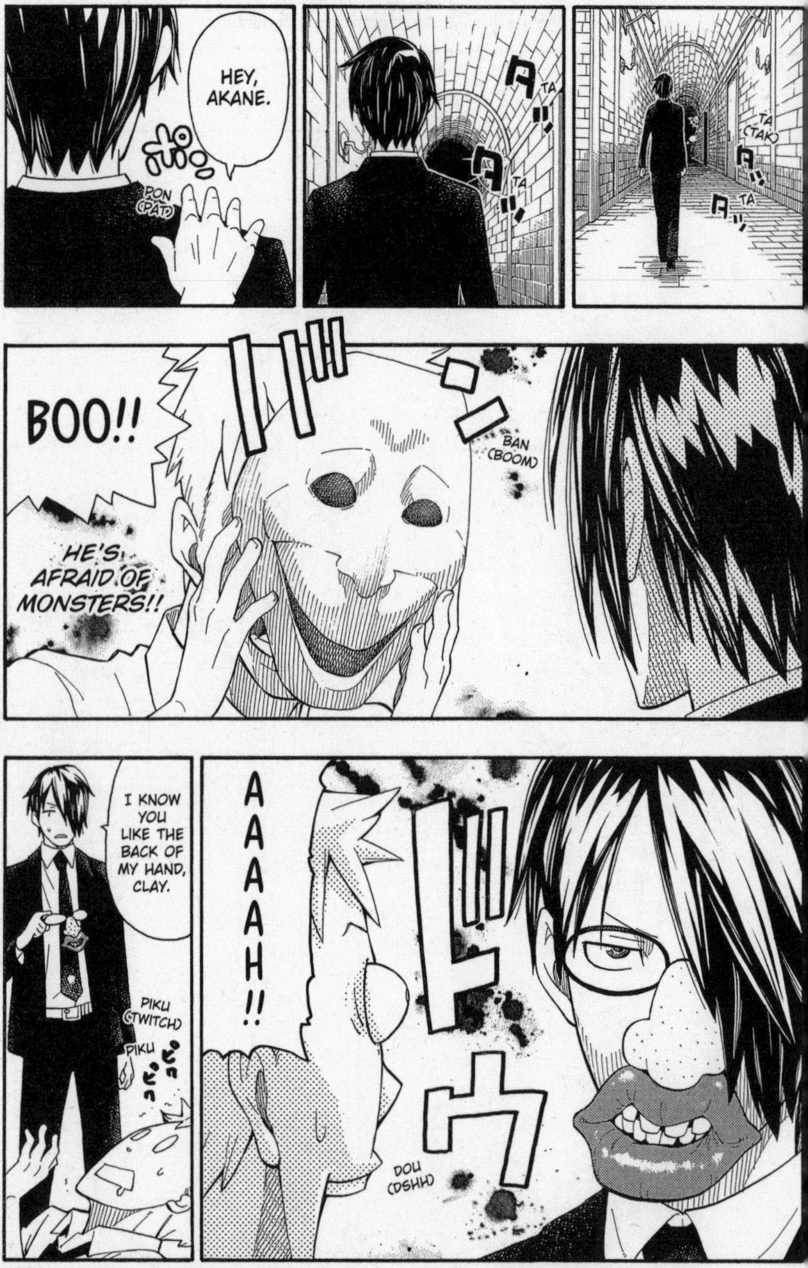
TA (TAK)
TA
TA
TA
HEY, AKANE.
PON (PAT)
BAN (BOOM)
BOO!!
HE'S AFRAID OF MONSTERS!!
AAAAAH!!
DOU (DSHH)
I KNOW YOU LIKE THE BACK OF MY HAND, CLAY.
PIKU (TWITCH)
PIKU

A JOT SHAKEN

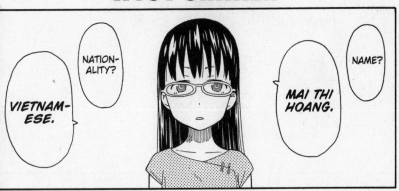

NATION-ALITY?

VIETNAM-ESE.

MAI THI HOANG.

NAME?

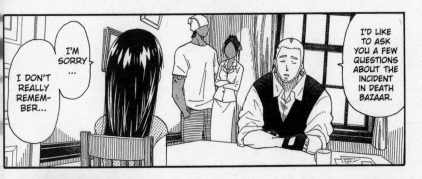

I'M SORRY...

I DON'T REALLY REMEMBER...

I'D LIKE TO ASK YOU A FEW QUESTIONS ABOUT THE INCIDENT IN DEATH BAZAAR.

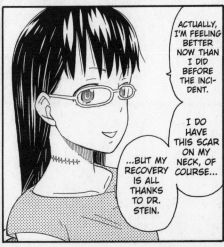

ACTUALLY, I'M FEELING BETTER NOW THAN I DID BEFORE THE INCIDENT.

I DO HAVE THIS SCAR ON MY NECK, OF COURSE...

...BUT MY RECOVERY IS ALL THANKS TO DR. STEIN.

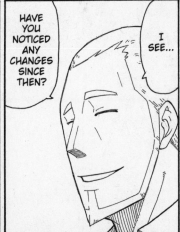

HAVE YOU NOTICED ANY CHANGES SINCE THEN?

I SEE...

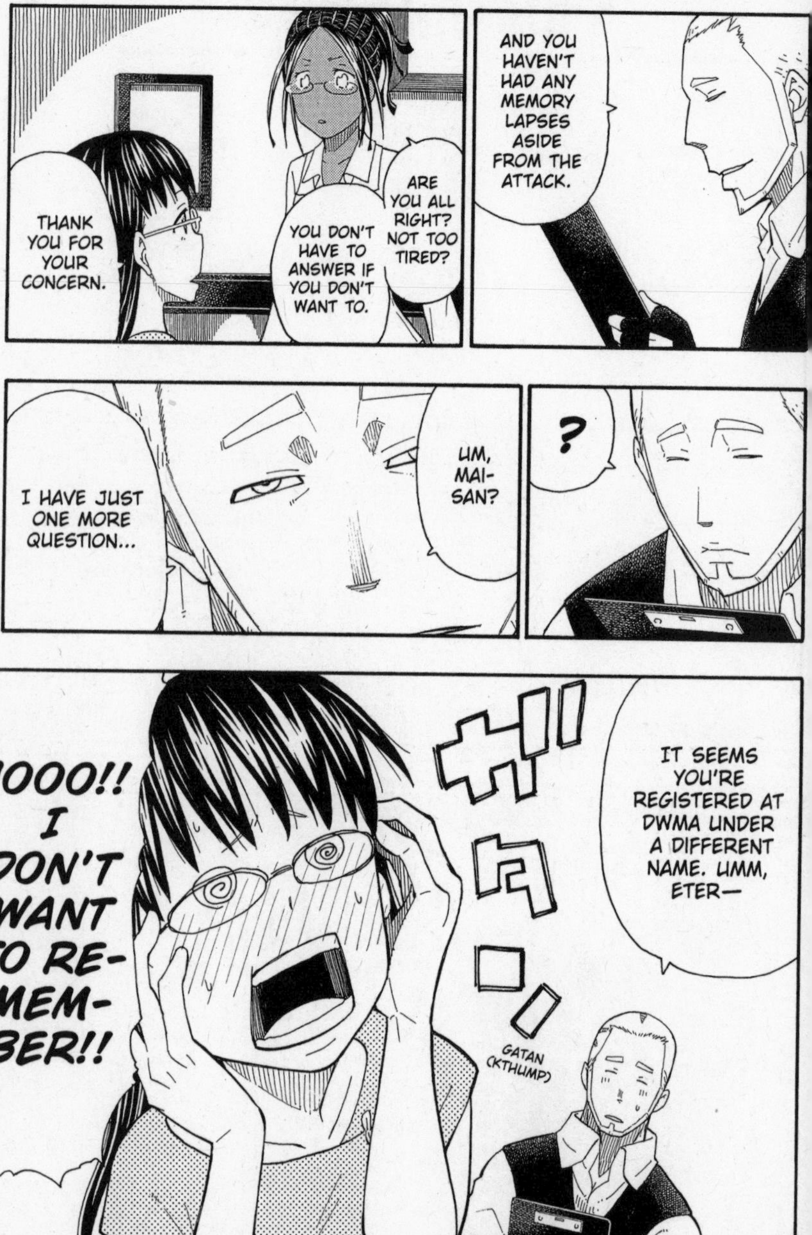
AND YOU HAVEN'T HAD ANY MEMORY LAPSES ASIDE FROM THE ATTACK.
ARE YOU ALL RIGHT? NOT TOO TIRED?
YOU DON'T HAVE TO ANSWER IF YOU DON'T WANT TO.
THANK YOU FOR YOUR CONCERN.
?
UM, MAI-SAN?
I HAVE JUST ONE MORE QUESTION...
IT SEEMS YOU'RE REGISTERED AT DWMA UNDER A DIFFERENT NAME. UMM, ETER—
GATAN (KTHUMP)
NOOO!! I DON'T WANT TO RE-MEM-BER!!

A JOT UNFAMILIAR

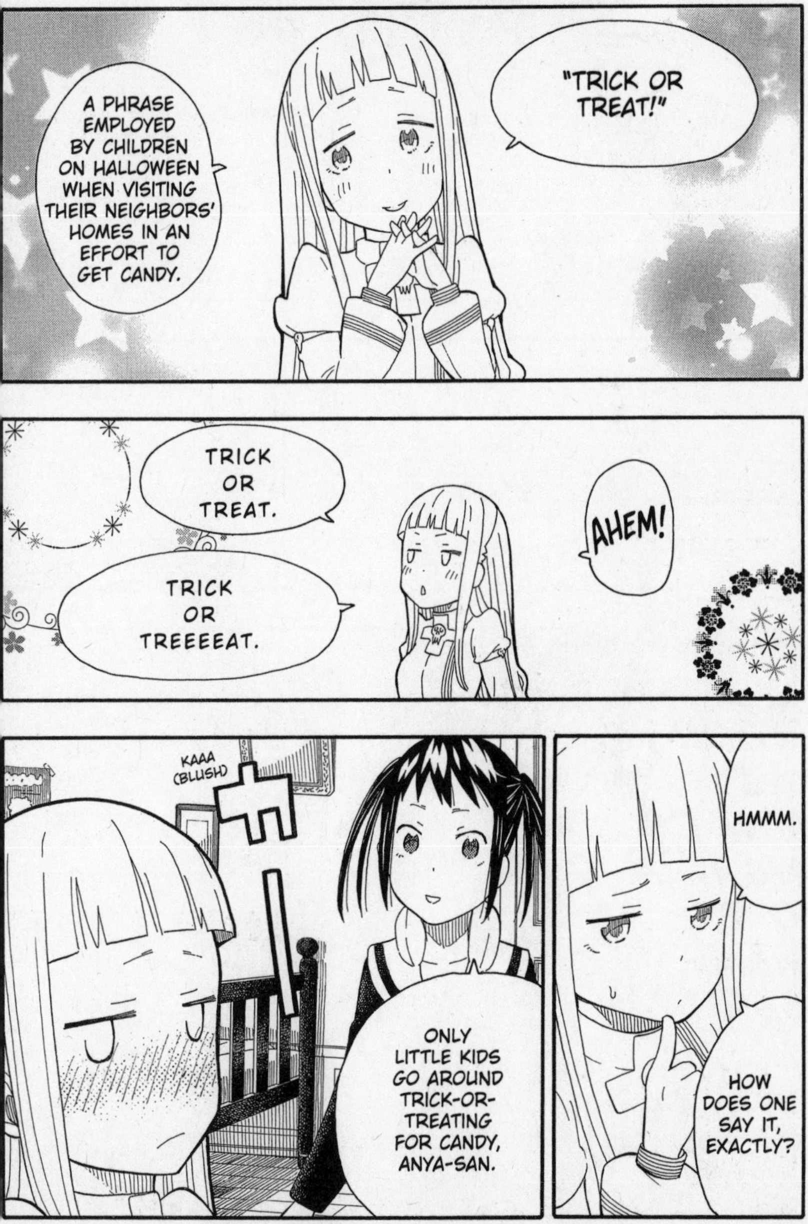
"TRICK OR TREAT!"
A PHRASE EMPLOYED BY CHILDREN ON HALLOWEEN WHEN VISITING THEIR NEIGHBORS' HOMES IN AN EFFORT TO GET CANDY.
AHEM!
TRICK OR TREAT.
TRICK OR TREEEEAT.
HMMM.
HOW DOES ONE SAY IT, EXACTLY?
ONLY LITTLE KIDS GO AROUND TRICK-OR-TREATING FOR CANDY, ANYA-SAN.
KAAA (BLUSH)

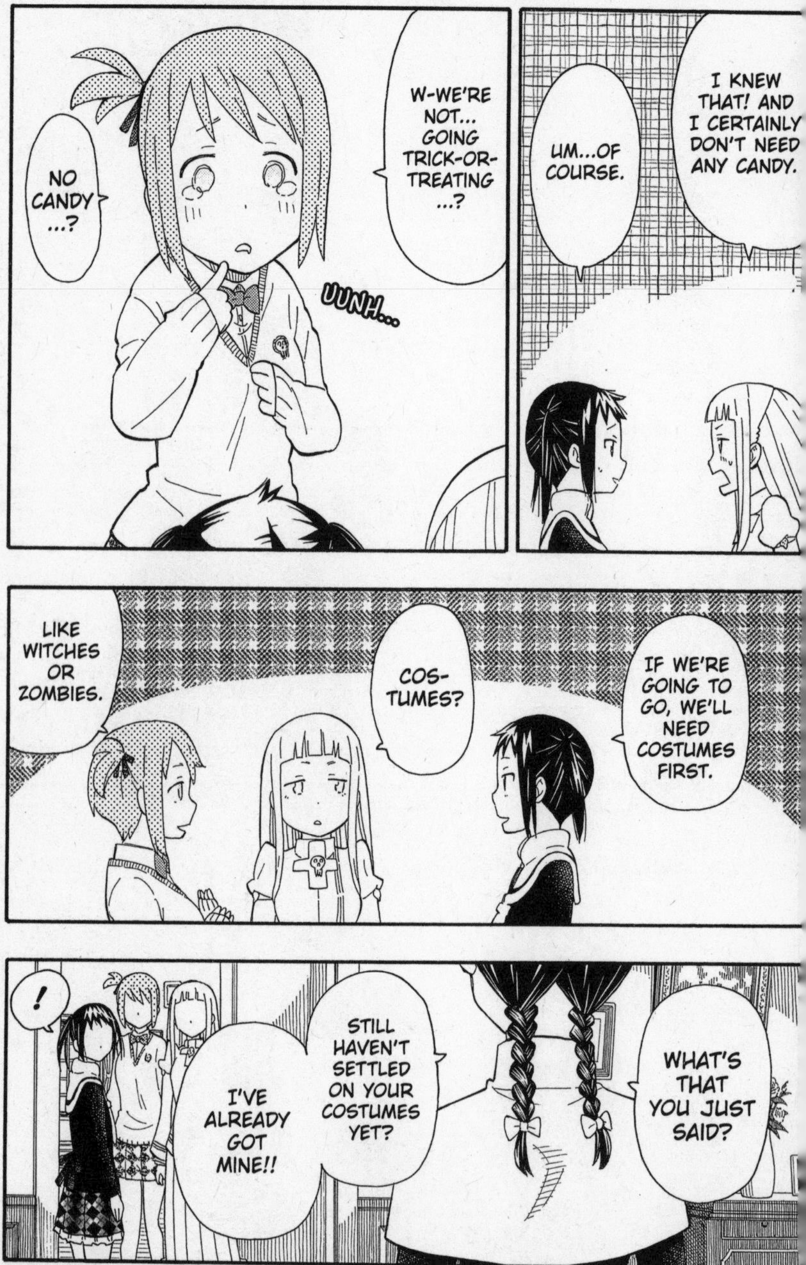
I KNEW THAT! AND I CERTAINLY DON'T NEED ANY CANDY.
UM...OF COURSE.
W-WE'RE NOT... GOING TRICK-OR-TREATING ...?
NO CANDY ...?
UUNH...
IF WE'RE GOING TO GO, WE'LL NEED COSTUMES FIRST.
COS-TUMES?
LIKE WITCHES OR ZOMBIES.
WHAT'S THAT YOU JUST SAID?
STILL HAVEN'T SETTLED ON YOUR COSTUMES YET?
I'VE ALREADY GOT MINE!!
!

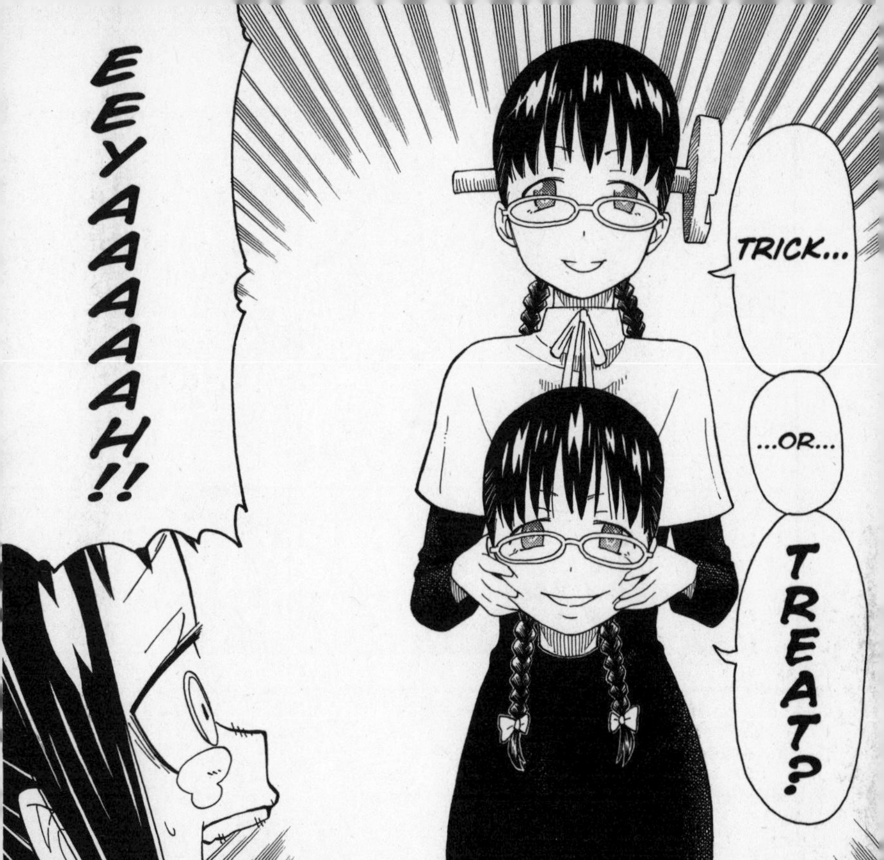
TRICK...
...OR...
TREAT?
EEYAAAAAAAH!!
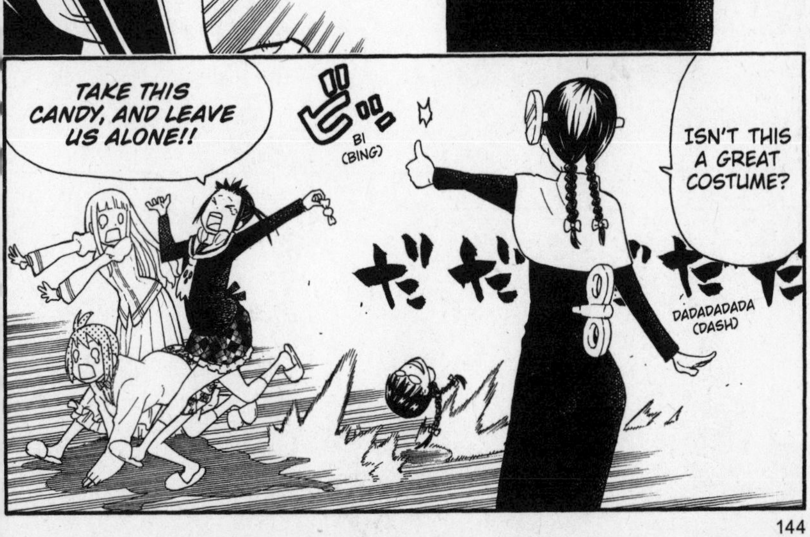
ISN'T THIS A GREAT COSTUME?
BI (BING)
TAKE THIS CANDY, AND LEAVE US ALONE!!
DADADADADA (DASH)

A JOT OF YOUR TIME, AKANE-KUN?

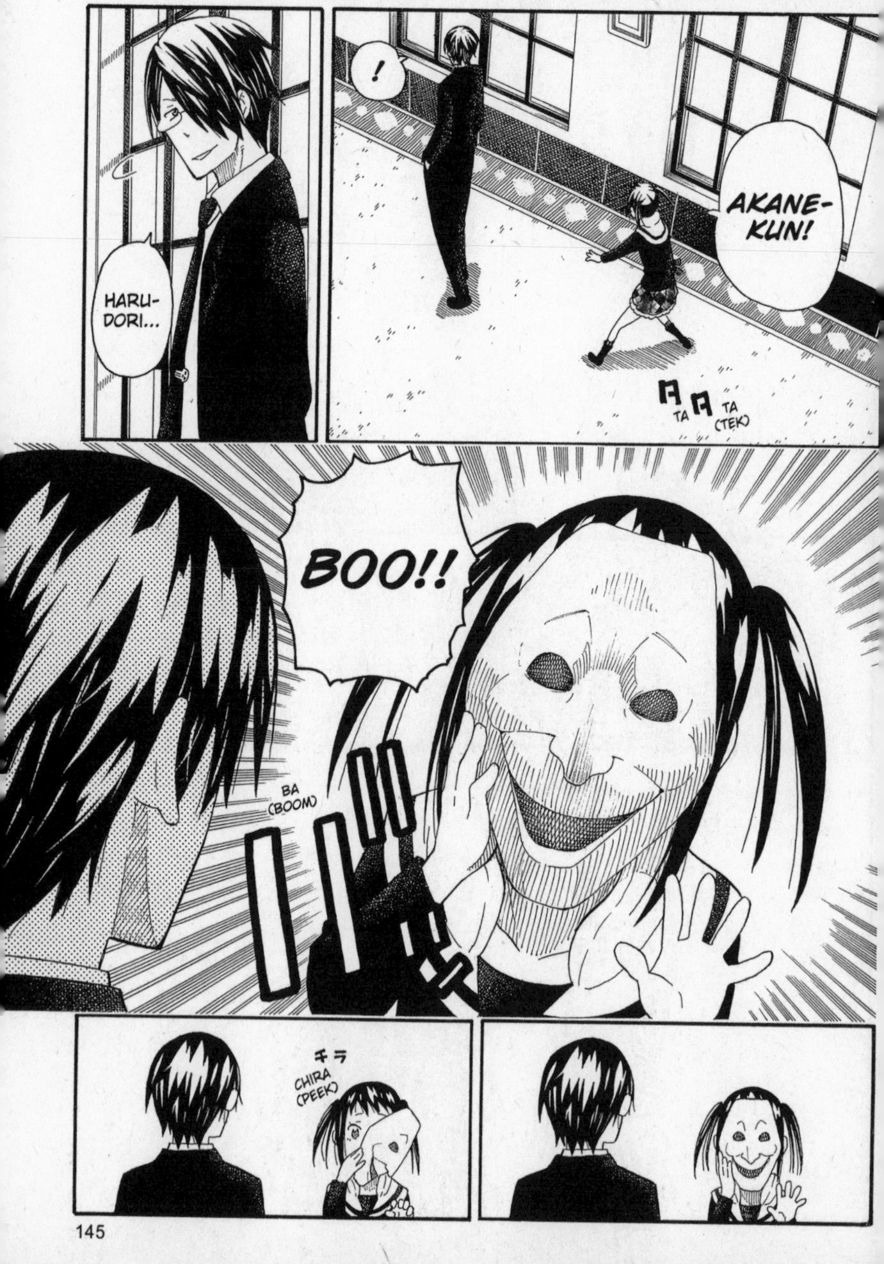
AKANE-KUN!
TA TA TA (TEK)
!
HARU-DORI...
BOO!!
BA (BOOM)
チラ
CHIRA (PEEK)

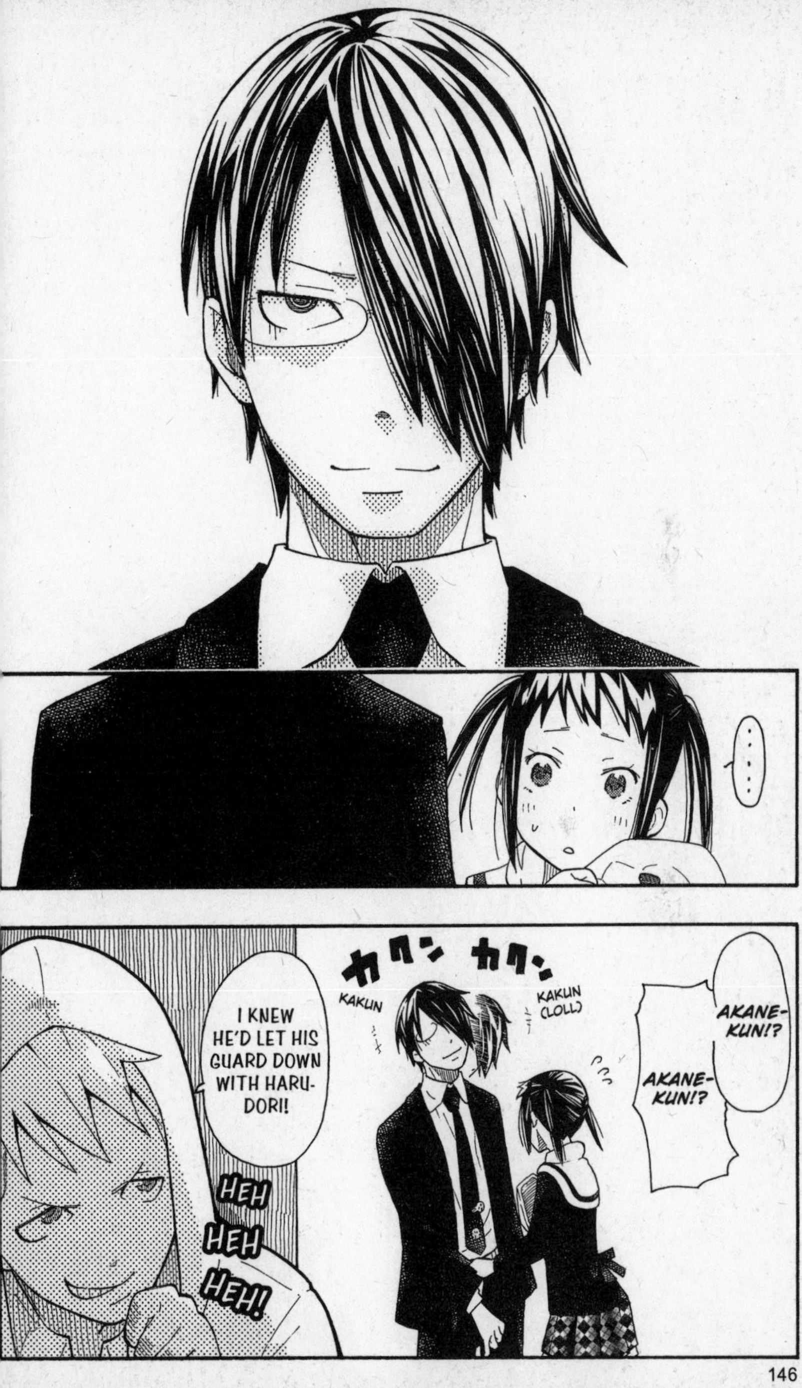
......
AKANE-KUN!?
AKANE-KUN!?
カクン カクン
KAKUN (LOLL)
KAKUN
I KNEW HE'D LET HIS GUARD DOWN WITH HARU-DORI!
HEH HEH HEH!

SOUL EATER NOT!

CHAPTER 25: PREPARATIONS!

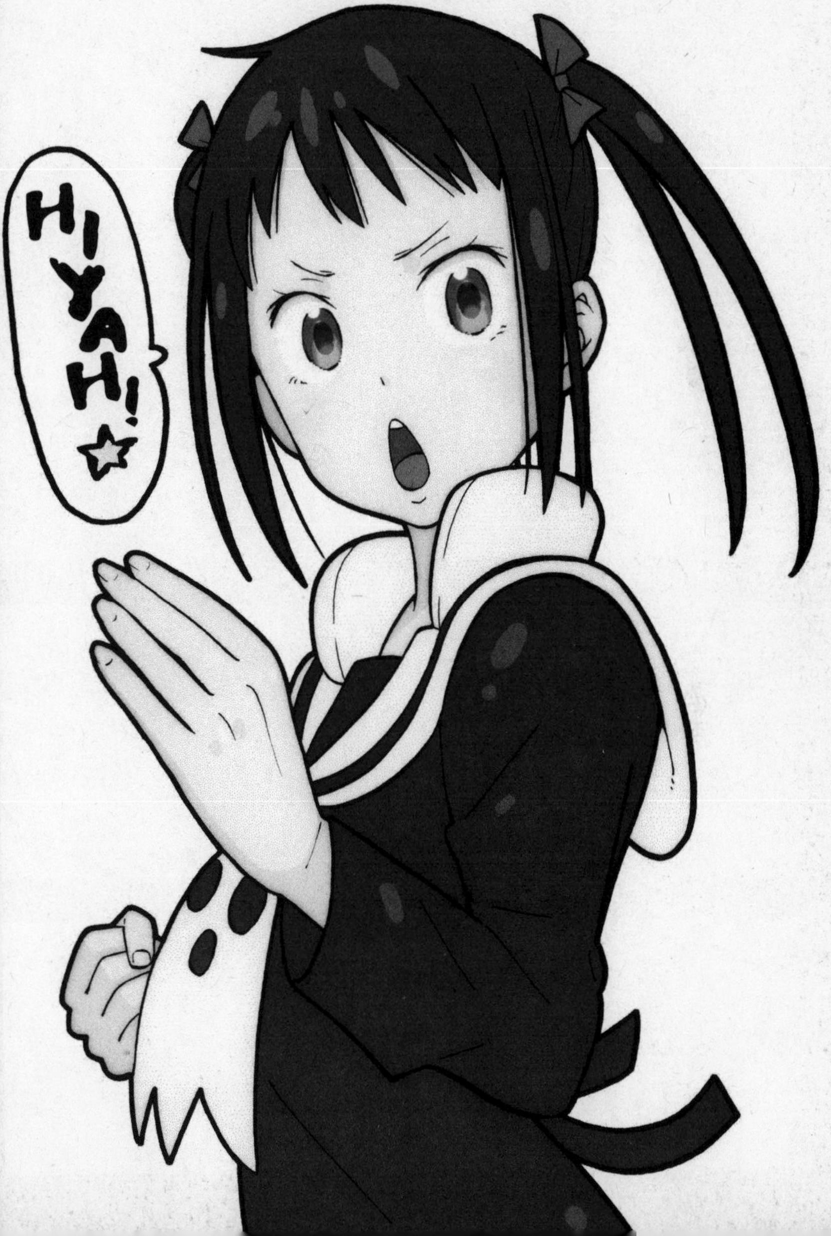
HIYAH!☆

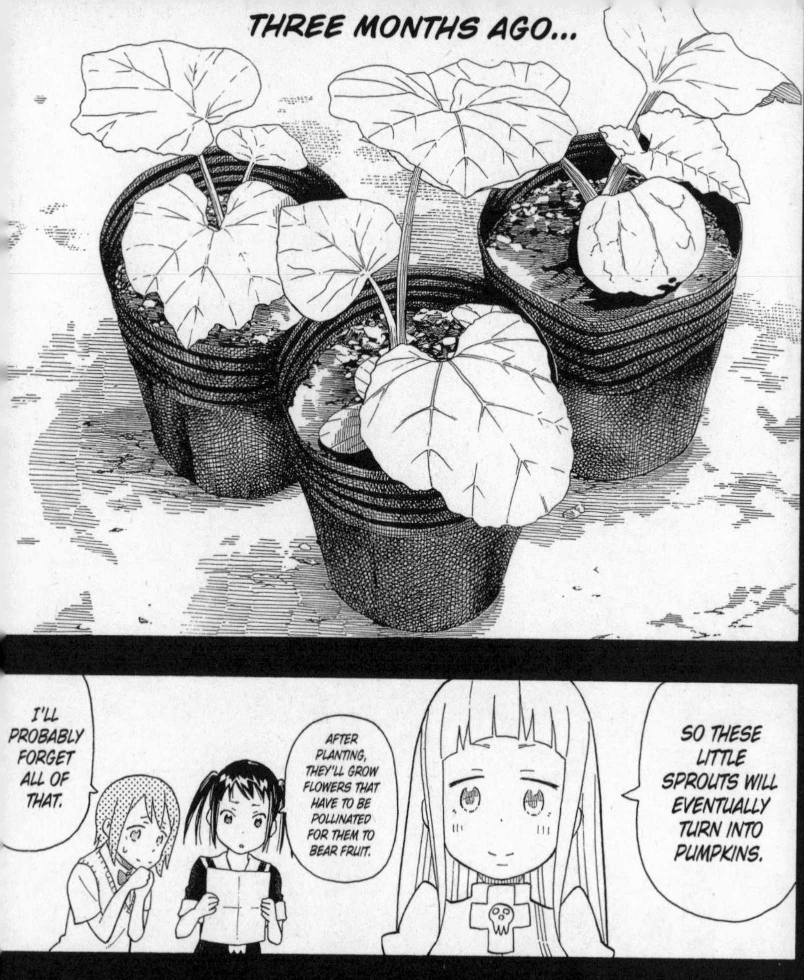
THREE MONTHS AGO...
SO THESE LITTLE SPROUTS WILL EVENTUALLY TURN INTO PUMPKINS.
AFTER PLANTING, THEY'LL GROW FLOWERS THAT HAVE TO BE POLLINATED FOR THEM TO BEAR FRUIT.
I'LL PROBABLY FORGET ALL OF THAT.
スク
SUKU
スク
SUKU (GROW)
スク
SUKU

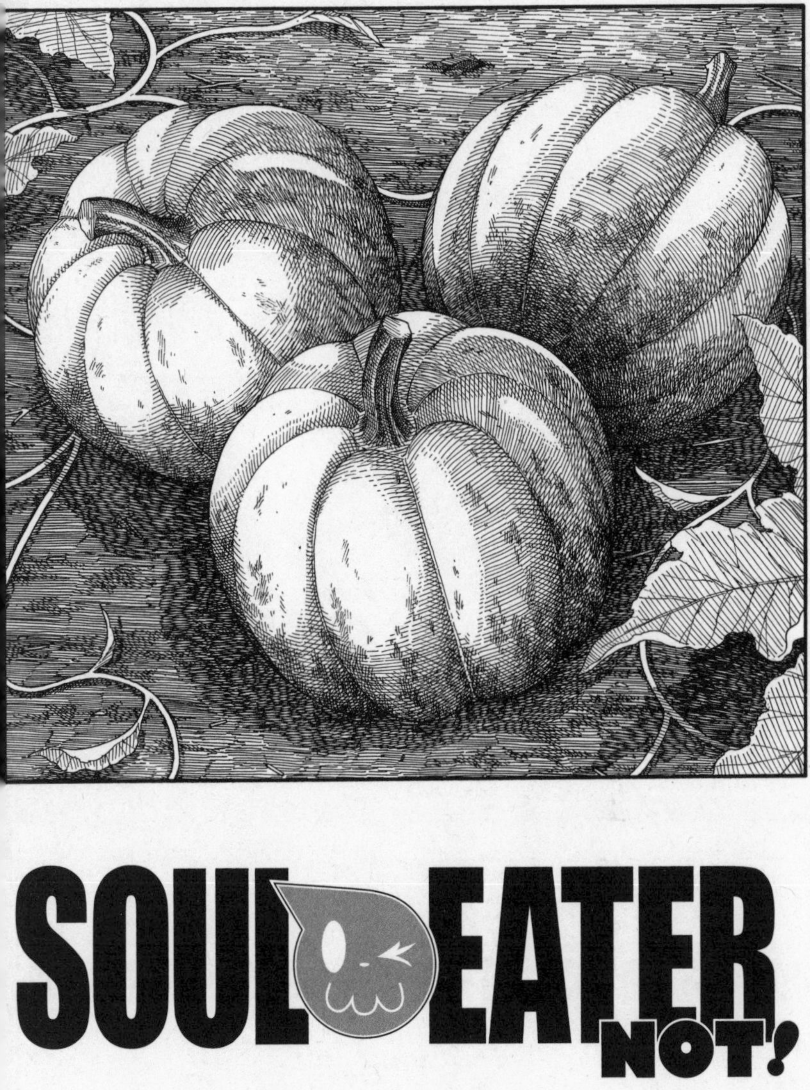

SOUL EATER NOT!

CHAPTER 25: PREPARATIONS!

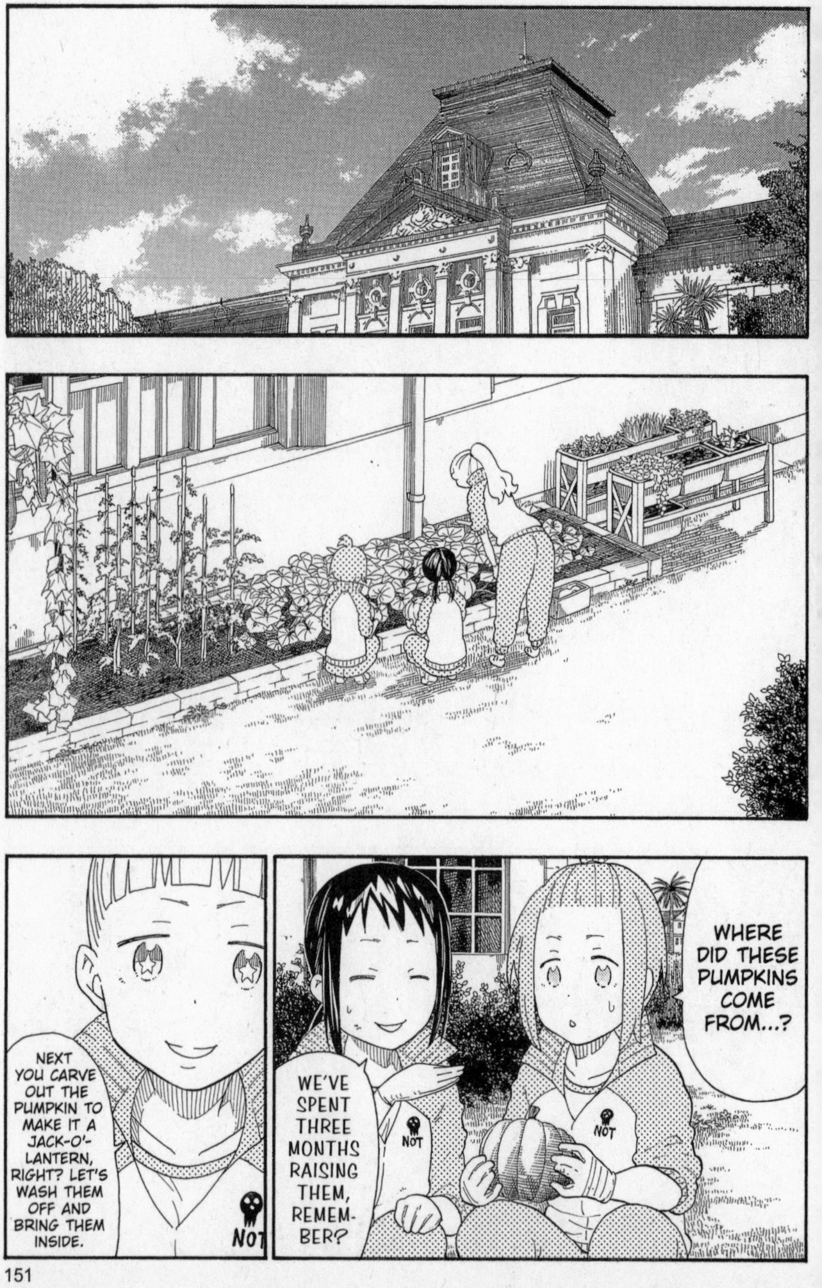
WHERE DID THESE PUMPKINS COME FROM...?
WE'VE SPENT THREE MONTHS RAISING THEM, REMEMBER?
NOT
NOT
NEXT YOU CARVE OUT THE PUMPKIN TO MAKE IT A JACK-O'-LANTERN, RIGHT? LET'S WASH THEM OFF AND BRING THEM INSIDE.
NOT

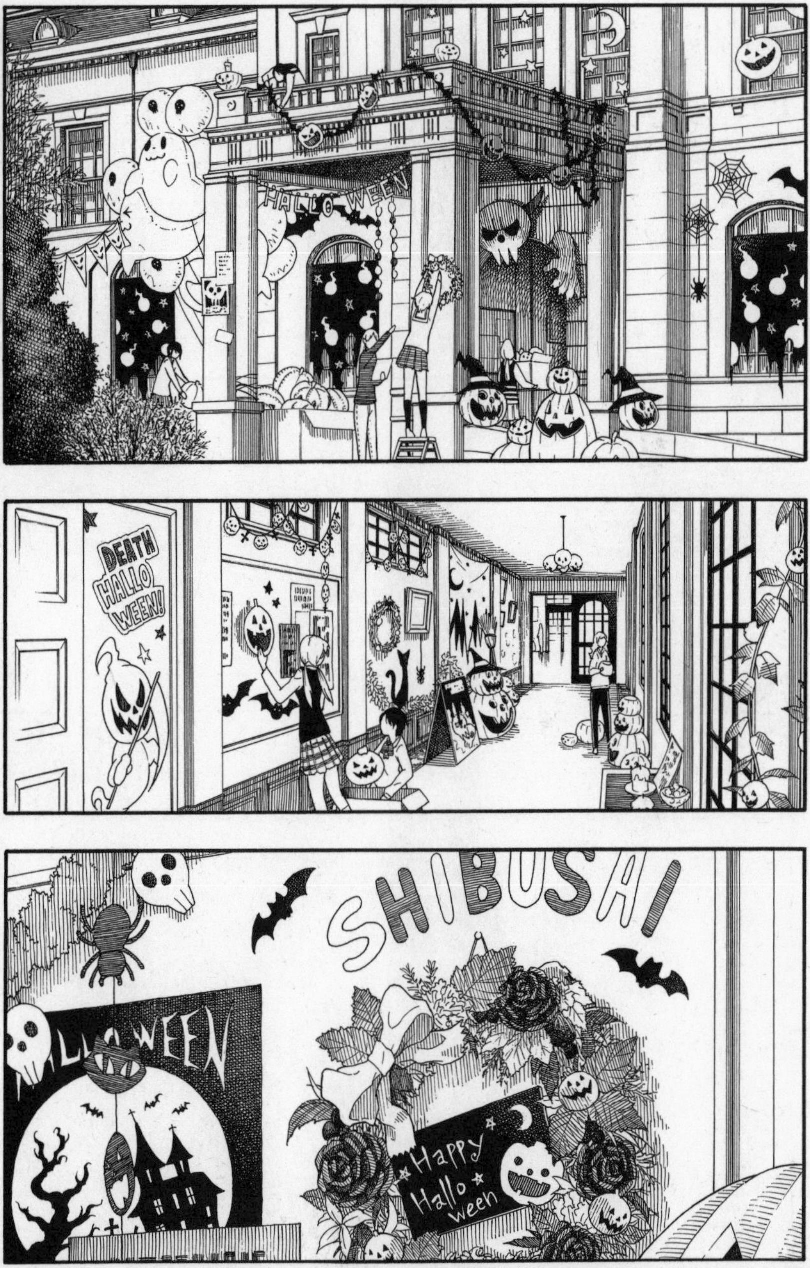
HALLO WEEN
DEATH HALLO WEEN!
SHIBUSAI
WEEN
Happy Hallo ween

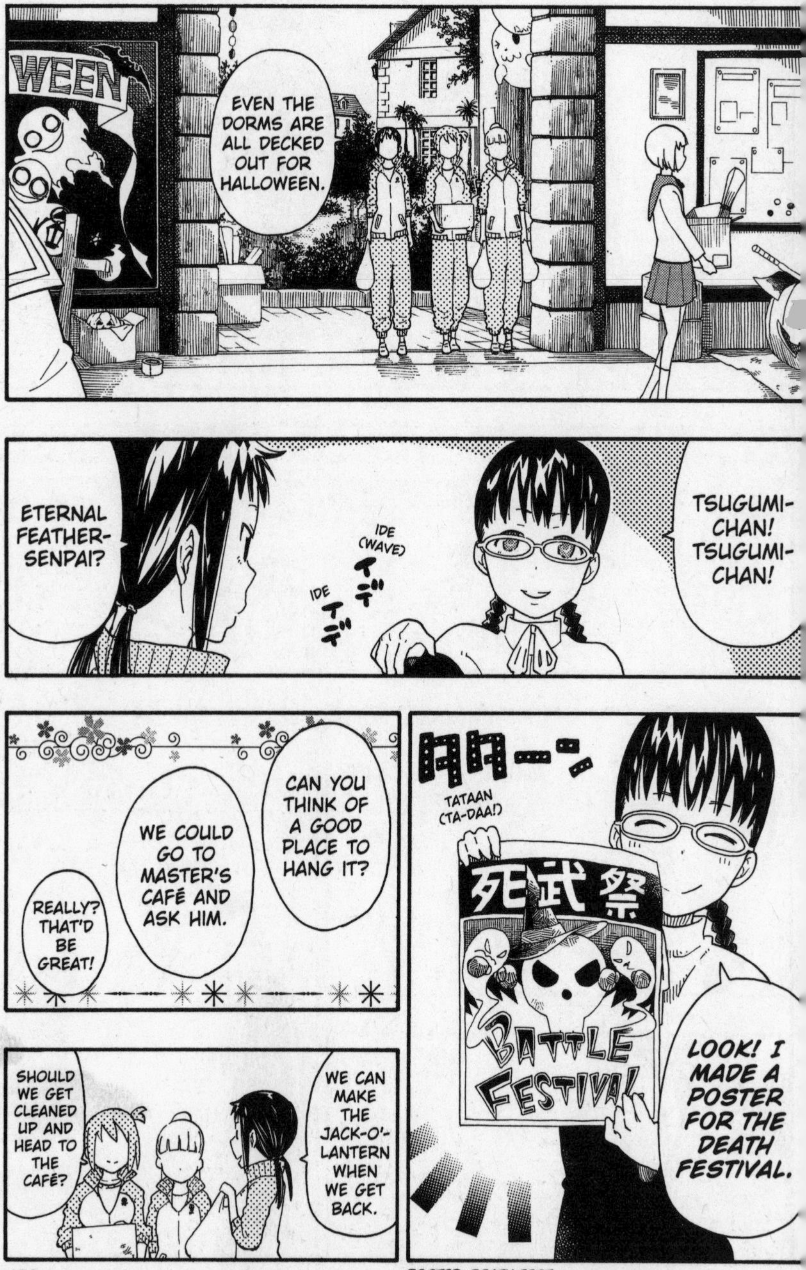
WEEN
EVEN THE DORMS ARE ALL DECKED OUT FOR HALLOWEEN.
TSUGUMI-CHAN! TSUGUMI-CHAN!
イデ IDE (WAVE)
イデ IDE
ETERNAL FEATHER-SENPAI?
タターン TATAAN (TA-DAA!)
死武祭
BATTLE FESTIVAL
LOOK! I MADE A POSTER FOR THE DEATH FESTIVAL.
CAN YOU THINK OF A GOOD PLACE TO HANG IT?
WE COULD GO TO MASTER'S CAFÉ AND ASK HIM.
REALLY? THAT'D BE GREAT!
WE CAN MAKE THE JACK-O'-LANTERN WHEN WE GET BACK.
SHOULD WE GET CLEANED UP AND HEAD TO THE CAFÉ?

POSTER: DEATH FEST

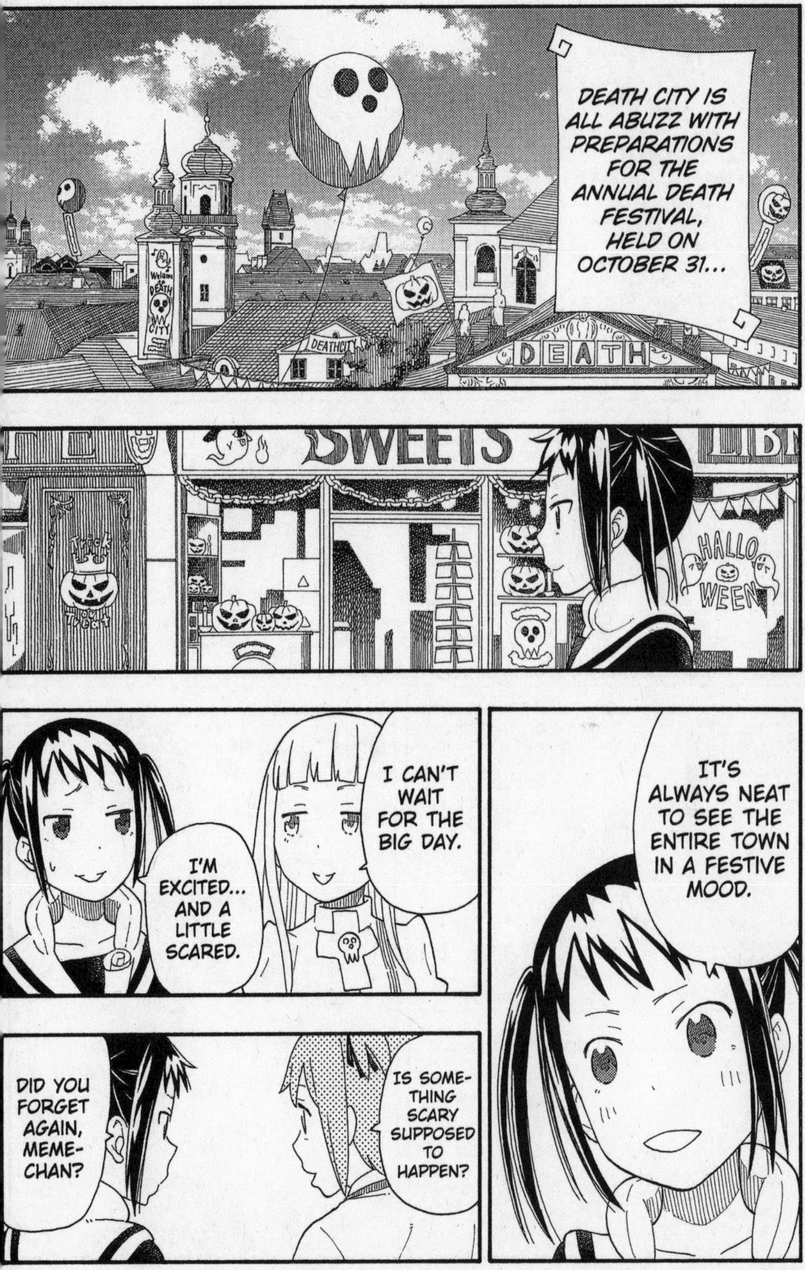
DEATH CITY IS ALL ABUZZ WITH PREPARATIONS FOR THE ANNUAL DEATH FESTIVAL, HELD ON OCTOBER 31…
DEATHCITY
DEATH
SWEETS
HALLO WEEN
IT'S ALWAYS NEAT TO SEE THE ENTIRE TOWN IN A FESTIVE MOOD.
I CAN'T WAIT FOR THE BIG DAY.
I'M EXCITED… AND A LITTLE SCARED.
IS SOME-THING SCARY SUPPOSED TO HAPPEN?
DID YOU FORGET AGAIN, MEME-CHAN?

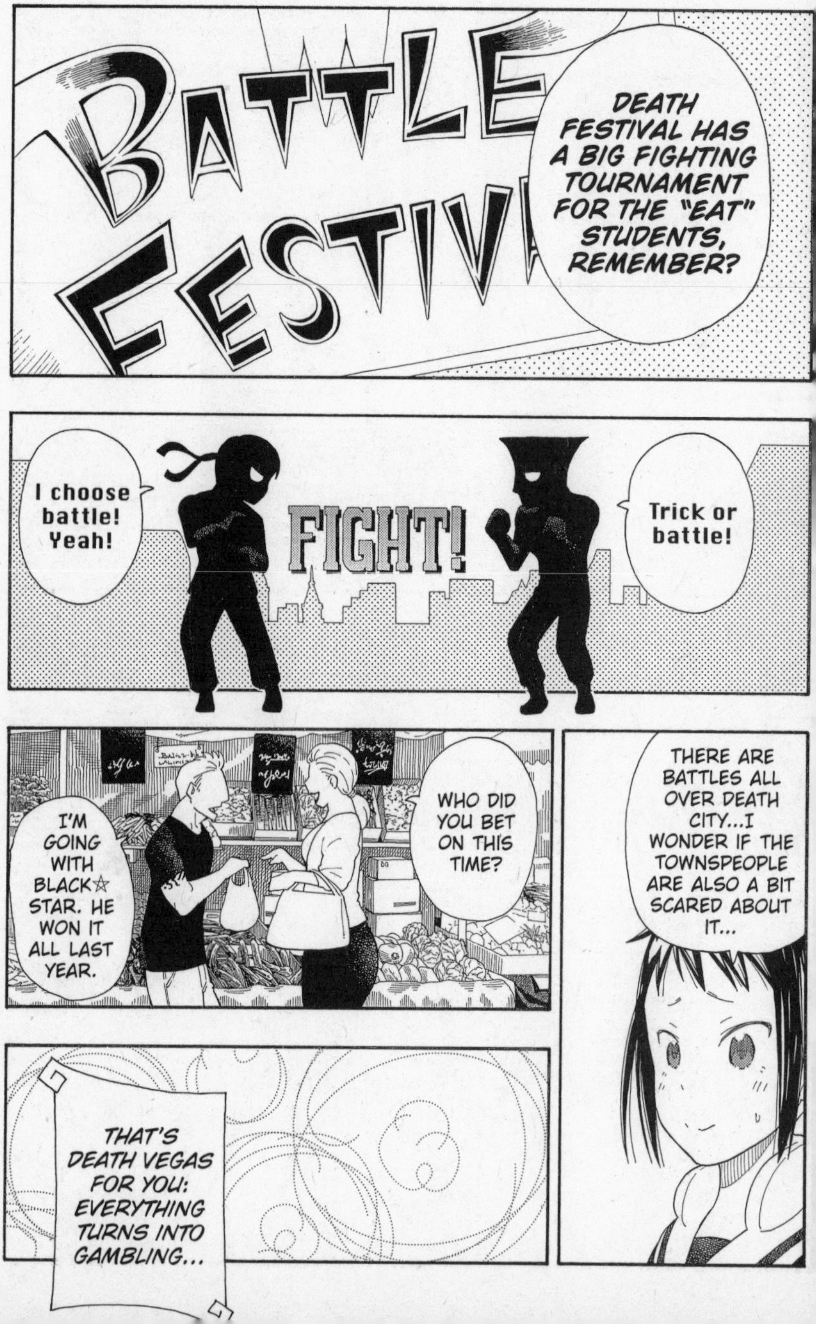
DEATH FESTIVAL HAS A BIG FIGHTING TOURNAMENT FOR THE "EAT" STUDENTS, REMEMBER?
BATTLE FESTIV
Trick or battle!
FIGHT!
I choose battle! Yeah!
THERE ARE BATTLES ALL OVER DEATH CITY...I WONDER IF THE TOWNSPEOPLE ARE ALSO A BIT SCARED ABOUT IT...
WHO DID YOU BET ON THIS TIME?
I'M GOING WITH BLACK☆STAR. HE WON IT ALL LAST YEAR.
THAT'S DEATH VEGAS FOR YOU: EVERYTHING TURNS INTO GAMBLING...

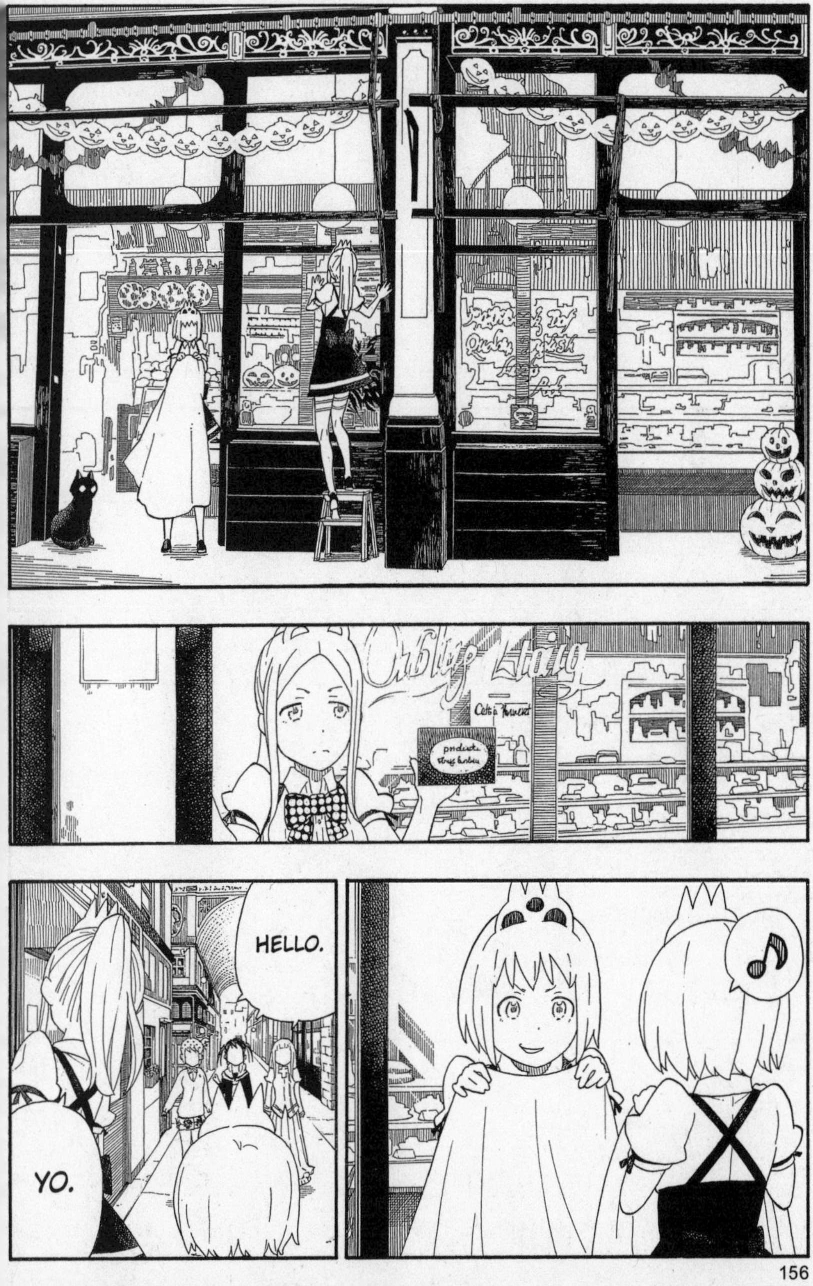
HELLO.
YO.

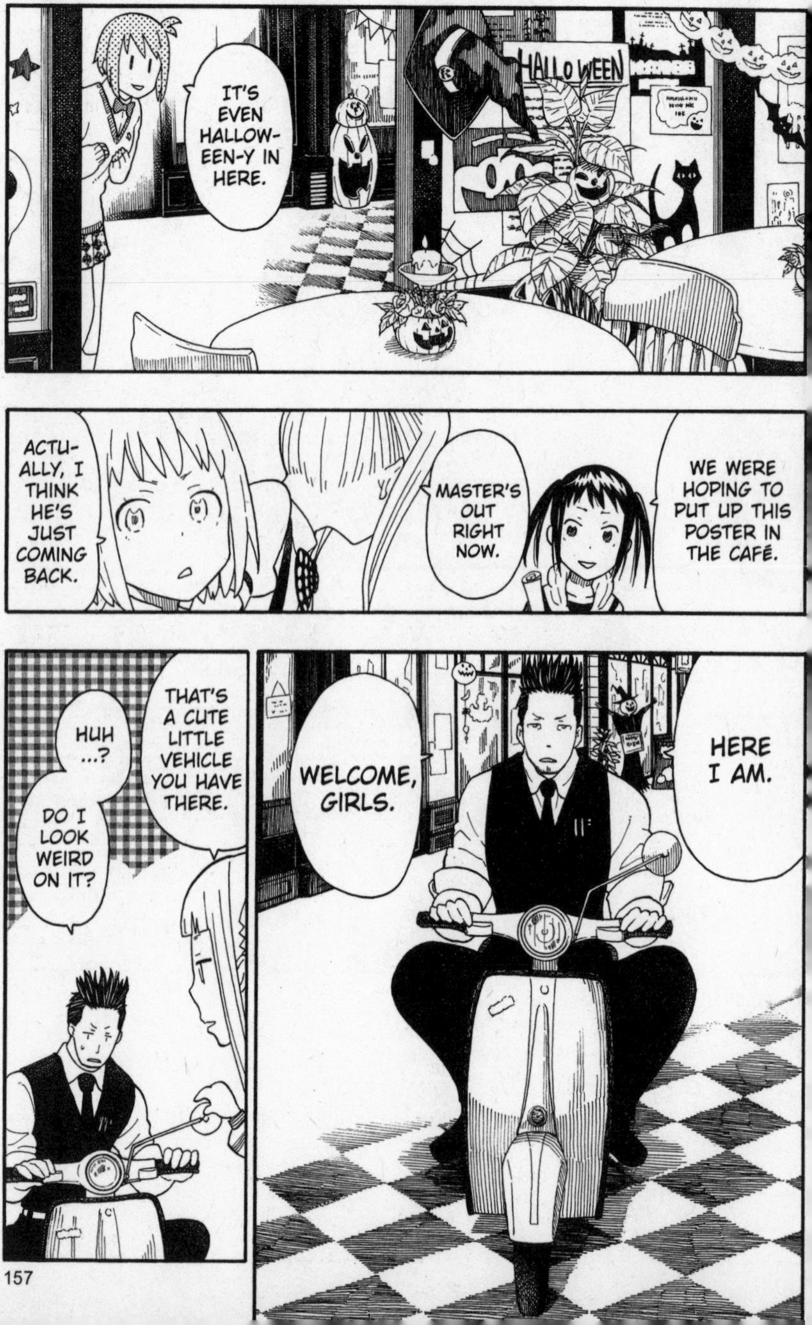
IT'S EVEN HALLOW-EEN-Y IN HERE.
WE WERE HOPING TO PUT UP THIS POSTER IN THE CAFÉ.
MASTER'S OUT RIGHT NOW.
ACTU-ALLY, I THINK HE'S JUST COMING BACK.
HERE I AM.
WELCOME, GIRLS.
THAT'S A CUTE LITTLE VEHICLE YOU HAVE THERE.
HUH ...?
DO I LOOK WEIRD ON IT?
HALLOWEEN

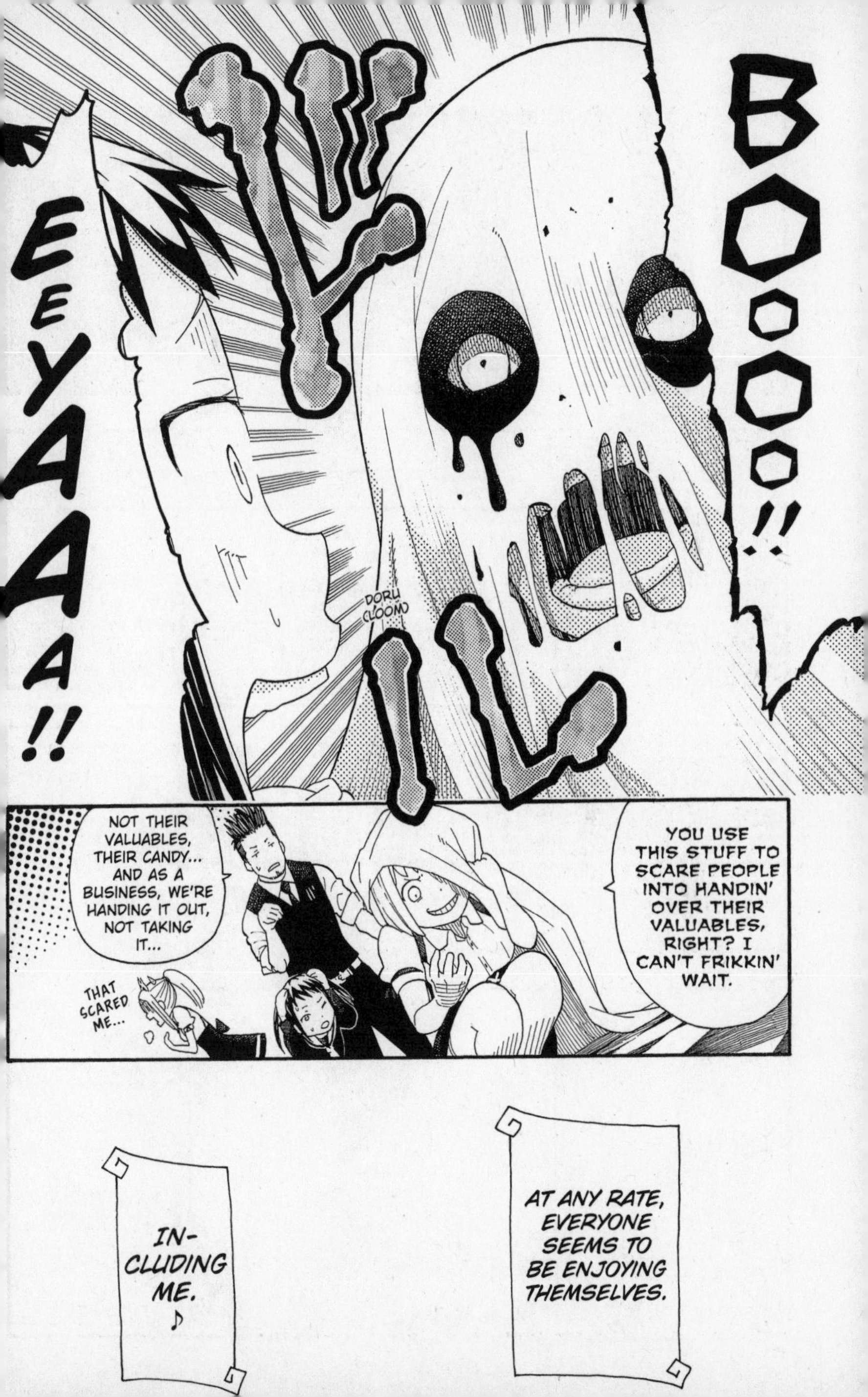
BOOOOO!!
EEYAAA!!
DORU (LOOM)
YOU USE THIS STUFF TO SCARE PEOPLE INTO HANDIN' OVER THEIR VALUABLES, RIGHT? I CAN'T FRIKKIN' WAIT.
NOT THEIR VALUABLES, THEIR CANDY... AND AS A BUSINESS, WE'RE HANDING IT OUT, NOT TAKING IT...
THAT SCARED ME...
AT ANY RATE, EVERYONE SEEMS TO BE ENJOYING THEMSELVES.
IN-CLUDING ME. ♪

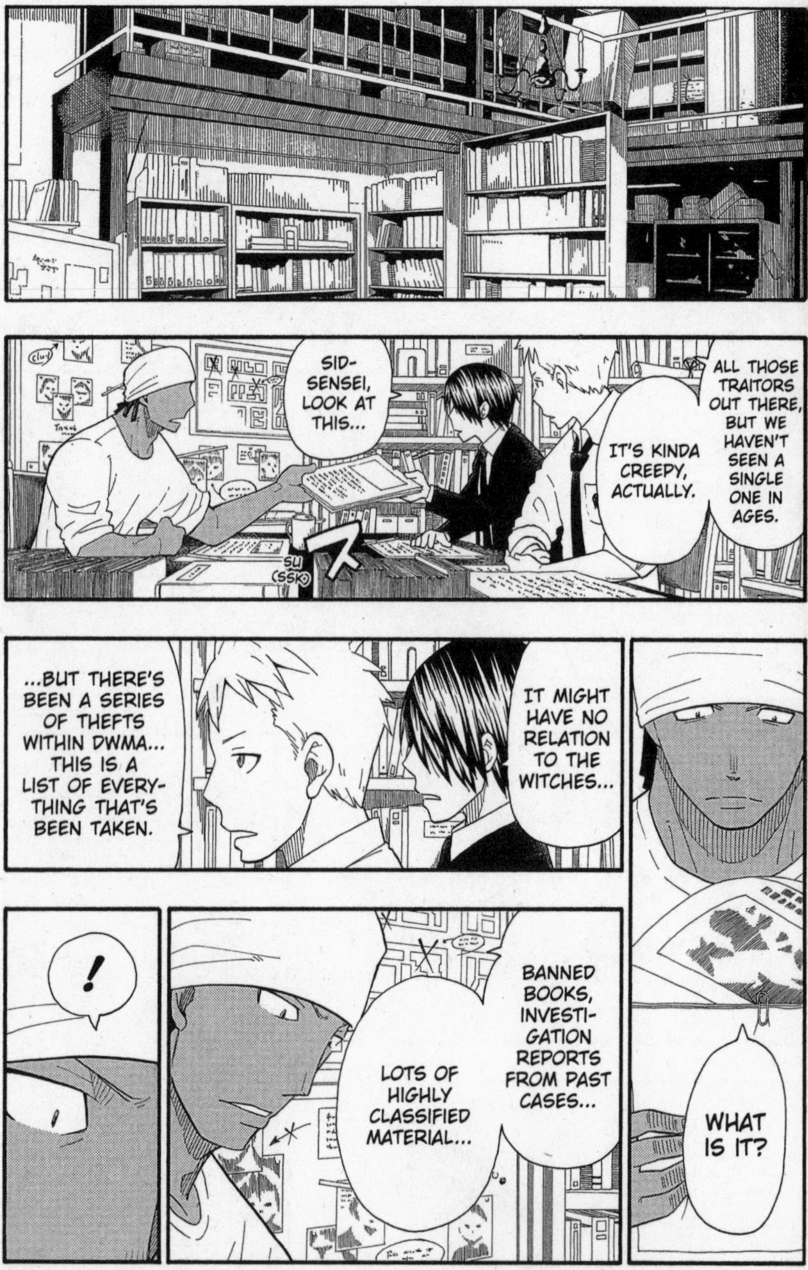
ALL THOSE TRAITORS OUT THERE, BUT WE HAVEN'T SEEN A SINGLE ONE IN AGES.
IT'S KINDA CREEPY, ACTUALLY.
SID-SENSEI, LOOK AT THIS...
SU (SSK)
WHAT IS IT?
IT MIGHT HAVE NO RELATION TO THE WITCHES...
...BUT THERE'S BEEN A SERIES OF THEFTS WITHIN DWMA... THIS IS A LIST OF EVERYTHING THAT'S BEEN TAKEN.
BANNED BOOKS, INVESTIGATION REPORTS FROM PAST CASES...
LOTS OF HIGHLY CLASSIFIED MATERIAL...
!

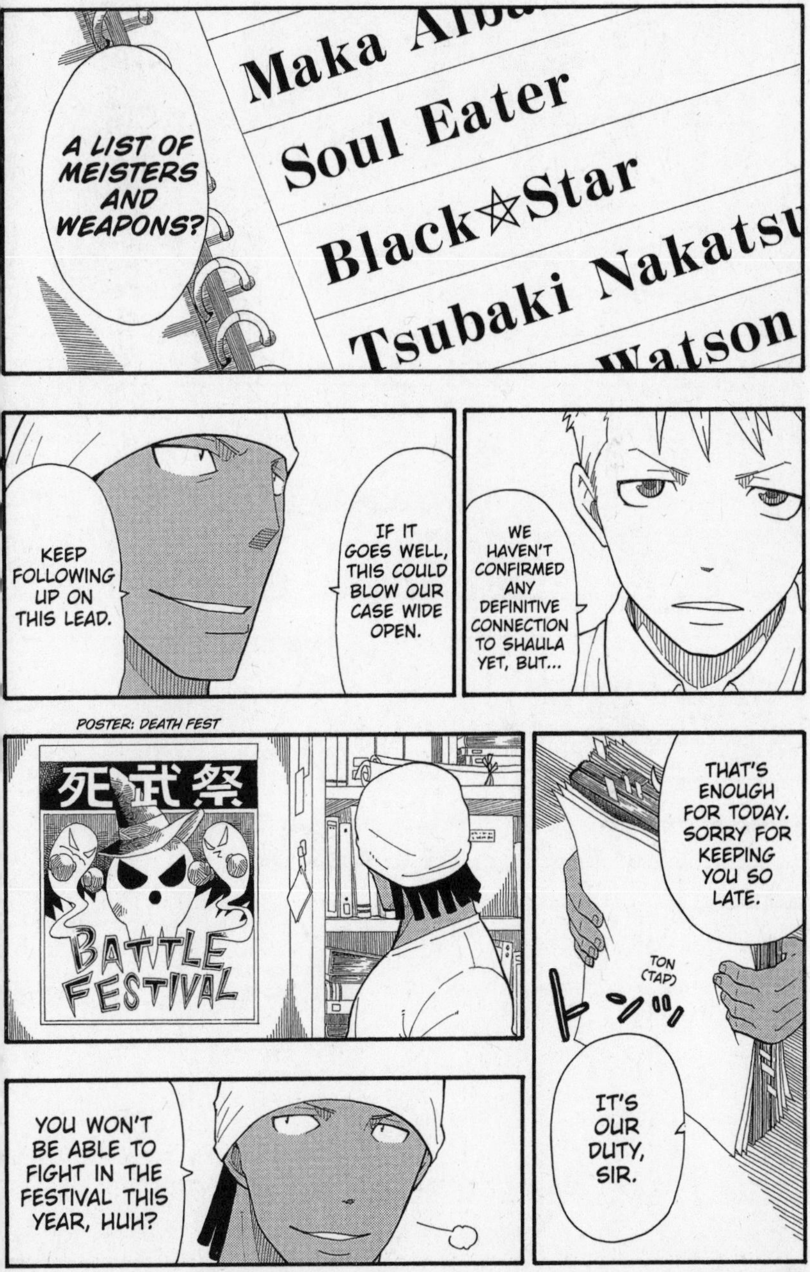
A LIST OF MEISTERS AND WEAPONS?
Maka Alb
Soul Eater
Black☆Star
Tsubaki Nakatsu
Watson
WE HAVEN'T CONFIRMED ANY DEFINITIVE CONNECTION TO SHAULA YET, BUT...
IF IT GOES WELL, THIS COULD BLOW OUR CASE WIDE OPEN.
KEEP FOLLOWING UP ON THIS LEAD.
THAT'S ENOUGH FOR TODAY. SORRY FOR KEEPING YOU SO LATE.
TON (TAP)
IT'S OUR DUTY, SIR.
POSTER: DEATH FEST
死武祭
BATTLE FESTIVAL
YOU WON'T BE ABLE TO FIGHT IN THE FESTIVAL THIS YEAR, HUH?

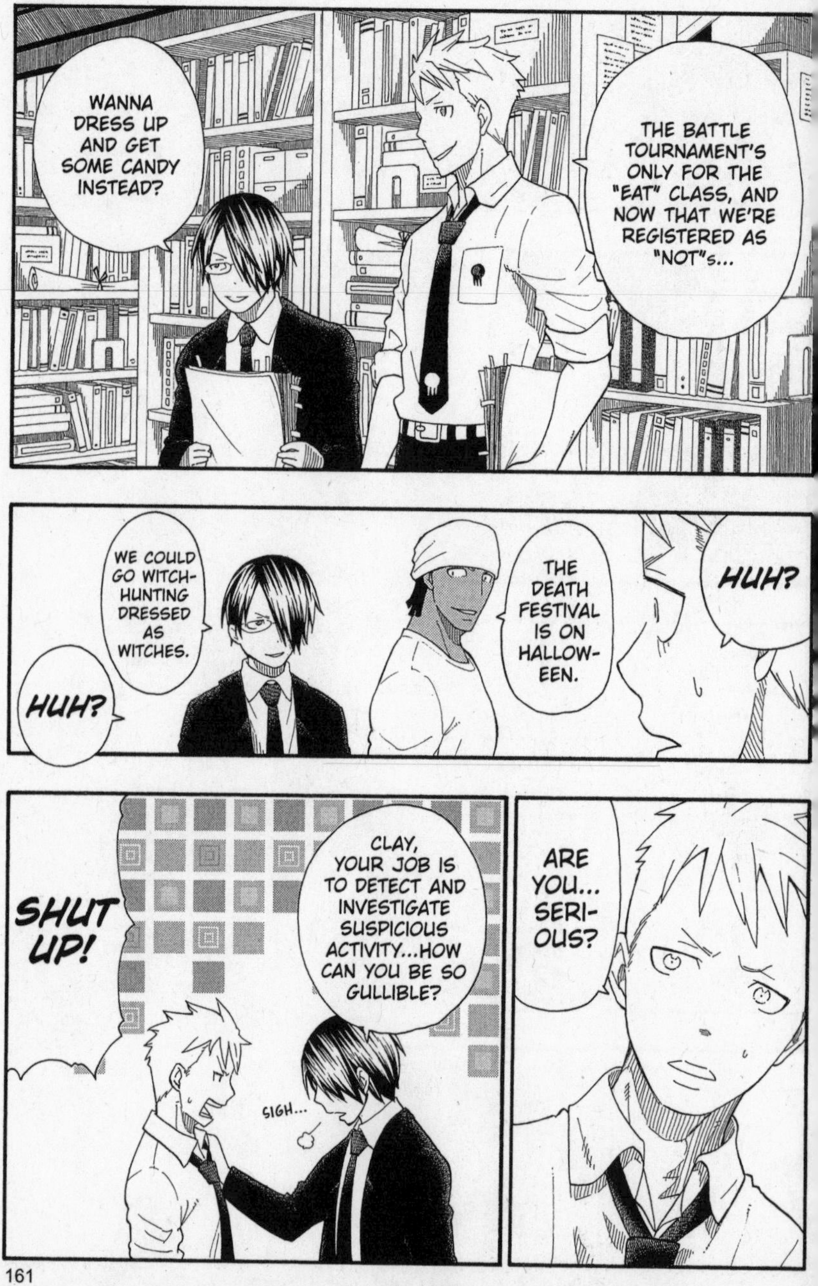
THE BATTLE TOURNAMENT'S ONLY FOR THE "EAT" CLASS, AND NOW THAT WE'RE REGISTERED AS "NOT"s...
WANNA DRESS UP AND GET SOME CANDY INSTEAD?
HUH?
THE DEATH FESTIVAL IS ON HALLOW-EEN.
WE COULD GO WITCH-HUNTING DRESSED AS WITCHES.
HUH?
ARE YOU... SERI-OUS?
CLAY, YOUR JOB IS TO DETECT AND INVESTIGATE SUSPICIOUS ACTIVITY...HOW CAN YOU BE SO GULLIBLE?
SHUT UP!
SIGH...

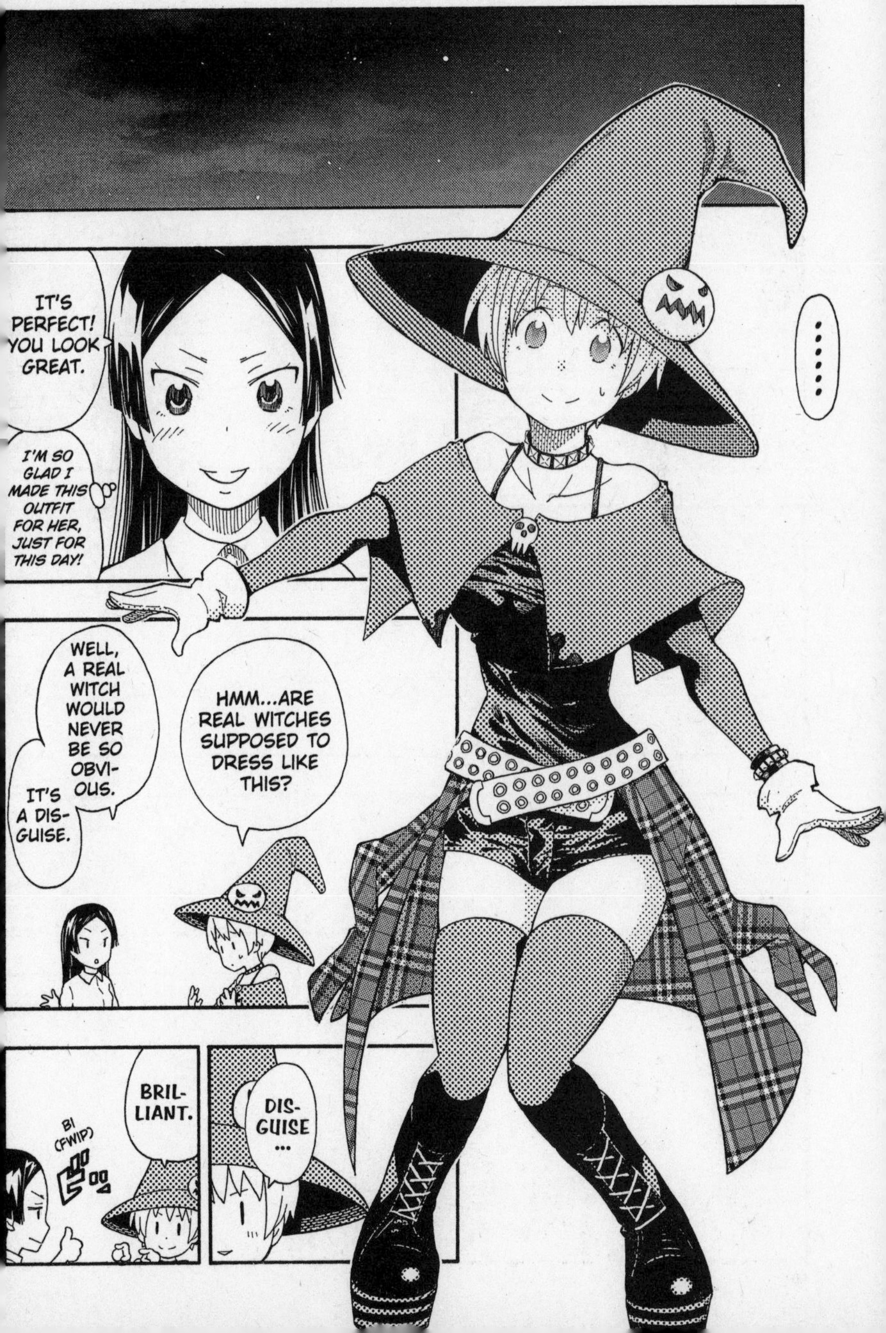

......
IT'S PERFECT! YOU LOOK GREAT.
I'M SO GLAD I MADE THIS OUTFIT FOR HER, JUST FOR THIS DAY!
HMM...ARE REAL WITCHES SUPPOSED TO DRESS LIKE THIS?
WELL, A REAL WITCH WOULD NEVER BE SO OBVI-OUS.
IT'S A DIS-GUISE.
DIS-GUISE...
BRIL-LIANT.
BI (FWIP)

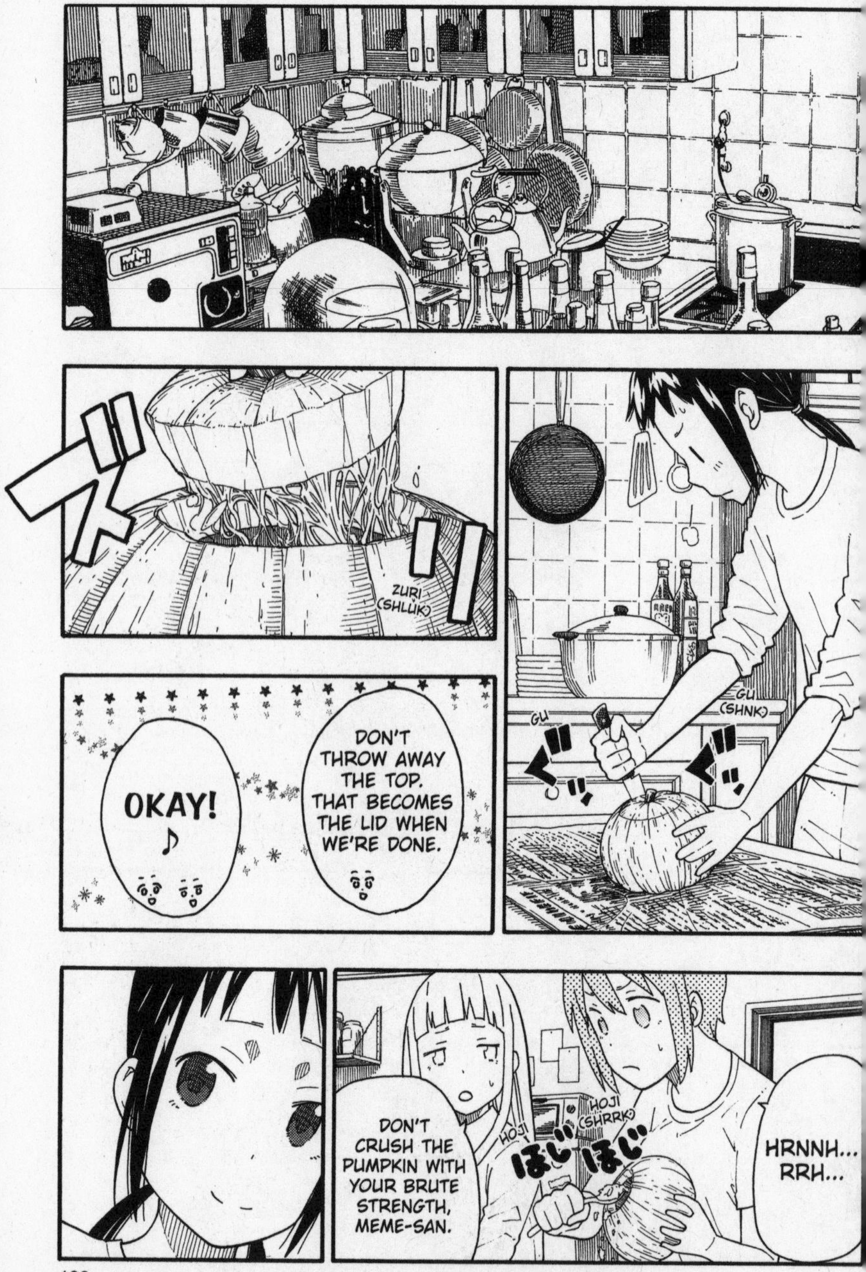
GU (SHNK)
GU
ZURI (SHLUK)
DON'T THROW AWAY THE TOP. THAT BECOMES THE LID WHEN WE'RE DONE.
OKAY! ♪
HRNNH... RRH...
HOJI (SHRRK)
HOJI
ほじほじ
DON'T CRUSH THE PUMPKIN WITH YOUR BRUTE STRENGTH, MEME-SAN.

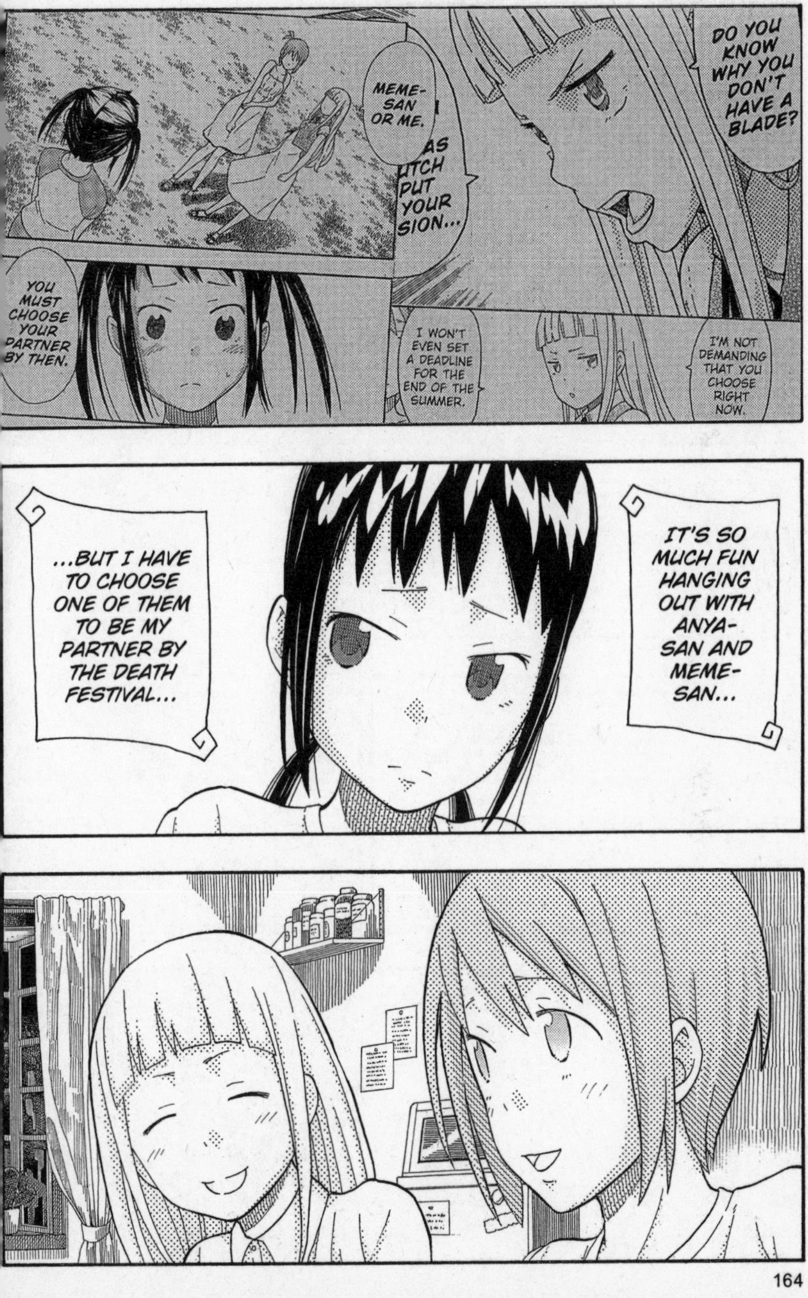
DO YOU KNOW WHY YOU DON'T HAVE A BLADE?
AS UTCH PUT YOUR SION...
MEME-SAN OR ME.
I'M NOT DEMANDING THAT YOU CHOOSE RIGHT NOW.
I WON'T EVEN SET A DEADLINE FOR THE END OF THE SUMMER.
YOU MUST CHOOSE YOUR PARTNER BY THEN.
IT'S SO MUCH FUN HANGING OUT WITH ANYA-SAN AND MEME-SAN...
...BUT I HAVE TO CHOOSE ONE OF THEM TO BE MY PARTNER BY THE DEATH FESTIVAL...

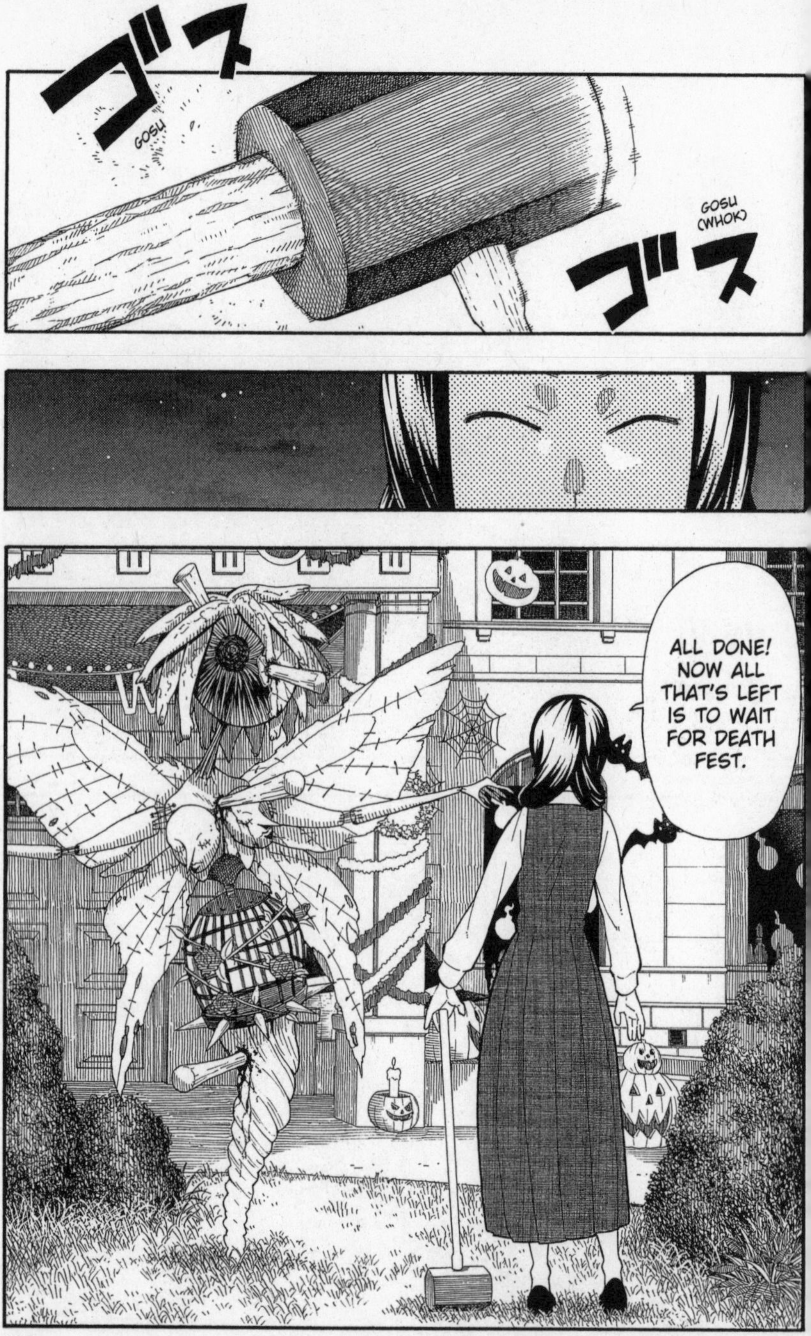
ゴス
GOSU
GOSU (WHOK)
ゴス
ALL DONE! NOW ALL THAT'S LEFT IS TO WAIT FOR DEATH FEST.

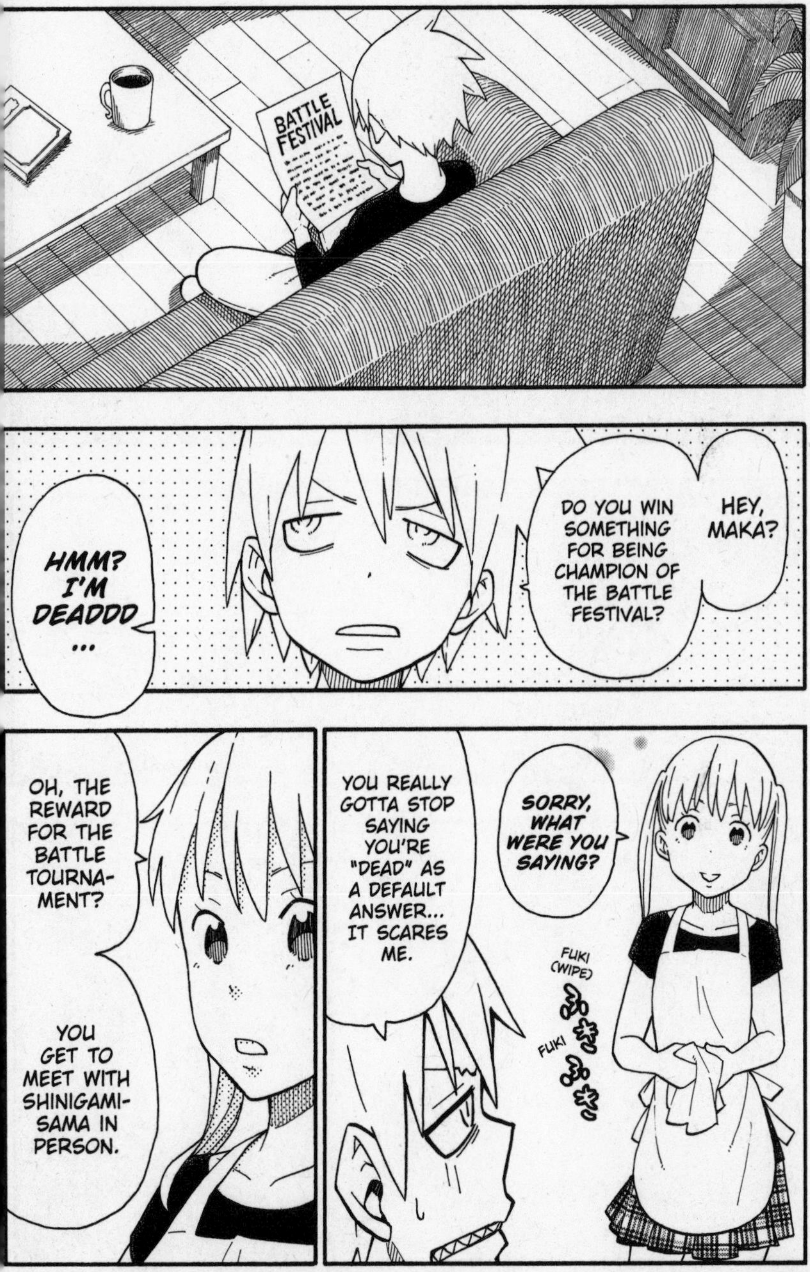
BATTLE FESTIVAL
HEY, MAKA?
DO YOU WIN SOMETHING FOR BEING CHAMPION OF THE BATTLE FESTIVAL?
HMM? I'M DEADDD ...
SORRY, WHAT WERE YOU SAYING?
YOU REALLY GOTTA STOP SAYING YOU'RE "DEAD" AS A DEFAULT ANSWER... IT SCARES ME.
FUKI (WIPE)
FUKI
OH, THE REWARD FOR THE BATTLE TOURNA-MENT?
YOU GET TO MEET WITH SHINIGAMI-SAMA IN PERSON.

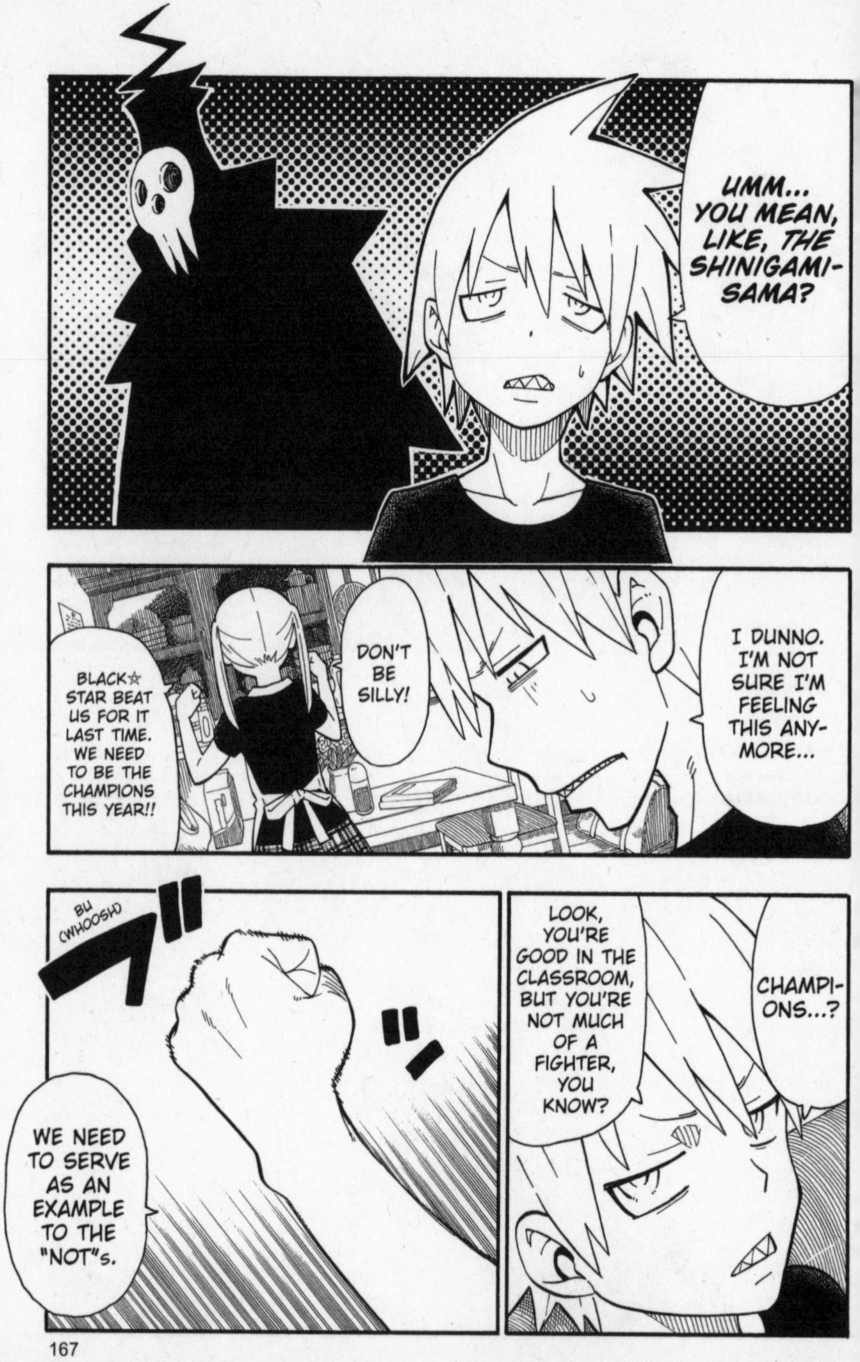
UMM... YOU MEAN, LIKE, THE SHINIGAMI-SAMA?
I DUNNO. I'M NOT SURE I'M FEELING THIS ANYMORE...
DON'T BE SILLY!
BLACK☆STAR BEAT US FOR IT LAST TIME. WE NEED TO BE THE CHAMPIONS THIS YEAR!!
CHAMPIONS...?
LOOK, YOU'RE GOOD IN THE CLASSROOM, BUT YOU'RE NOT MUCH OF A FIGHTER, YOU KNOW?
BU (WHOOSH)
WE NEED TO SERVE AS AN EXAMPLE TO THE "NOT"s.

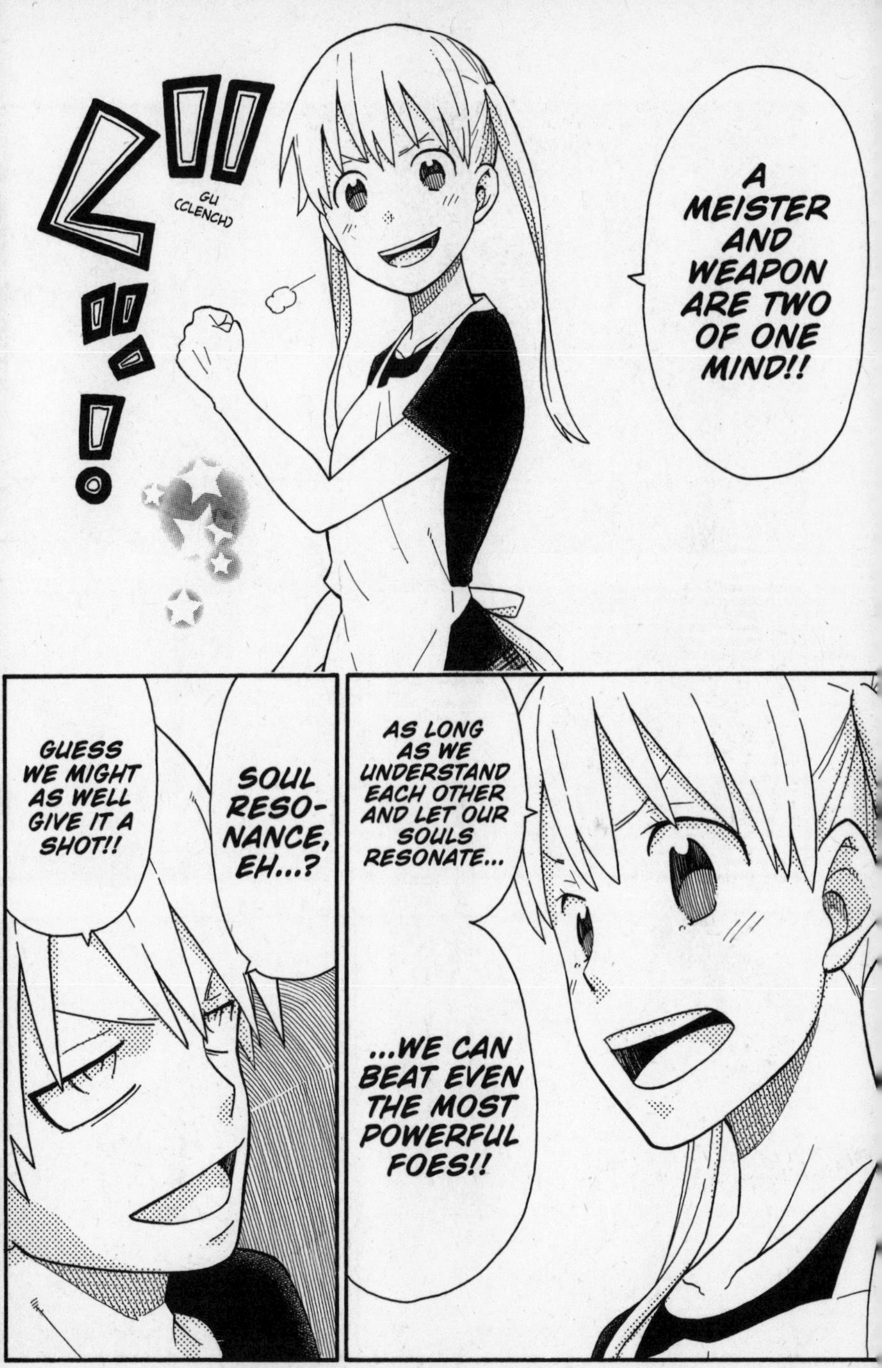
A MEISTER AND WEAPON ARE TWO OF ONE MIND!!
GU (CLENCH)
AS LONG AS WE UNDERSTAND EACH OTHER AND LET OUR SOULS RESONATE...
...WE CAN BEAT EVEN THE MOST POWERFUL FOES!!
SOUL RESONANCE, EH...?
GUESS WE MIGHT AS WELL GIVE IT A SHOT!!

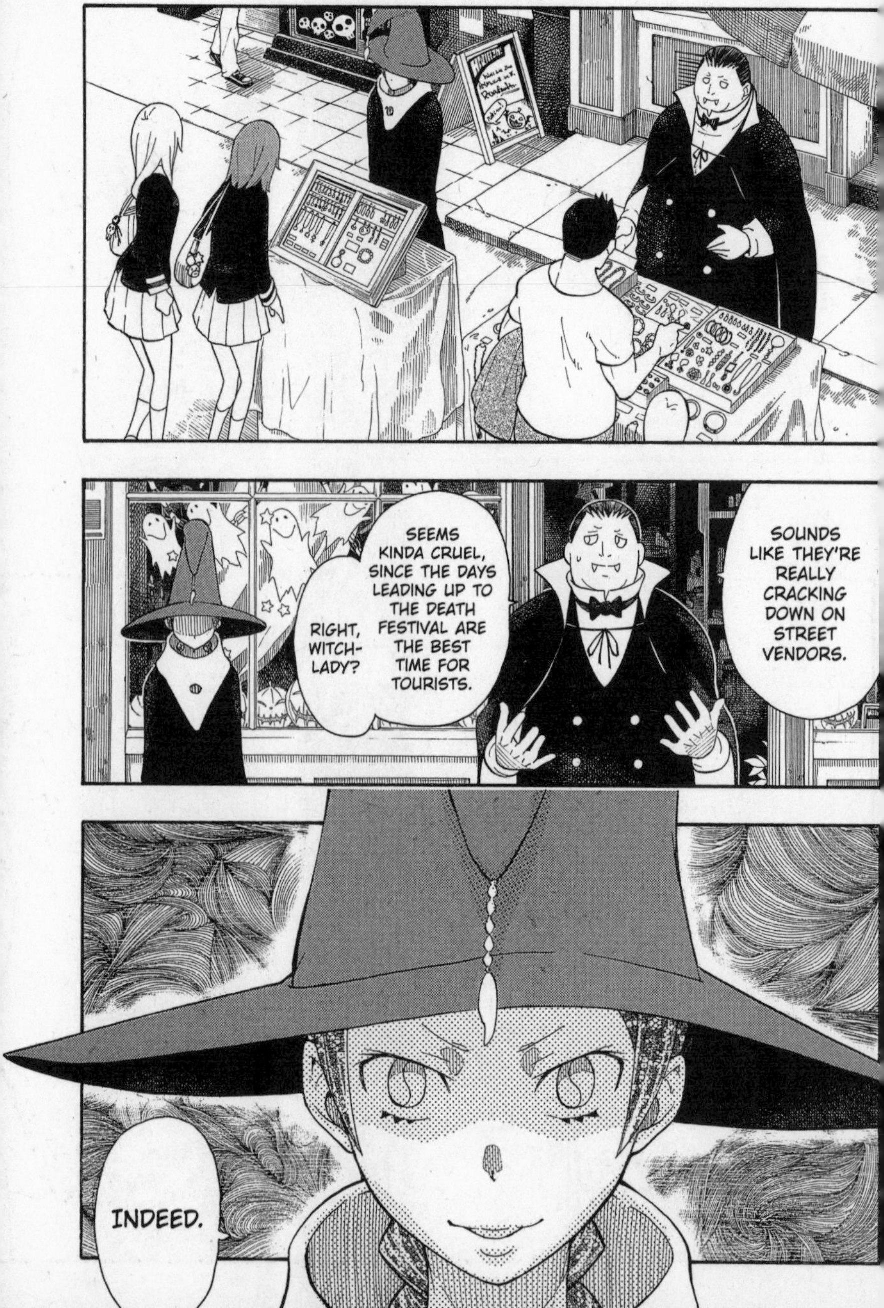
SOUNDS LIKE THEY'RE REALLY CRACKING DOWN ON STREET VENDORS.
SEEMS KINDA CRUEL, SINCE THE DAYS LEADING UP TO THE DEATH FESTIVAL ARE THE BEST TIME FOR TOURISTS.
RIGHT, WITCH-LADY?
INDEED.

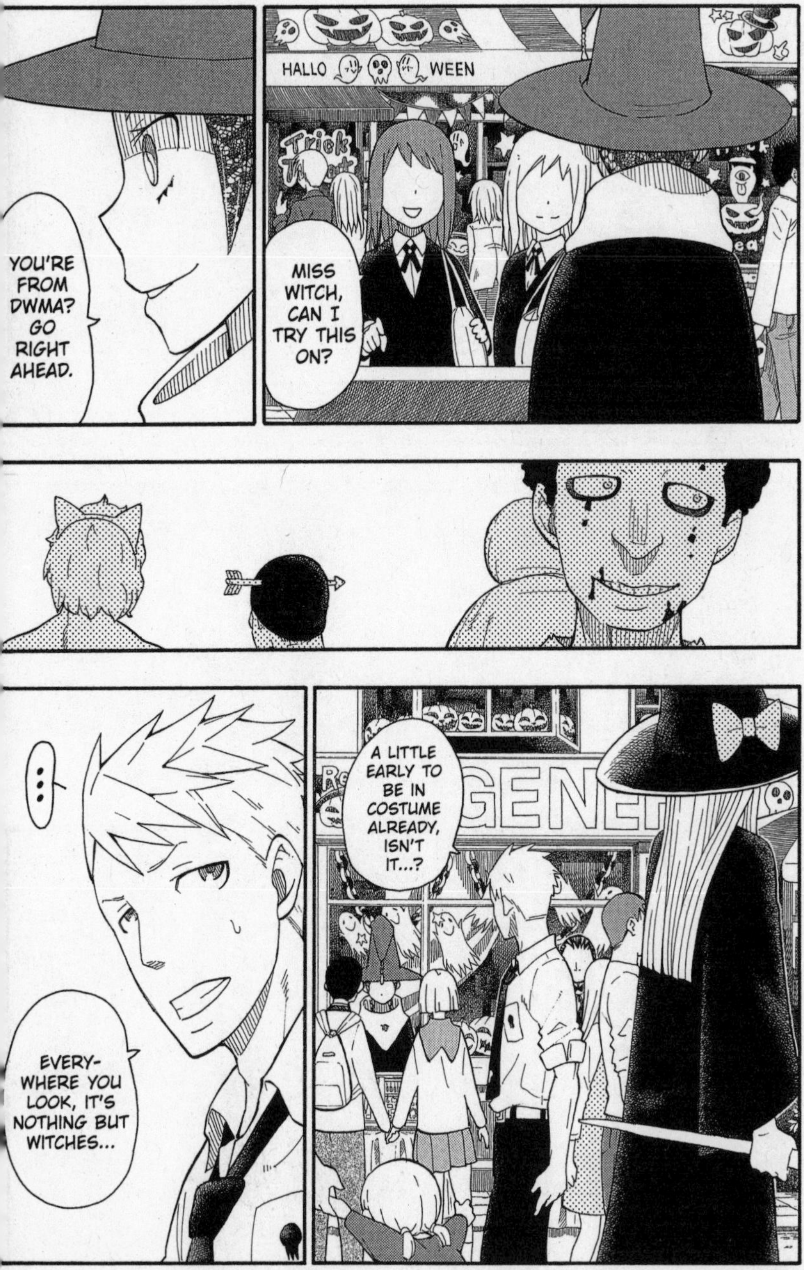
HALLO WEEN
MISS WITCH, CAN I TRY THIS ON?
YOU'RE FROM DWMA? GO RIGHT AHEAD.
A LITTLE EARLY TO BE IN COSTUME ALREADY, ISN'T IT...?
...
EVERY-WHERE YOU LOOK, IT'S NOTHING BUT WITCHES...

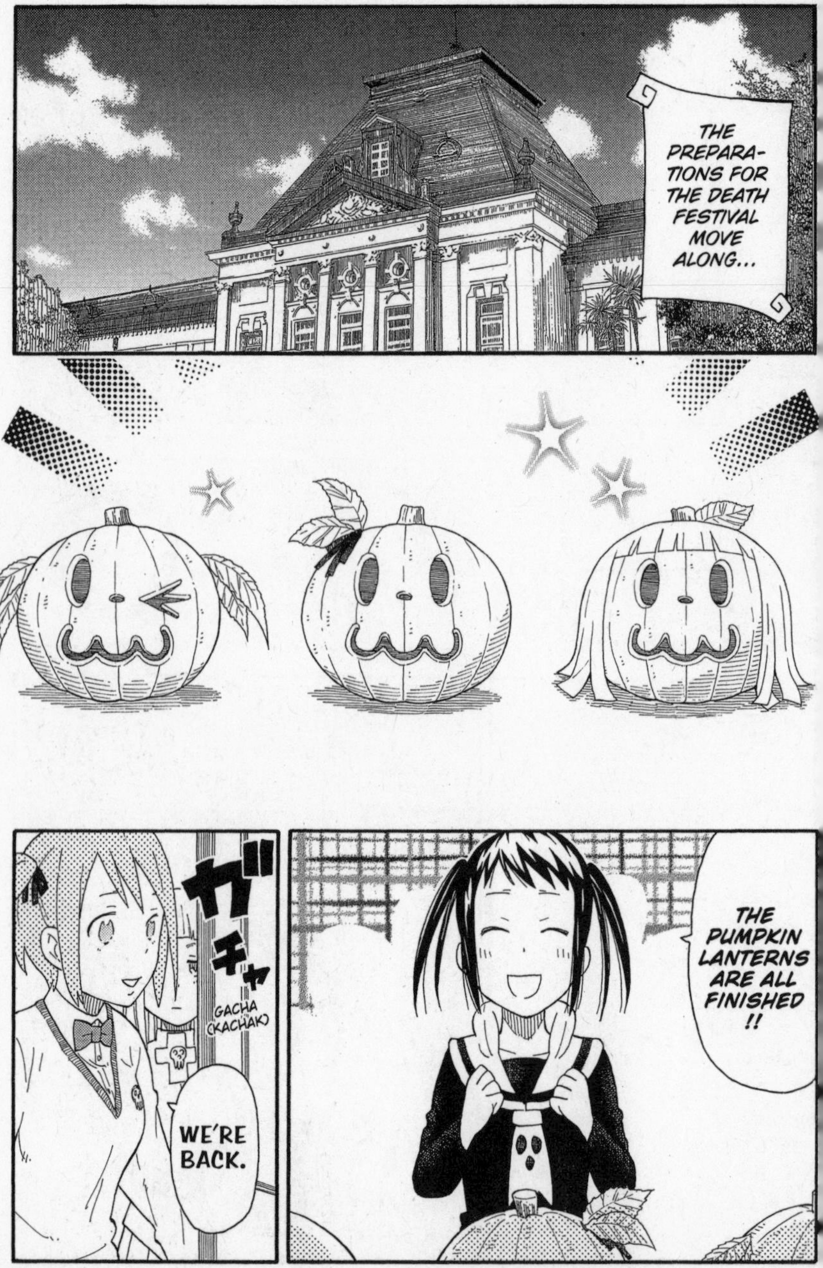
THE PREPARATIONS FOR THE DEATH FESTIVAL MOVE ALONG...
THE PUMPKIN LANTERNS ARE ALL FINISHED!!
ガチャ
GACHA (KACHAK)
WE'RE BACK.

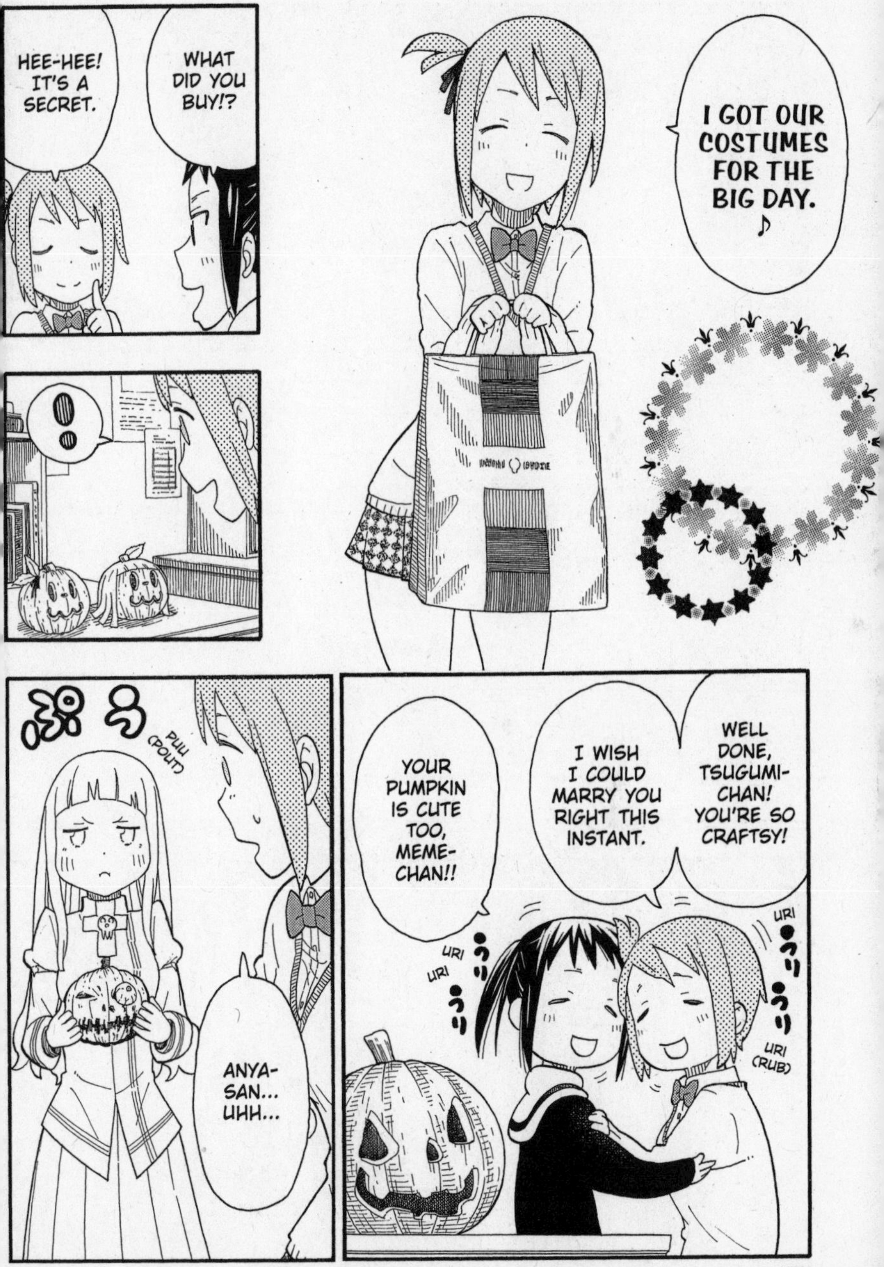

I GOT OUR COSTUMES FOR THE BIG DAY. ♪
WHAT DID YOU BUY!?
HEE-HEE! IT'S A SECRET.
!
WELL DONE, TSUGUMI-CHAN! YOU'RE SO CRAFTSY!
I WISH I COULD MARRY YOU RIGHT THIS INSTANT.
YOUR PUMPKIN IS CUTE TOO, MEME-CHAN!!
URI
URI (RUB)
URI
URI
PUU (POUT)
ANYA-SAN... UHH...

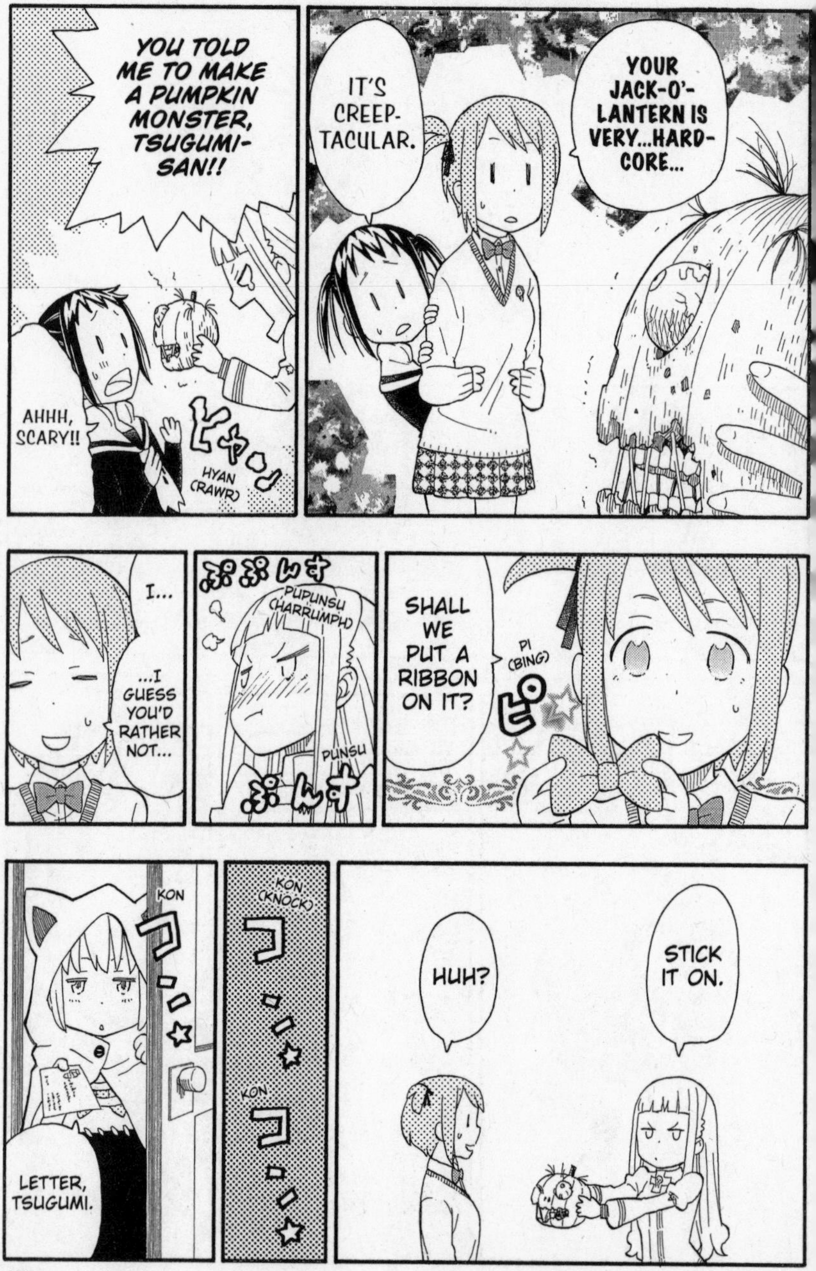
YOUR JACK-O'-LANTERN IS VERY...HARD-CORE...
IT'S CREEP-TACULAR.
YOU TOLD ME TO MAKE A PUMPKIN MONSTER, TSUGUMI-SAN!!
HYAN (RAWR)
AHHH, SCARY!!
SHALL WE PUT A RIBBON ON IT?
PI (BING)
PUPUNSU (HARRUMPH)
PUNSU
I...
...I GUESS YOU'D RATHER NOT...
STICK IT ON.
HUH?
KON (KNOCK)
KON
KON
LETTER, TSUGUMI.

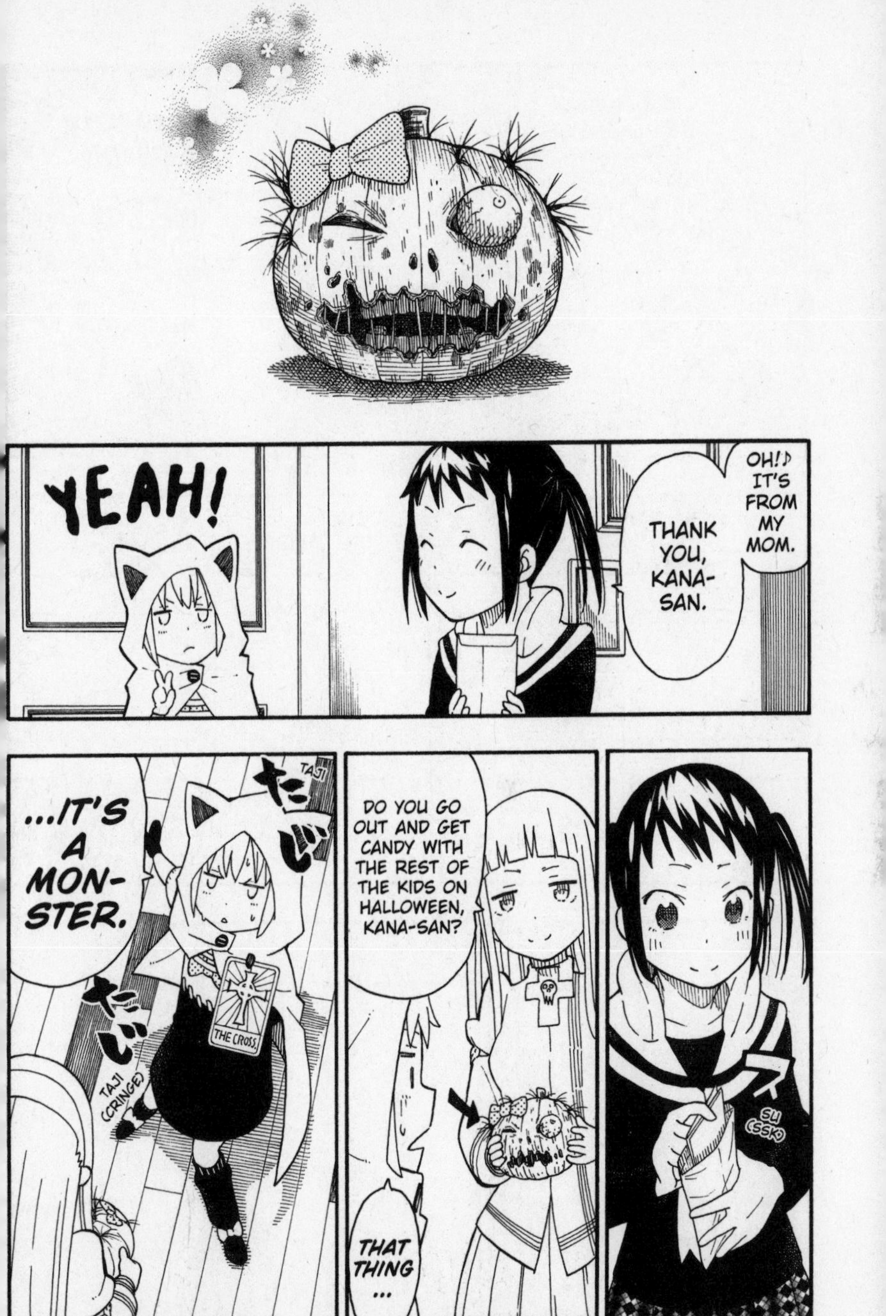
OH!♪ IT'S FROM MY MOM.
THANK YOU, KANA-SAN.
YEAH!
SU (SSK)
DO YOU GO OUT AND GET CANDY WITH THE REST OF THE KIDS ON HALLOWEEN, KANA-SAN?
THAT THING...
TAJI
...IT'S A MONSTER.
THE CROSS
TAJI (CRINGE)

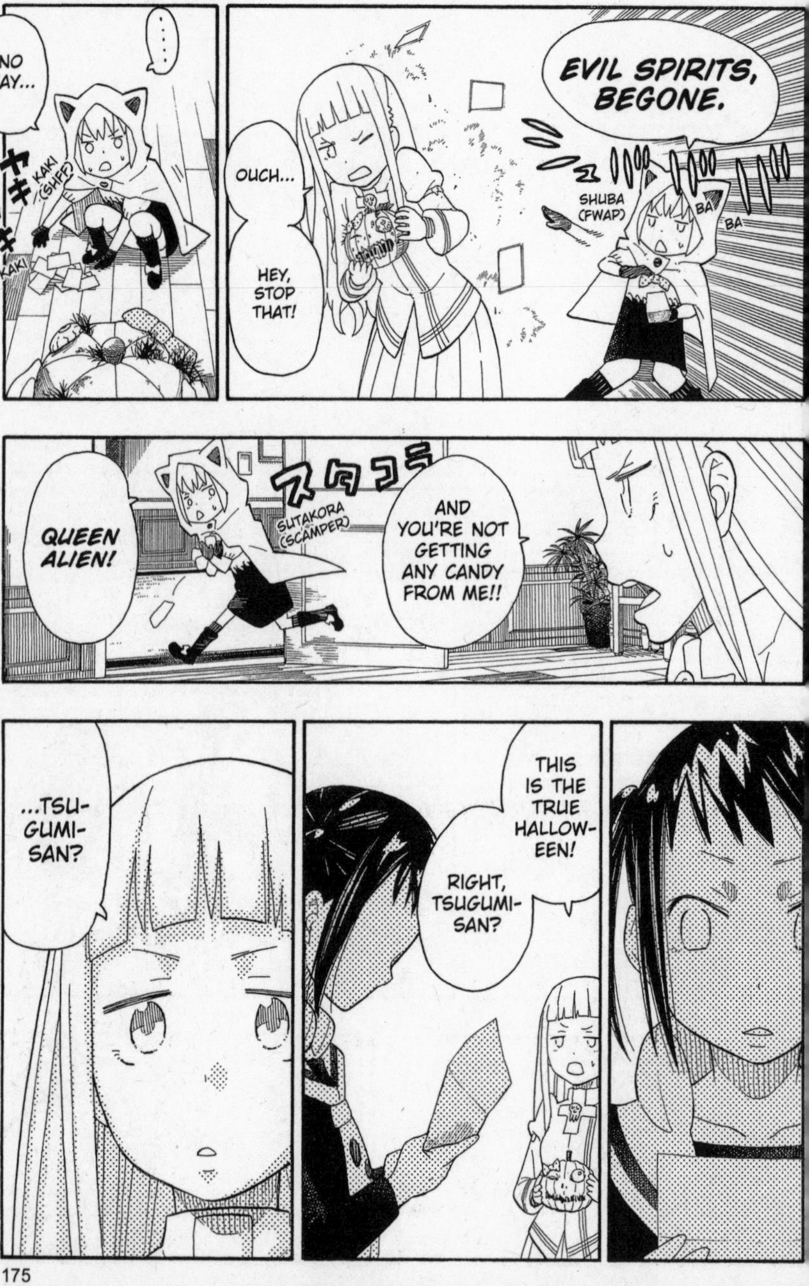
EVIL SPIRITS, BEGONE.
SHUBA (FWAP)
BA
BA
OUCH...
HEY, STOP THAT!
NO WAY...
...
KAKI (SHFF)
KAKI
AND YOU'RE NOT GETTING ANY CANDY FROM ME!!
SUTAKORA (SCAMPER)
QUEEN ALIEN!
THIS IS THE TRUE HALLOW-EEN!
RIGHT, TSUGUMI-SAN?
...TSU-GUMI-SAN?

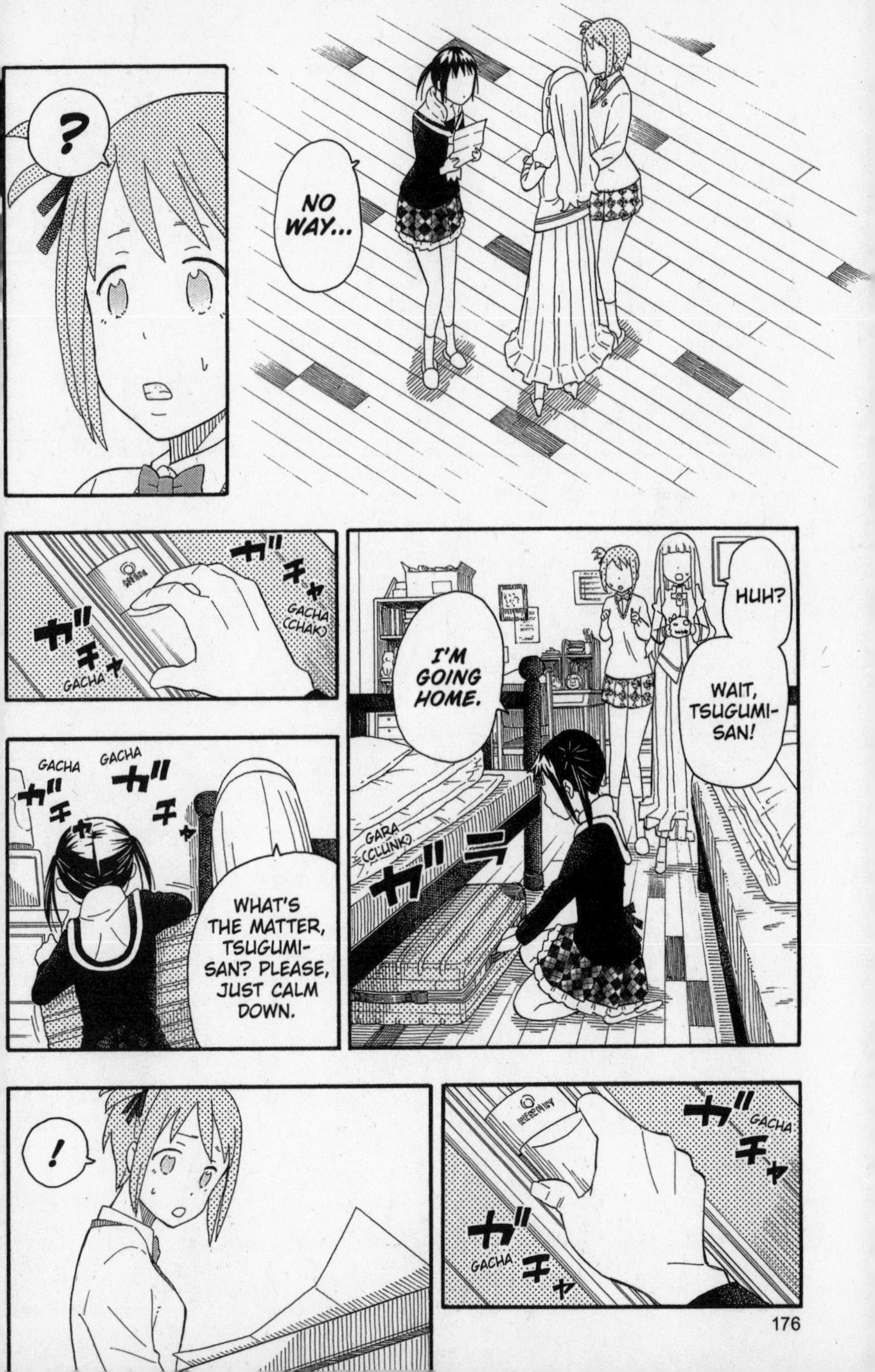
NO WAY...
?
HUH?
WAIT, TSUGUMI-SAN!
I'M GOING HOME.
GARA (CLUNK)
GACHA (CHAK)
GACHA
GACHA
GACHA
WHAT'S THE MATTER, TSUGUMI-SAN? PLEASE, JUST CALM DOWN.
GACHA
GACHA
!

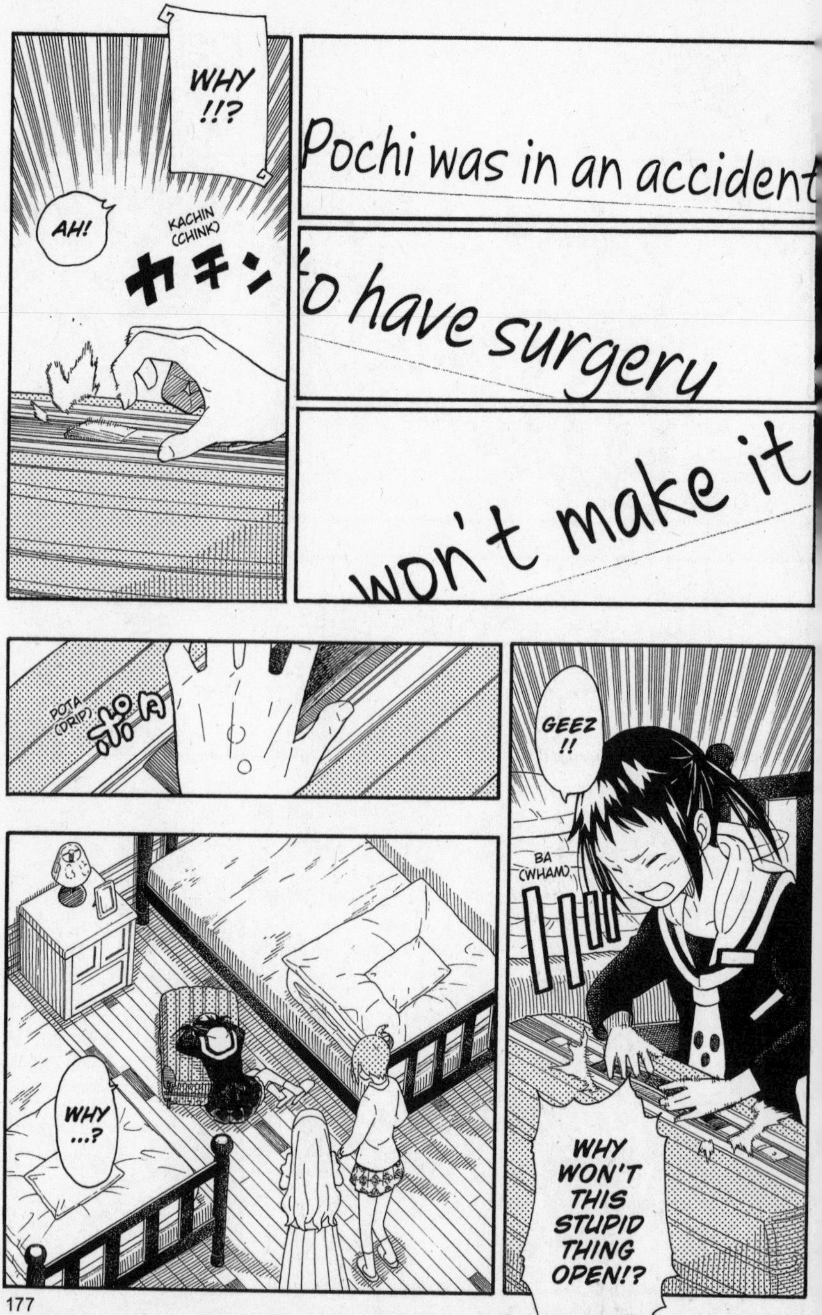
Pochi was in an accident
to have surgery
won't make it
WHY !!?
AH!
KACHIN (CHINK)
カチン
GEEZ !!
BA (WHAM)
WHY WON'T THIS STUPID THING OPEN!?
POTA (DRIP)
ポタ
WHY ...?

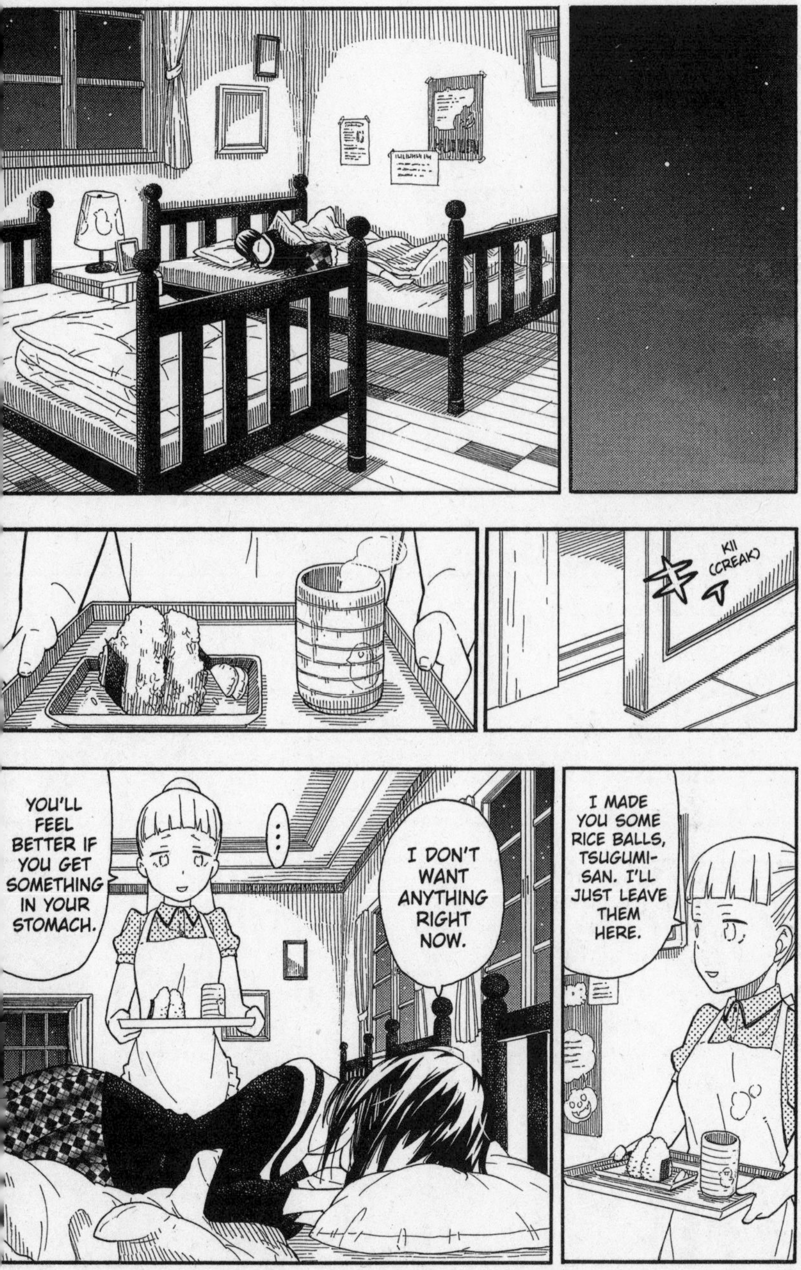
KII
(CREAK)
I MADE YOU SOME RICE BALLS, TSUGUMI-SAN. I'LL JUST LEAVE THEM HERE.
I DON'T WANT ANYTHING RIGHT NOW.
...
YOU'LL FEEL BETTER IF YOU GET SOMETHING IN YOUR STOMACH.

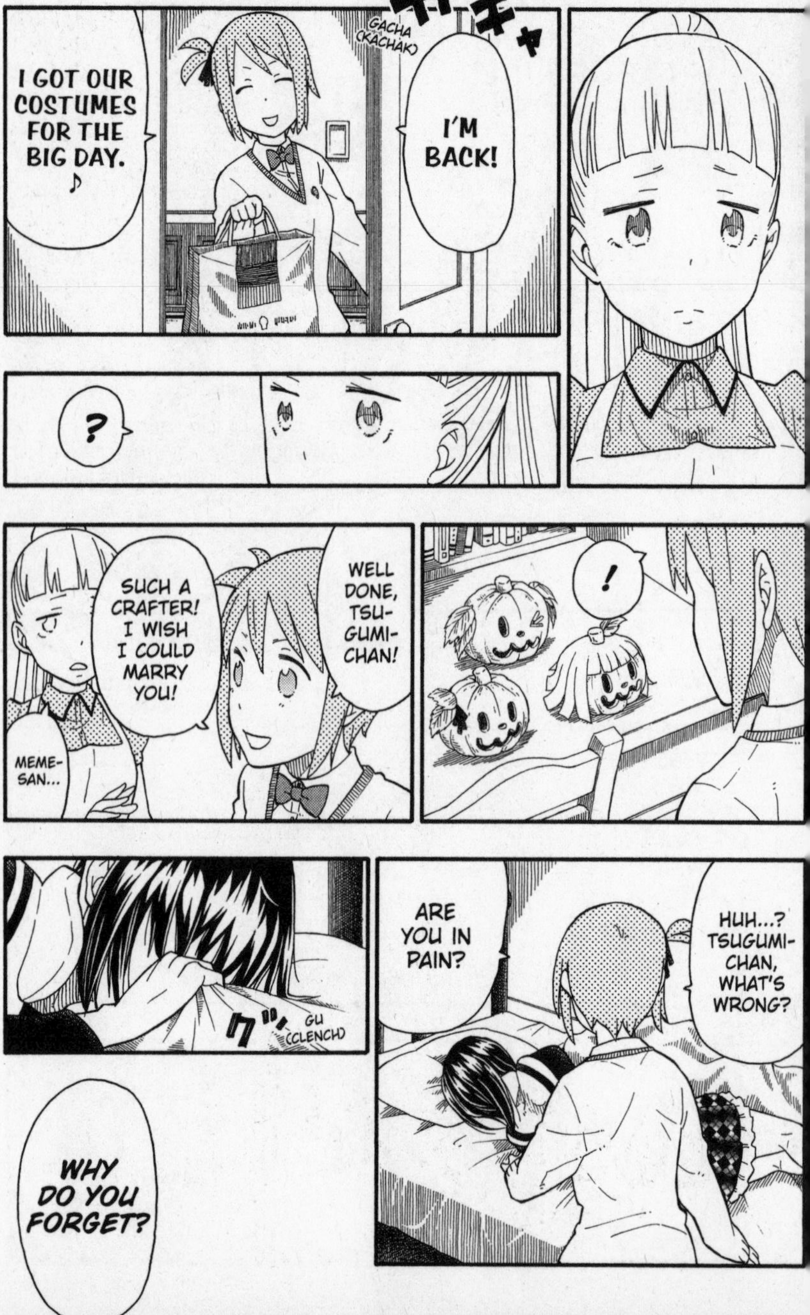
GACHA (KACHAK)
I'M BACK!
I GOT OUR COSTUMES FOR THE BIG DAY. ♪
?
!
WELL DONE, TSUGUMI-CHAN!
SUCH A CRAFTER! I WISH I COULD MARRY YOU!
MEME-SAN...
HUH...? TSUGUMI-CHAN, WHAT'S WRONG?
ARE YOU IN PAIN?
GU (CLENCH)
WHY DO YOU FORGET?

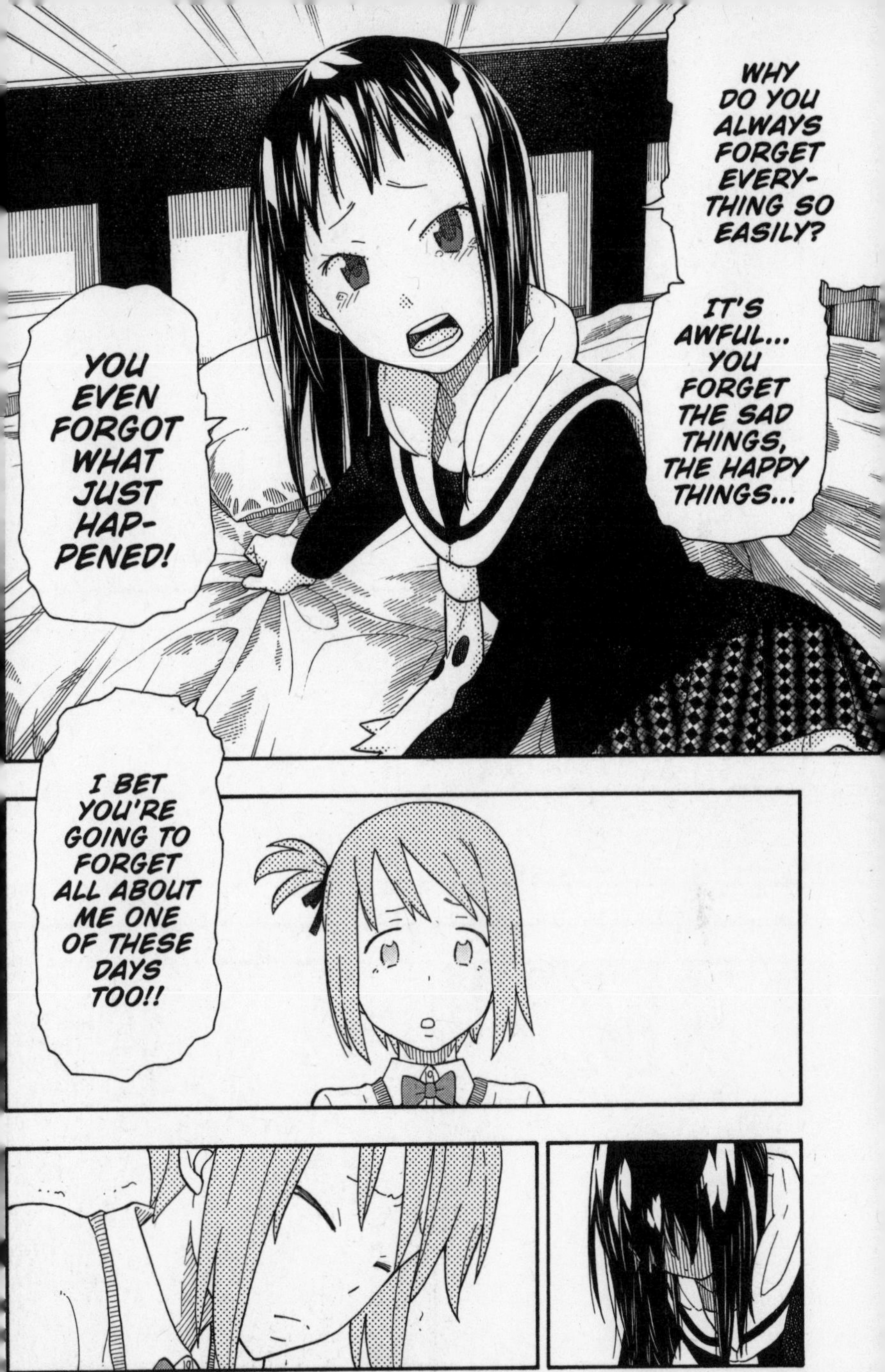
WHY DO YOU ALWAYS FORGET EVERY-THING SO EASILY?
IT'S AWFUL... YOU FORGET THE SAD THINGS, THE HAPPY THINGS...
YOU EVEN FORGOT WHAT JUST HAP-PENED!
I BET YOU'RE GOING TO FORGET ALL ABOUT ME ONE OF THESE DAYS TOO!!
...

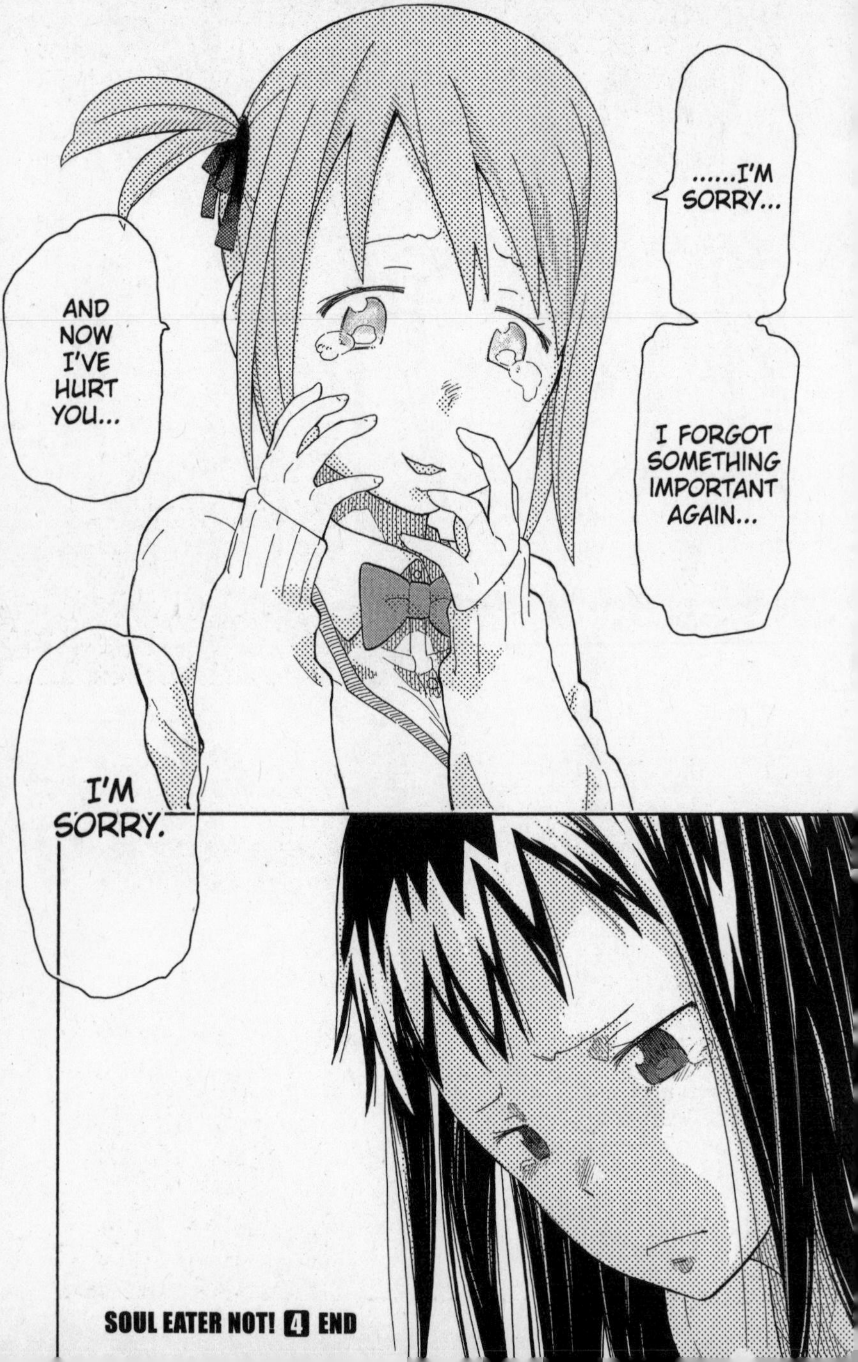
......I'M SORRY...
I FORGOT SOMETHING IMPORTANT AGAIN...
AND NOW I'VE HURT YOU...
I'M SORRY.
SOUL EATER NOT! 4 END

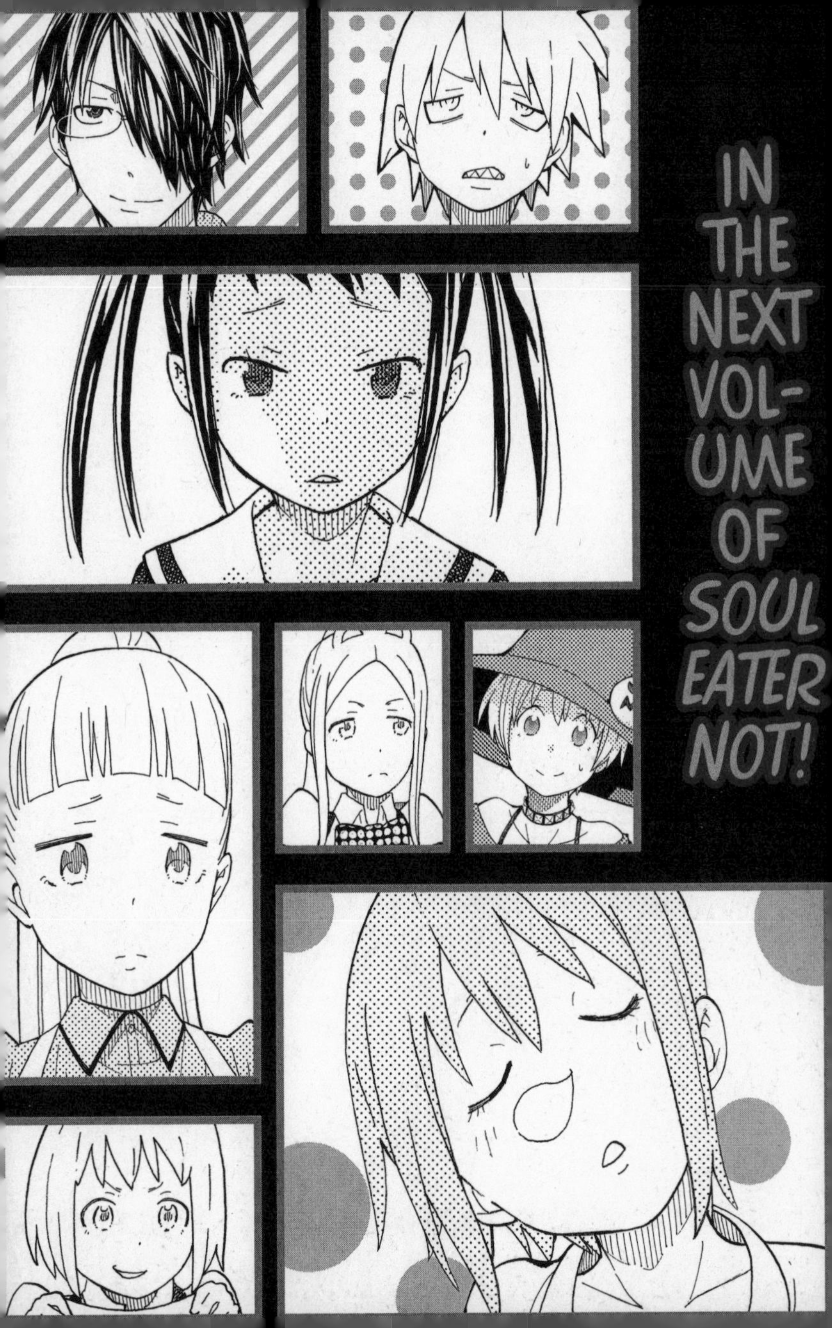
IN THE NEXT VOL-UME OF SOUL EATER NOT!

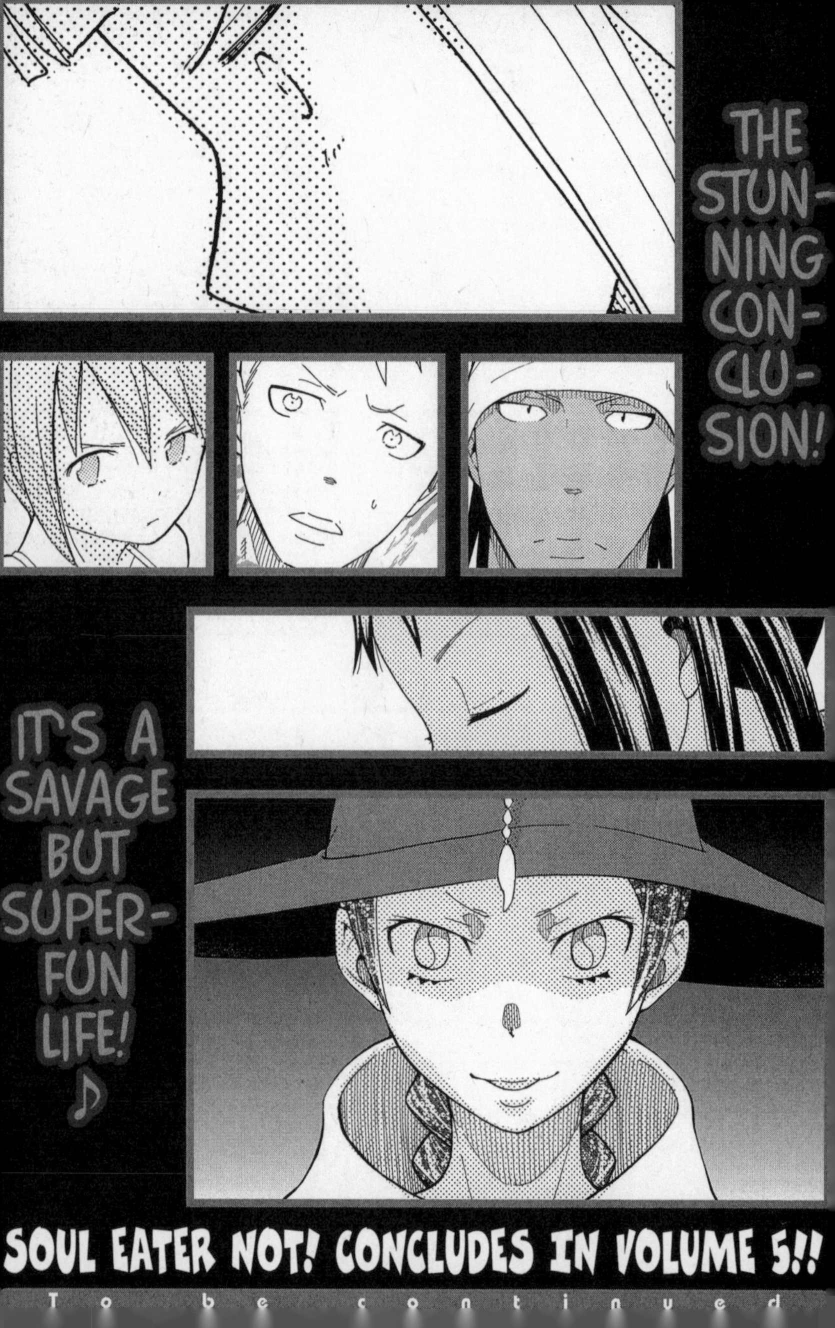
THE STUN-NING CON-CLU-SION!
IT'S A SAVAGE BUT SUPER-FUN LIFE! ♪
SOUL EATER NOT! CONCLUDES IN VOLUME 5!!
To be continued

後書きマンガ
あつし屋
ノット支店

Afterword Manga Atsushiya Not! Location

Title designed by:
Me (Mouth)

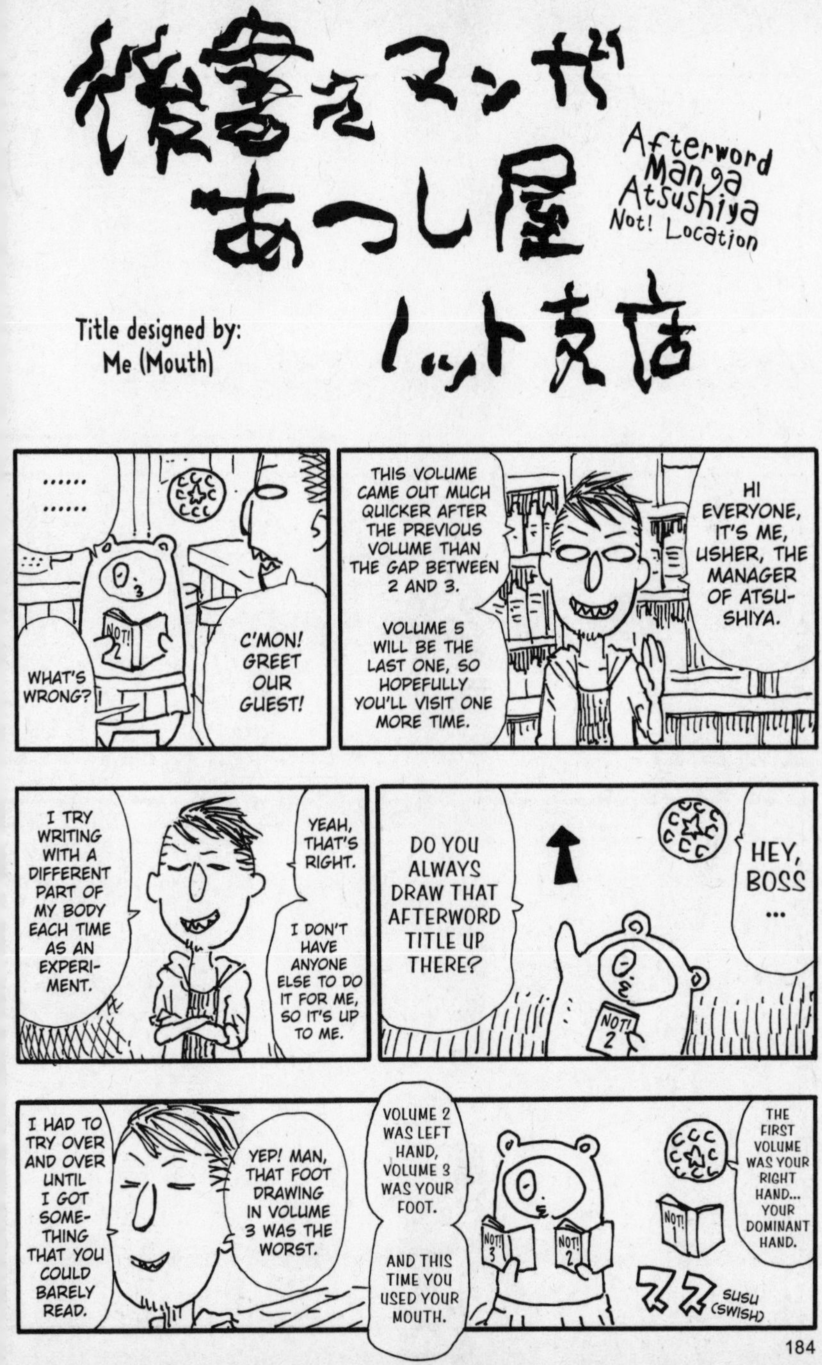
HI EVERYONE, IT'S ME, USHER, THE MANAGER OF ATSU-SHIYA.
THIS VOLUME CAME OUT MUCH QUICKER AFTER THE PREVIOUS VOLUME THAN THE GAP BETWEEN 2 AND 3.
VOLUME 5 WILL BE THE LAST ONE, SO HOPEFULLY YOU'LL VISIT ONE MORE TIME.
......
......
C'MON! GREET OUR GUEST!
WHAT'S WRONG?
HEY, BOSS ...
DO YOU ALWAYS DRAW THAT AFTERWORD TITLE UP THERE?
YEAH, THAT'S RIGHT.
I DON'T HAVE ANYONE ELSE TO DO IT FOR ME, SO IT'S UP TO ME.
I TRY WRITING WITH A DIFFERENT PART OF MY BODY EACH TIME AS AN EXPERI-MENT.
THE FIRST VOLUME WAS YOUR RIGHT HAND... YOUR DOMINANT HAND.
SUSU (SWISH)
VOLUME 2 WAS LEFT HAND, VOLUME 3 WAS YOUR FOOT.
AND THIS TIME YOU USED YOUR MOUTH.
YEP! MAN, THAT FOOT DRAWING IN VOLUME 3 WAS THE WORST.
I HAD TO TRY OVER AND OVER UNTIL I GOT SOME-THING THAT YOU COULD BARELY READ.

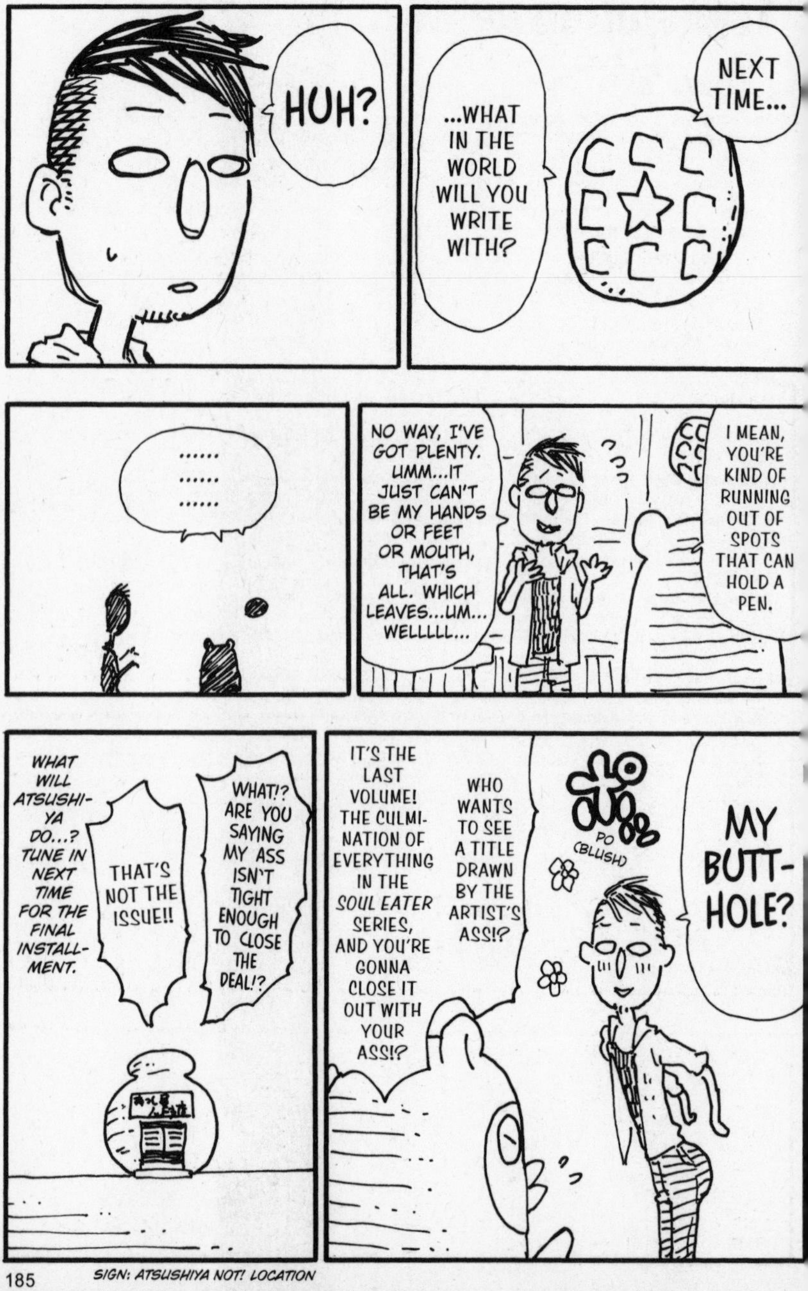
NEXT TIME...
...WHAT IN THE WORLD WILL YOU WRITE WITH?
HUH?
I MEAN, YOU'RE KIND OF RUNNING OUT OF SPOTS THAT CAN HOLD A PEN.
NO WAY, I'VE GOT PLENTY. UMM...IT JUST CAN'T BE MY HANDS OR FEET OR MOUTH, THAT'S ALL. WHICH LEAVES...UM... WELLLLL...
......
......
......
MY BUTT-HOLE?
PO (BLUSH)
WHO WANTS TO SEE A TITLE DRAWN BY THE ARTIST'S ASS!?
IT'S THE LAST VOLUME! THE CULMINATION OF EVERYTHING IN THE *SOUL EATER* SERIES, AND YOU'RE GONNA CLOSE IT OUT WITH YOUR ASS!?
WHAT!? ARE YOU SAYING MY ASS ISN'T TIGHT ENOUGH TO CLOSE THE DEAL!?
THAT'S NOT THE ISSUE!!
WHAT WILL ATSUSHIYA DO...? TUNE IN NEXT TIME FOR THE FINAL INSTALLMENT.

SIGN: ATSUSHIYA NOT! LOCATION

Translation Notes

Common Honorifics

no honorific: Indicates familiarity or closeness; if used without permission or reason, addressing someone in this manner would constitute an insult.

-san: The Japanese equivalent of Mr./Mrs./Miss. If a situation calls for politeness, this is the fail-safe honorific.

-sama: Conveys great respect; may also indicate that the social status of the speaker is lower than that of the addressee.

-kun: Used most often when referring to boys, this indicates affection or familiarity. Occasionally used by older men among their peers, but it may also be used by anyone referring to a person of lower standing.

-chan: An affectionate honorific indicating familiarity used mostly in reference to girls; also used in reference to cute persons or animals of either gender.

-senpai: A suffix used to address upperclassmen or more experienced coworkers.

-sensei: A respectful term for teachers, artists, or high-level professionals.

Page 69
Ganguro: Used here as a pun on "Anglo-Saxon," *Ganguro* describes a fashion trend that developed in Japan in rebellion against the traditional notion of Japanese beauty. Common trademarks of the style include a dark tan, bleached or dyed hair, white eye and lip makeup, and brightly-colored clothing and accessories.

Page 114
Takenoko-zoku: The *Takenoko-zoku* (Bamboo Shoot Tribe) was a youth subculture centered around Tokyo in the late '70s to early '80s. Teenagers formed tight-knit dance troupes that would put on street performances to disco music played on boom boxes.

Page 184
Title writing: Because the art of calligraphy requires a lot of practice, there are established calligraphers who can be commissioned to provide title logos and the like when Japanese media companies (whether film, TV, books, etc.) want to add this artistic touch to their product. It's a big deal, and the name of the calligrapher is always printed just below the title.

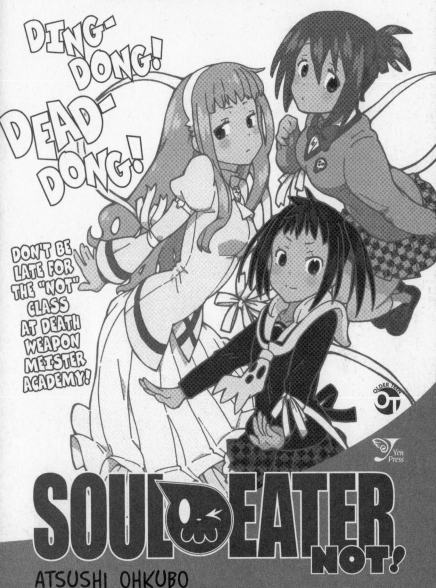

READ THE LATEST INSTALLMENT SIMULTANEOUSLY WITH JAPAN!

NEW CHAPTERS AVAILABLE MONTHLY FROM YOUR FAVORITE EBOOK RETAILER AND IN THE YEN PRESS APP!

DING-DONG! DEAD-DONG!

DON'T BE LATE FOR THE "NOT" CLASS AT DEATH WEAPON MEISTER ACADEMY!

OLDER TEEN
OT

Yen Press

SOUL EATER NOT!

ATSUSHI OHKUBO

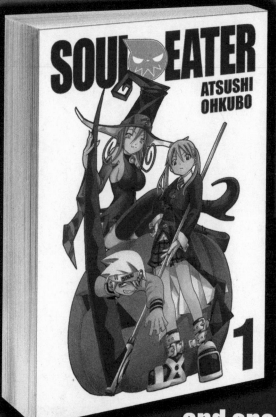

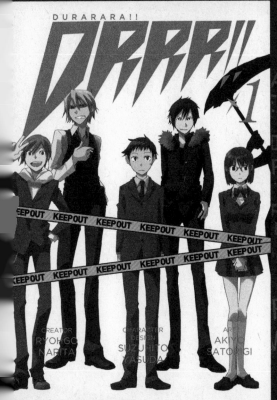

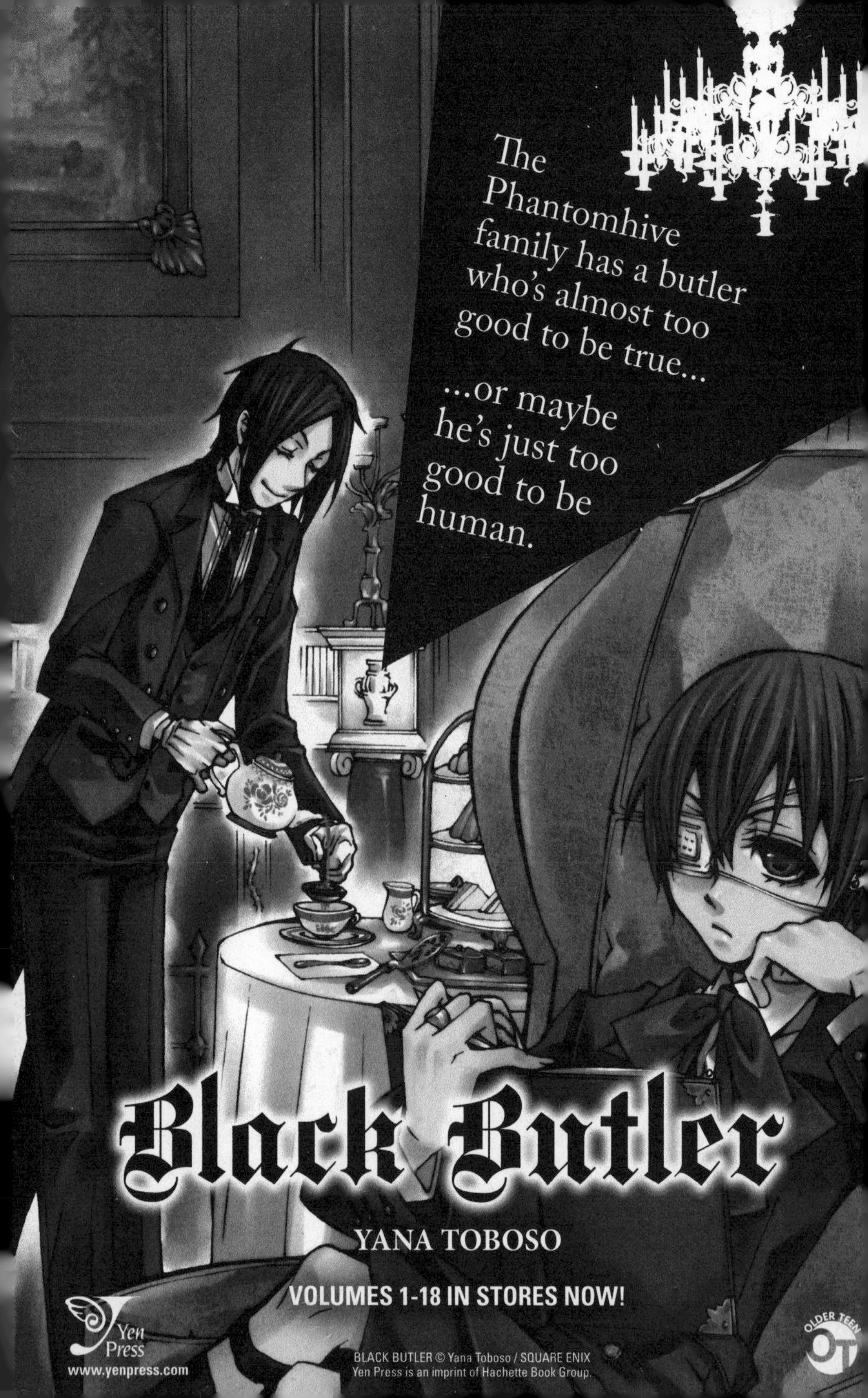
The Phantomhive family has a butler who's almost too good to be true...
...or maybe he's just too good to be human.
Black Butler
YANA TOBOSO
VOLUMES 1-18 IN STORES NOW!
Yen Press
www.yenpress.com
BLACK BUTLER © Yana Toboso / SQUARE ENIX
Yen Press is an imprint of Hachette Book Group.
OLDER TEEN
OT

SOUL EATER

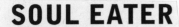

ATSUSHI OHKUBO

Translation: Stephen Paul

Lettering: Abigail Blackman

This book is a work of fiction. Names, characters, places, and incidents are the product of the author's imagination or are used fictitiously. Any resemblance to actual events, locales, or persons, living or dead, is coincidental.

SOUL EATER NOT! Vol. 4 © 2014 Atsushi Ohkubo / SQUARE ENIX. First published in Japan in 2014 by SQUARE ENIX CO., LTD. English translation rights arranged with SQUARE ENIX CO., LTD. and Hachette Book Group through Tuttle-Mori Agency, Inc.

Translation © 2014 by SQUARE ENIX CO., LTD.

Yen Press
Hachette Book Group
1290 Avenue of the Americas
New York, NY 10104

www.HachetteBookGroup.com
www.YenPress.com

Yen Press is an imprint of Hachette Book Group, Inc. The Yen Press name and logo are trademarks of Hachette Book Group, Inc.

First Yen Press Edition: November 2014

ISBN: 978-0-316-29816-2

10 9 8 7 6 5 4 3 2 1

BVG

Printed in the United States of America